iPhone

covers iOS 6
3rd edition updated for iPhone 5

In easy steps is an imprint of In Easy Steps Limited
4 Chapel Court · 42 Holly Walk · Leamington Spa
Warwickshire · United Kingdom · CV32 4YS
www.ineasysteps.com

Third Edition

In Easy Steps Limited supports The Forest Stewardship Council (FSC), the leading international forest certification organisation. All our titles that are printed on Greenpeace approved FSC certified paper carry the FSC logo.

Printed and bound in the United Kingdom

ISBN 978-1-84078-529-6

Contents

1 iPhone 5

iPhone 5 is a sophisticated and highly capable smartphone which is able to make calls, send text and multimedia messages, browse the web, keep contacts and calendars synchronized with desktop Macs or PCs, take and store video images and still photos, play games and keep you organized professionally and personally.

A Very Smart Smartphone!

Why has there been so much hype surrounding the iPhone? Cellular phones have been around for years. Many of them can play music, movies, browse the web. So what's so special about the Apple iPhone?

Apple's first generation iPhone was launched in June 2007. Because of the advance publicity there was a feeding frenzy when launch day came, with customers queuing for many hours to get their hands on an iPhone.

There are several reasons for the excitement, including the Apple brand (stylish, functional and innovative). People already loved the iPod so a cell phone with iPod capabilities and a wide screen had major appeal. The sheer simplicity of operation, using a touch screen rather than a plethora of buttons, had major appeal.

So this was a cell phone unlike any other. In addition to the usual telephony capabilities, this phone could play music, videos, YouTube and more. It could be used as a diary with easy synchronization to Microsoft Outlook or Apple Calendar. It would handle email (including Exchange Server) more easily. Its SMS program made messaging a breeze. Its browser made browsing the web easier than with previous smartphones.

In addition, there were applications such as Weather, Stocks, Maps and others. Despite criticisms from some quarters regarding the poor camera (2 megapixels in the first and second generation iPhones) and lack of video, along with the inability for the user to add more applications, the first generation iPhone was a huge success.

The second generation iPhone was launched in July 2008 and brought with it 3G, a much faster data network connection. In June 2009 the 3GS ("S" stands for "speed") was launched. The new iPhone 3GS brought with it the ability to capture video, Voice Control, which enables users to control the iPhone 3GS using voice commands, and numerous other features.

The 4G iPhone was launched in June 2010 and brought with it many refinements such as dual cameras, camera flash, FaceTime, Siri, higher resolution Retina Display screen and many other improvements over the previous models. The 4GS was launched in Summer 2011, and September 2012 saw the arrival of iPhone 5.

What Does It Do?

It would be easier to ask what it *doesn't* do! The iPhone, even as a basic cell phone, before you start adding applications, has many functions – probably enough for most people without actually having to add more apps of your own. But, since there are *thousands* of applications available for download, you can extend the functionality of the iPhone way beyond this. The iPhone is more like a small computer since you can store files, email, connect to other desktop computers, view documents including Word and PDF files, play games, look up recipes, manage your time, and many other functions.

Hot tip

The iPhone is more like a computer than a standard cell phone.

Work

Make phone calls
Manage your diary
Check email
Check Visual Voicemail
Maintain your contacts list
Check stocks and shares
Take Voice Memos
Takes notes using Notes
Do the math with Calculator

Expand your iPhone

Buy music, films and audiobooks
Customize your iPhone 5
Buy apps or download free apps
Store files
Open Word and other docs
Connect to desktop Mac or PC
Turn iPhone into a remote control
Find recipes
Play games

Play

Send SMS or MMS
Chat using Skype and other apps
Look at photos and videos
Never get lost again! Use Maps and GPS
See weather in multiple locations
Clock, alarm and stop-watch
Calculator
Listen to music or watch videos
Browse the web

iPhone 5 Specifications

Cellular and wireless capabilities

The iPhone 5 is a Quad band phone which uses GSM and GPRS/EDGE.

There is also built-in Wi-Fi (802.11b/g) and Bluetooth. The iPhone also includes Global Positioning System (GPS) software, making it easy to geotag your pictures and videos. iPhone 5 also uses 3G and 4G networks where available.

Battery

Unlike most cell phones, the user cannot take the battery out for replacement. The iPhone uses a built-in battery which is charged using a USB connection to the computer, or using the lightning charger supplied by Apple.

Beware

You cannot remove the iPhone battery. This has to be carried out by Apple.

What do you get from a full charge?

Activity	Hours
Talk time	7 (3G)
Standby	300
Internet use	10 (Wi-Fi) 6 (3G)
Video playback	10
Audio playback	40

Internal storage

The iPhone uses internal flash drive storage. There is no SD or other card slot so the internal flash memory is all the storage you have – use it wisely!

iPhone 5 is available with 16 GB, 32 GB or 64 GB storage capacity.

If you intend to keep videos as well as music on your iPhone it may be wise to opt for the higher capacity iPhone. In terms of color, you can get the iPhone in Black & Slate or White & Silver.

What can I do with the storage space?

	16GB	32GB	64GB
Songs	3,500	7,000	14,000
Videos	20 hours	40 hours	80 hours
Photos	20,000	25,000	50,000

Sensors in the iPhone

There are four sensors in the iPhone: the Three-Axis Gyro, the Accelerometer, Proximity Sensor and the Ambient Light Sensor.

The *Accelerometer* enables the phone to detect rotation and position. This is important when switching from portrait to landscape viewing. The Accelerometer is also used in many of the iPhone game apps such as *Labyrinth* (below) which uses the Accelerometer to good effect – as you tilt the iPhone the ball bearing moves across a virtual board.

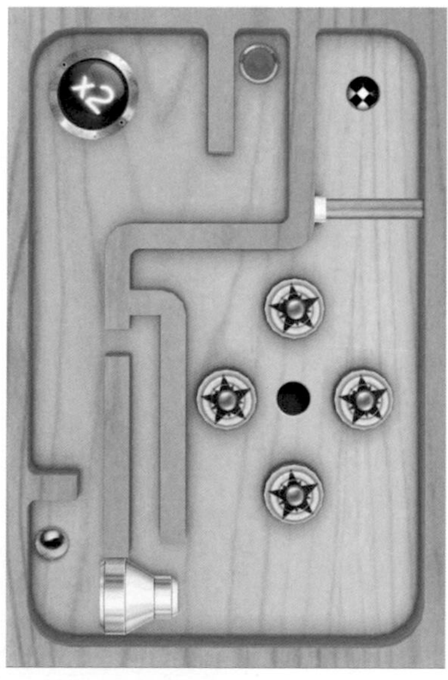

The *Proximity Sensor* switches off the iPhone screen when you make a call – it senses that the phone is close to the ear, saving valuable power. The *Ambient Light Sensor* adjusts the iPhone screen to the ambient lighting, again saving energy if a bright screen is not required.

The iPhone Itself

Unlike most cell phones, the iPhone is unusual since it has very few physical buttons.

Hot tip

Press the Sleep/Wake (On/Off) button as soon as you have finished using the iPhone – this helps conserve battery power.

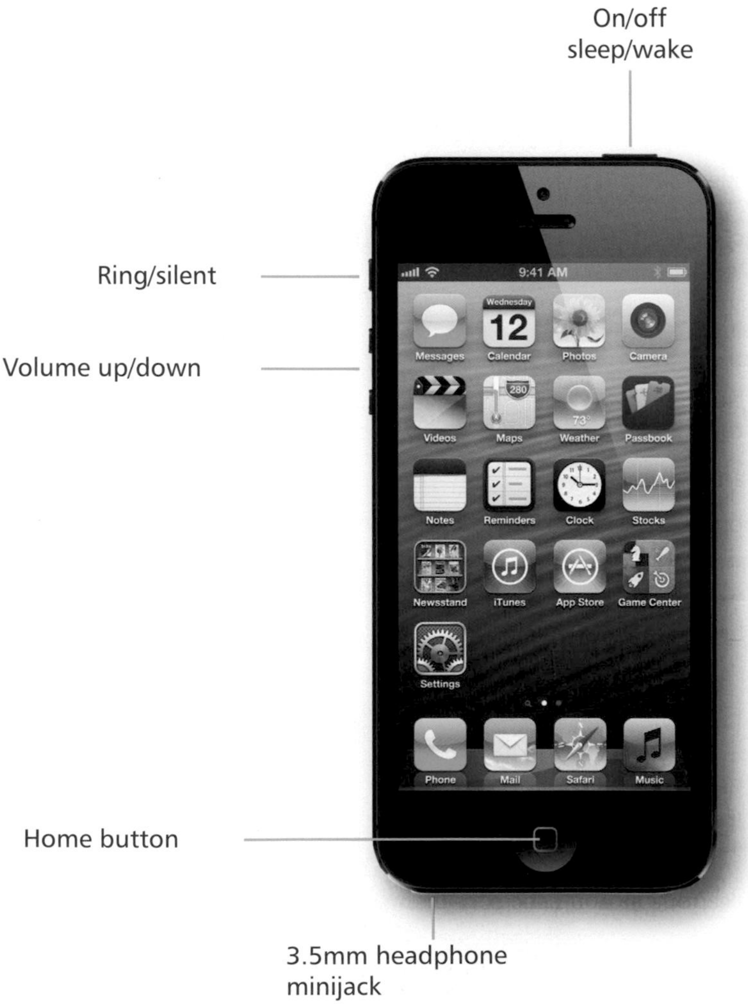

Buttons you need to know on the iPhone

- Sleep/Wake (On/Off)
- Ring/Silent
- Volume controls
- Home button

On/off sleep/wake

Ring/silent

Volume up/down

Home button

3.5mm headphone minijack

Sleep/Wake

Press and briefly hold this button if your iPhone is switched off. You will see the Apple logo and the loading screen will start up. You will then be taken to the Home screen (opposite page).

If you wish to put your phone away, press the Sleep/Wake button to put your phone to sleep. This button is also useful if you wish to forward a caller to Voicemail.

Ring/Silent

You often want your phone on silent, during meetings for example. The Ring/Silent button can be toggled up and down. When you see the red line, this means the iPhone is on silent.

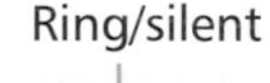

This position is Sounds OFF (mute)
Flip up for Sounds ON

The Home button

This does what the name suggests and brings you back to the Home page from wherever you are. If you are browsing applications in another screen, pressing the Home button will bring you right back to the Home page. If you are using an app, pressing Home will close the app. If you are on a phone call, pressing the Home button lets you access your email or other apps.

Press here to return to the Home screen or quit an application

Hot tip

Pressing the The Home button quits an app, and if you press again it will take you back to the Home Screen.

Other Buttons on the iPhone

Volume controls

Volume is controlled using two separate buttons – a **+** and **–** button (increase and decrease volume respectively). You can easily adjust the volume of the audio output when you are listening to the Music app, or when you are making a phone call. If you cannot hear the caller very well try increasing the volume.

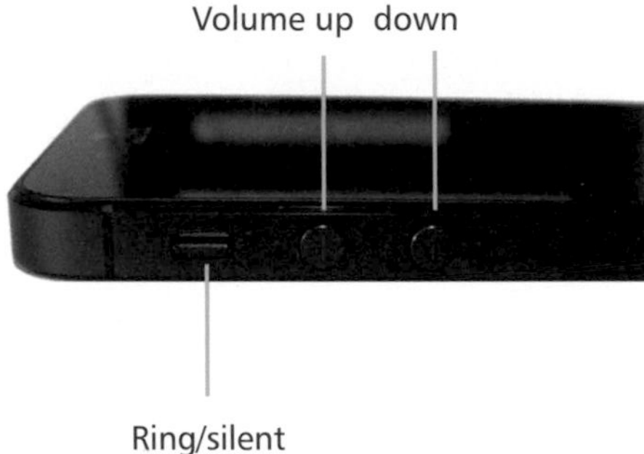

The Nano SIM slot

The iPhone 5 uses a nano SIM (much smaller than micro SIM which is used in older iPhone models). Apple provides a SIM removal tool in the iPhone box.

Insert SIM tool into this hole and push down. The SIM card holder will pop up and you can remove or insert a SIM card

Lightning connector, speaker, microphone, and headset jack

These are located at the bottom of the iPhone.

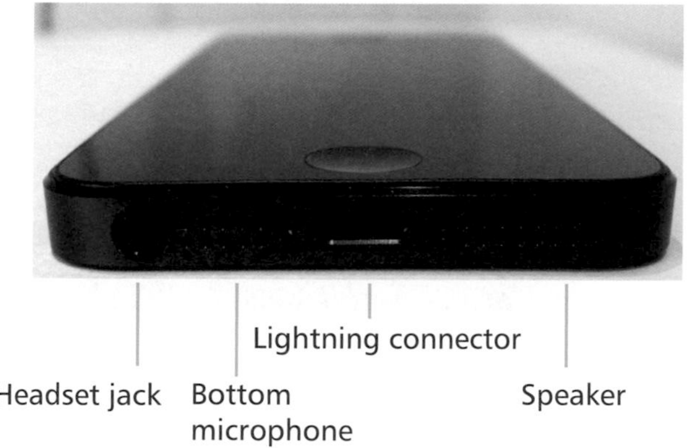

Back view of the iPhone 5

This shows the location of the main camera and the LED flash (flash is not available for the front camera).

The Home Screen

What's on the Home Screen?

When you turn the iPhone on you will see some icons which are fixed, such as the top bar with the time and battery charge indicator, as well as the dock at the bottom which holds four apps. By default, your iPhone will have Phone, Mail, Safari and Music on the bottom dock. You can move these off the dock if you want, but Apple puts these here because they are the most commonly-used apps, and having them on the dock makes them easy to find.

Just above the dock you will see a magnifying glass and two or more dots. The dots represent each of your screens – the more apps you install, the more screens you will need to accommodate them (you are allowed 11 in all). The illustration here shows an iPhone with two screens, and the Home Screen is the one we are viewing. If you flicked to the next screen, the second dot would be white and the first one would be black. In effect, these are meant to let you know where you are at any time.

Hot tip

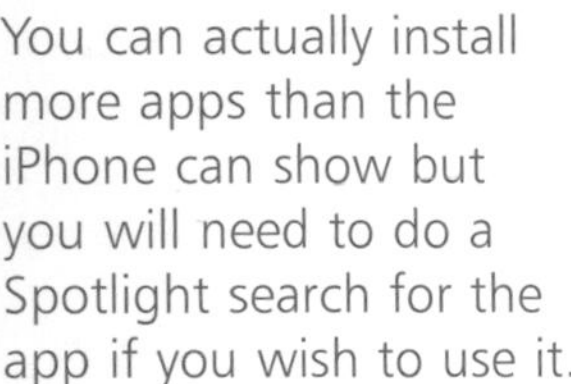

You can actually install more apps than the iPhone can show but you will need to do a Spotlight search for the app if you wish to use it.

Beware

The Battery indicator is fairly crude. For a more accurate guide, try switching on Battery % in Settings.

Hot tip

Spotlight searching works like a dream on the iPhone – use it if you want to find appointments, contacts and other items.

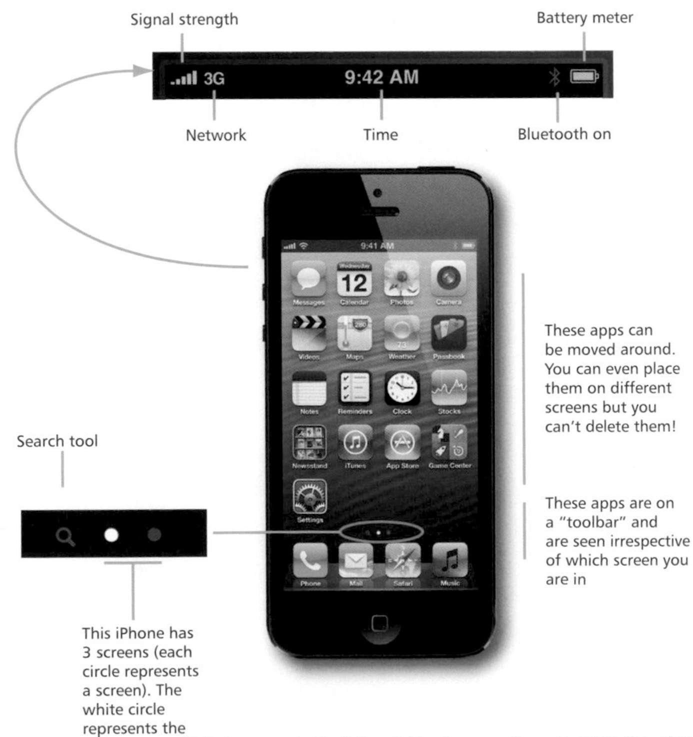
Signal strength
Battery meter
3G
9:42 AM
Network
Time
Bluetooth on
These apps can be moved around. You can even place them on different screens but you can't delete them!
Search tool
These apps are on a "toolbar" and are seen irrespective of which screen you are in
This iPhone has 3 screens (each circle represents a screen). The white circle represents the active screen (flick the screen to the left or right using your finger to get to the other screens)

Default Applications

The iPhone comes with applications that are part of the operating system. The core set here cannot be deleted.

Messages

Notes

Calendar

Photos

Calculator

Clock

Camera

Settings

Maps

iTunes Store

Phone

Weather

Stocks

App Store

Email

VoiceMemos

Safari

Game Center

Music

Videos

Newsstand

Reminders

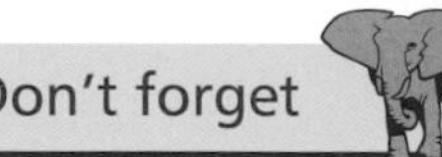

You cannot delete any of the standard apps – only the ones you add yourself.

Software version iOS 6

iOS 6 brings with it many new features across the entire range of iOS devices.

Maps

These are now provided by TomTom and include 3D Flyover, turn-by-turn navigation and several new features. At the time of writing there are problems with the Maps app (old data included in the maps, for example) but these glitches will be corrected as Apple updates the app.

Flyover view

Turn-by-turn navigation

Improved Siri

Including the ability to open apps using Siri.

Facebook integration

Facebook is solidly integrated into iOS 6 devices making it easier to post updates from many apps without having to log in to Facebook each time.

Share Photo Streams

You can elect to share photos with specific individuals running iOS 6.

Passbook

This app lets you store boarding passes, coupons and many other types of information so they are all available in one single location.

FaceTime

You can now have FaceTime chats using cellular data (previously FaceTime was limited to Wi-Fi connections only).

Phone improvements

When you receive a phone call you can elect to send to Voicemail, reply to the caller with a text message, and set up reminders to call them back later.

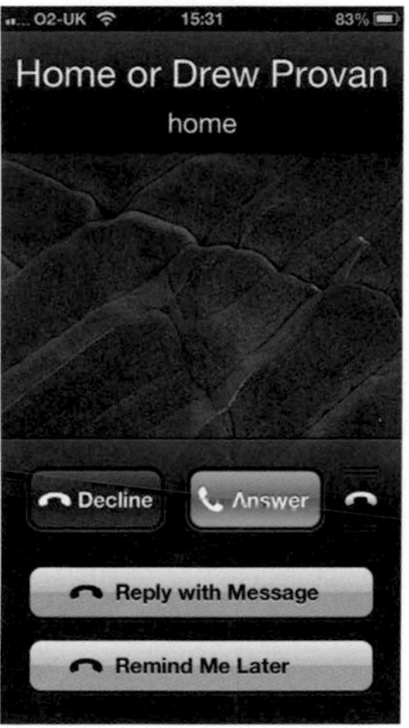

Do Not Disturb

This allows you to silence the iPhone at specific times, for example during the night. You can configure Do Not Disturb so that the iPhone will ring *only* if a family member or other specific individual calls.

Safari

You can browse Safari on one device and pick up where you left off due to iCloud syncing.

Camera

You can now take panoramas which are stitched together effortlessly.

The Touch Screen Display

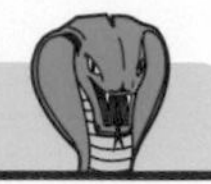

Beware

The touch screen works best using skin contact. You can buy special gloves that will work but standard gloves cannot be used.

The iPhone uses a touch-sensitive screen for input, using gestures and a virtual keyboard. The screen is 3.5 inches (diagonal) and has a resolution of 1136 x 640-pixel resolution at 326 PPI (Pixels Per Inch) – Apple has called this the *Retina Display* because the resolution is so high. This results in great clarity when viewing the browser or watching movies on the iPhone. Although the iPhone has a fingerprint-resistant coating it still gets grubby. A number of companies make screen protectors (sticky plastic sheets that cover the entire screen) but they are probably not necessary since the screen is made from scratch-resistant glass. You can also protect the other parts of the iPhone from scratching by using a protective case.

Touch screen features

The screen is able to detect touch using skin. If you wear gloves or try to tap the screen using a stylus nothing will happen – it responds best to skin.

Tapping

Tapping with one finger is used for lots of apps. It's a bit like clicking with the mouse. You tap apps to open them, to open hyperlinks, to select photo albums which then open, to enter text using the keyboard, and many other tasks.

Sliding

Sliding is another common action. When you first press the iPhone Home button you will see an option at the bottom of the screen to Slide to Unlock. Putting your finger on the arrow button then sliding all the way to the right will then take you to the Home Screen. You also use the slide action to answer phone calls and shut down the iPhone.

Dragging

This is used to move documents that occupy more than a screen's worth across the screen. Maps use this feature, as do web pages. Place your finger on the screen, keep it there and move the image to where you want it.

Pinching and spreading

If you are looking at a photo or text which you want to enlarge, you can spread two fingers apart and the image will become larger. Keep doing this until it's the size you want. If you want to zoom out and make the image smaller, pinch your fingers together.

Flicking

If you are faced with a long list, e.g. in Contacts, you can flick the list up or down by placing your finger at the bottom or top of the screen, keeping your finger on the screen, then flicking your finger downwards or upwards and the list will fly up or down.

Shake the iPhone

When entering text or copying and pasting, to undo what you have done, shake the iPhone. Shake again to redo.

Portrait or landscape mode

The iPhone is generally viewed in a portrait mode but for many tasks it is easier to turn the iPhone and work in landscape mode. If you're in Mail, or using Safari, the text will be larger. More importantly, the keys of the virtual keyboard will become larger making it easier to type accurately.

Entering text

The iPhone has predictive text, but this is unlike any you may have used before. The accuracy is astonishing. As you type, the iPhone will make suggestions before you complete a word. If you agree with the suggested word, tap the spacebar. If you disagree, tap the small "x" next to the word.

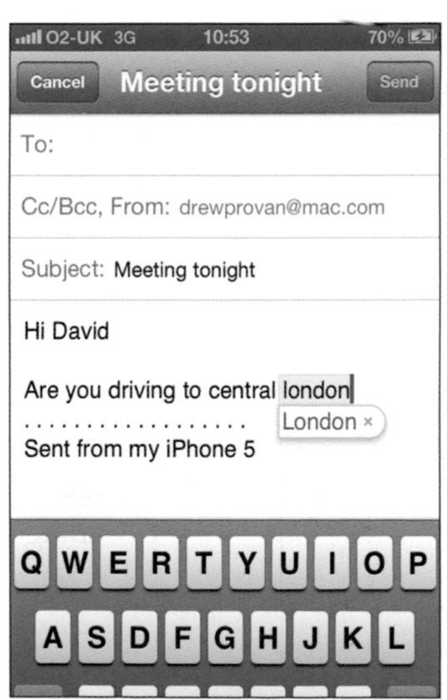

Accept the capitalized word by tapping the spacebar

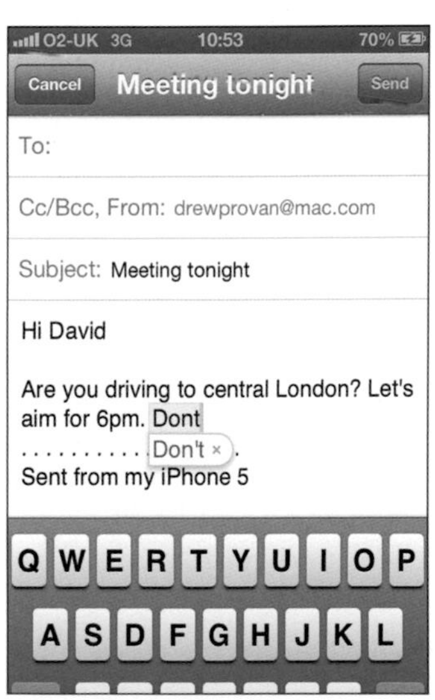

Accept the apostrophe by tapping the spacebar

Hot tip

You can shake your iPhone to skip audio tracks, undo and redo text, and more.

Hot tip

To accept a spelling suggestion tap the spacebar. Reject the suggestion by clicking the "x". Over time your iPhone will learn new words.

Hot tip

Tapping the spacebar with two fingers at the same time also inserts a period.

The Virtual Keyboard

Hot tip

The iPhone has done away with virtually all buttons and provides a software-based QWERTY keyboard. The keyboard becomes visible automatically when needed.

The keys are small but when you touch them they become larger, which increases accuracy. The letter "H" below has been pressed and has become much larger.

There are all the usual features of a computer keyboard, including spacebar, delete key, shift, numbers and symbols .?123 .

To correct a word, touch the word you want to correct and hold your finger on the word. You will see a magnifying glass. Move your finger to where you want the insertion point (|) to be, stop there and delete any wrong letters.

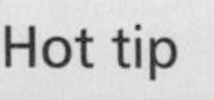

Hot tip

Some keys such as Currency and URL endings can be accessed by holding down the key. A pop-up will show the options.

The keyboard has automatic spellcheck and correction of misspelled words. It has a dynamic dictionary (learns new words). Some keys have multiple options if you hold them down, e.g. hold down the £ key and you'll see the other characters.

Where's Caps Lock?

It is frustrating hitting the Caps key for every letter if you want to type a complete word in upper case. But you can activate Caps Lock easily:

- Go to **Settings** > **General**
- Select **Keyboard**
- Make sure the **Caps Lock** slider is set to **ON**
- While you are there, make sure the other settings are on, for example "." **Shortcut** – this helps you add a period by tapping the spacebar twice (much like the BlackBerry)

Other settings for the keyboard

- **Auto-Correction** suggests the correct word. If it annoys you, switch it off
- **Auto-Capitalization** is great for putting capitals in names
- The "." **Shortcut** types a period every time you hit the spacebar twice. This saves time when typing long emails but if you prefer not to use this, switch it off. Here's another neat trick – you can also insert a period by tapping the spacebar with two fingers simultaneously

It's a good idea to activate Caps Lock. To use, just tap Shift twice – the shift button should turn blue if you have activated it properly in the Settings control panel.

Register Your iPhone

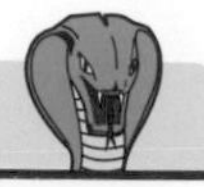

Beware

Unlike conventional cell phones, you have to register your iPhone with Apple before you can use it.

Before you can do anything on your iPhone you will need to activate it.

Once you switch on the new iPhone 5 (press the On/Off switch) you will be taken through a series of screens where you set up various options.

Even though the initial setup is carried out wirelessly, you should plug your iPhone 5 into your Mac or PC regularly to make sure you have a recent backup of the iPhone in case you lose or damage the iPhone.

If you have a recent backup it is very easy to plug a brand new iPhone 5 in to your Mac or PC and restore your files and apps, saving you a major headache!

The first screen you see is

Set the **location**

Enable **Location Services** (needed for Maps and many other apps) and join a **Wi-Fi** network

Choose whether to set the iPhone up as a new iPhone or restored from a previous backup (from your old iPhone)

Enter your **Apple ID** or create an account if you do not have an Apple ID (you will need an Apple ID to purchase apps)

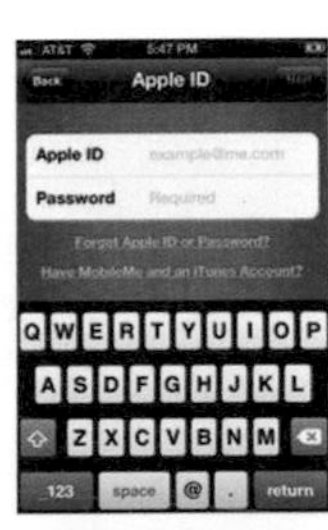

You can use **iCloud** storage if you want to (advisable to turn this on)

You will then be given the option to activate **Find My iPhone**. This is very useful in case your iPhone is lost or stolen

You can choose whether to use Siri or not. It is probably best to select **Use Siri**

Don't forget

You need to set yourself up with an Apple ID. Do this using iTunes or using the iPhone when you first set it up.

Synchronize Data with a PC

Syncing your iPhone 5 with a PC is easy. There are several ways to sync Contacts, Calendars, and other items (two-way) between your PC and iPhone 5:

1. iTunes sync using the wired route
2. iTunes sync using Wi-Fi option
3. Using iCloud (requires an iCloud account)

Sync between iPhone 5 and PC using the wired route

1. Connect your iPhone 5 to your PC using the Lightning cable that was supplied in the box
2. Open iTunes if it does not open automatically
3. Name your iPhone

4. Work your way across the tabs choosing exactly how you want to sync (for example, automatically), which music tracks, photos, podcasts, etc.

5. Click Sync and your iPhone 5 will be backed up and synced with your PC

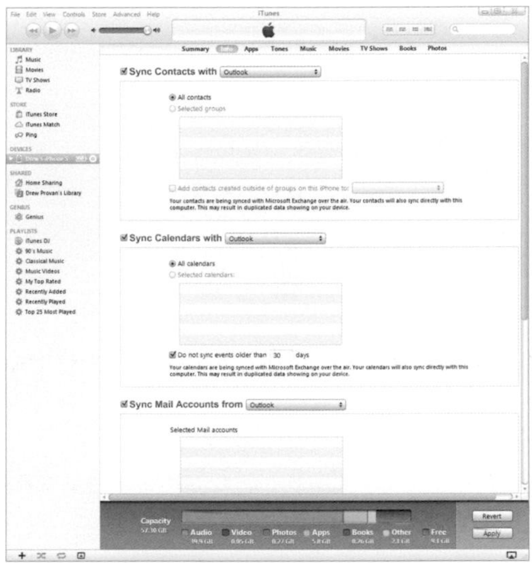

Sync between iPhone 5 and iTunes using the Wi-Fi route

1. Sync using the wired route as described above, for the first sync

2. Once you choose the option **Sync with this iPhone over Wi-Fi** option the iPhone will sync once a day as long as: the iPhone is connected to a power source, the iPhone and PC are connected to the same wireless network, and iTunes on the PC is running

iCloud sync

You can use iCloud to sync music tracks, apps, photos and other items. You will need an iCloud account in order to do this. You can choose whether to only allow iCloud sync when connected to a wireless network or allow the sync to be performed using the cellular network (if you have a limited data plan, e.g. 1 GB or less per month, try not to use the cellular iCloud sync method to avoid using up your data allowance).

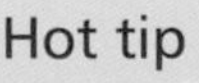

iCloud lets you sync emails, contacts, calendars and other items wirelessly (no need to physically plug the iPhone into the computer).

Synchronize Data with a Mac

You can change the sync options later if you no longer want to sync specific items.

Syncing data with the Mac is very straightforward

- Plug the iPhone into the Mac
- iTunes will open automatically
- Click on the iPhone icon on the left of the iTunes window
- Work your way through the tabs selecting what to sync

Each tab controls syncing of different items such as Music, Photos, Podcasts etc

This visual shows you how much space you have used, and with which items

How much space do I have left?

The picture above shows an iPhone plugged into the Mac. At the bottom of the iTunes window you can see a bar representing the total iPhone capacity. This one has about 9 GB free.

Be selective in the items you sync

The largest item on my iPhone is music, which takes up almost 39.8 GB. Each type of sync item (Music, Video, Photos, etc.) is given a different color, so you can see at a glance what's taking up the space. If you are running out of room because you have too many videos on the iPhone, you can go to the Video tab and deselect one or more videos then hit Apply. Those files will then be removed from the iPhone.

Uncheck videos then hit Apply to remove them from the iPhone

What can be synced?

- Contacts
- Calendars
- Email accounts
- Web page bookmarks
- Notes
- Ringtones
- Music and audiobooks
- Photos
- Podcasts
- Movies
- TV shows
- Music videos
- Applications from the app store

Back up and Restore

Hot tip

Plug your iPhone into your PC or Mac regularly. This ensures you have a recent backup file in the event your iPhone needs to be restored.

Each time you plug the iPhone into your computer it will back up your data, then it will synchronize your iPhone using the settings on your computer. If you have added new photos or music these will be sent to the iPhone.

If you look at the top of the iTunes window when you connect the phone you will see the iPhone being backed up, then synced.

This is what you see at the top of the iTunes window during the synchronization process:

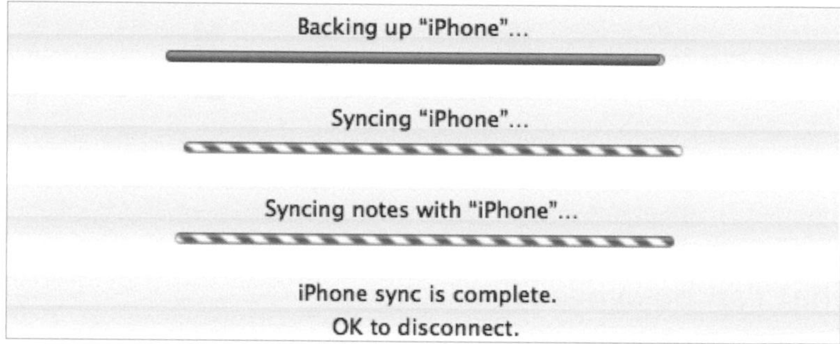

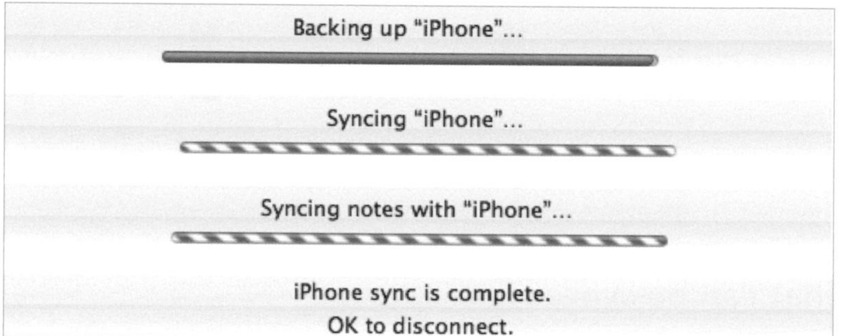

Normally things work well but occasionally the iPhone, like any electronic device, can misbehave. Just as you might restore Windows from a snapshot, so too can you restore the iPhone back to the last working version. If you are syncing your iPhone on a regular basis, you will have a recent backup from which to restore. If you have not been syncing and creating backups, you may have to erase the iPhone and reconfigure.

Hot tip

Unlike an iPod, where you have to eject it from the PC or Mac before unplugging, you don't have to eject the iPhone – simply unplug it.

To restore the iPhone from a backup

Right-click on the iPhone icon in the Devices window in iTunes. Choose **Restore from Backup....**

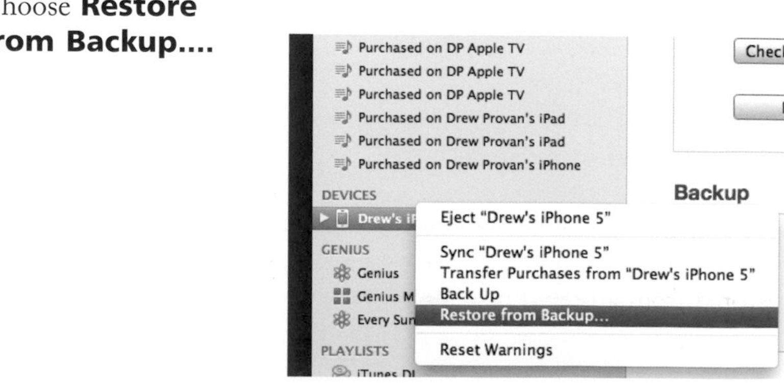

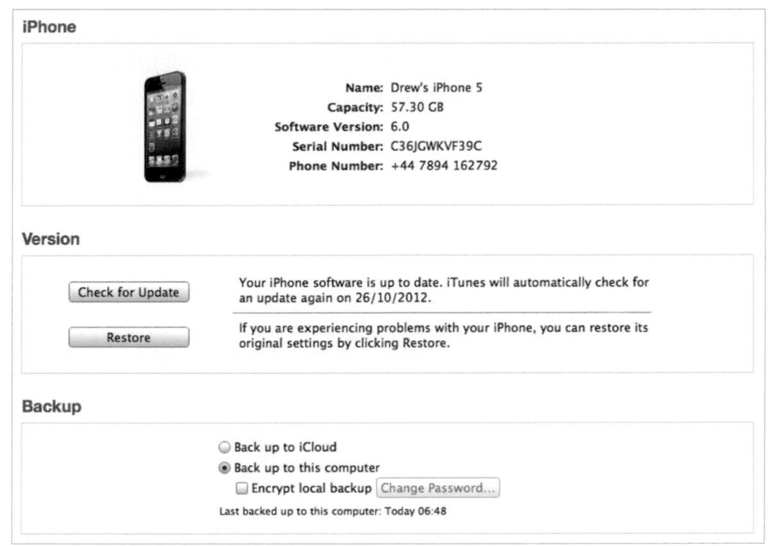

Click **Restore**:

Once you click **Restore** you will be led through the whole process, during which the iPhone will be erased and the latest saved iPhone state will be restored. Your iPhone should then function as normal.

It's a good idea to sync your iPhone with iTunes fairly often even if you do not sync music, video or apps. You can plug the iPhone into a wall charger, but you lack the backup files needed for a restore should your iPhone become unstable and need to be restored from a previous snapshot.

Airplane Mode

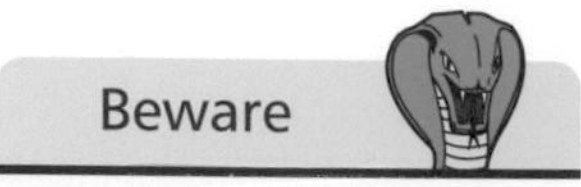

You must switch off Wi-Fi and Bluetooth on airplanes. This is a simple procedure using Airplane Mode.

When to use this mode

There are times when using the cellular or data networks is not allowed, for example when on an aircraft. Some cell phones allow you to switch off GPRS, EDGE, Wi-Fi, and Bluetooth individually before take-off. The iPhone has a single Airplane mode setting that switches off all these communications, making it safe for you to use your iPhone to watch movies or listen to music on the flight.

Airplane mode is also very useful if you want to conserve battery power, since using the cellular network, Wi-Fi and Bluetooth drains the power on the iPhone. If you don't need these, switch them off.

Where is it?

Go to **Settings** and slide the button beside **Airplane Mode** to the right.

Use Airplane Mode to reduce power consumption when your battery is running out.

How do you know Airplane Mode is switched on?

You can tell by the icon on the top left of the iPhone. You will see a picture of an airplane:

The other icons to look for include the cellular network icon, Wi-Fi and Bluetooth. It is very obvious when these are on.

Hot tip

You know you are in Airplane Mode by the plane icon at the top of the iPhone.

Headphones

Apple supplies headphones that look a bit like iPod headphones. But there is a major difference: the iPhone headphones have a control on the right earpiece cable. This control houses the microphone needed for phone conversations when the headphones are plugged in. The control also allows the audio volume to be adjusted to make it louder or quieter.

By clicking the control, audio will pause. Two clicks in quick succession will skip to the next track.

Hot tip

The iPhone headphones are highly sophisticated and can be used to make calls, and divert callers to voicemail.

Press here ONCE to pause audio or answer call (press again at end of call)

To decline call press and hold for ~2 seconds

To switch to incoming or on-hold call, press once

Press here TWICE to skip to next track

To use Voice Control, press and hold

(this tiny control unit also contains the microphone!)

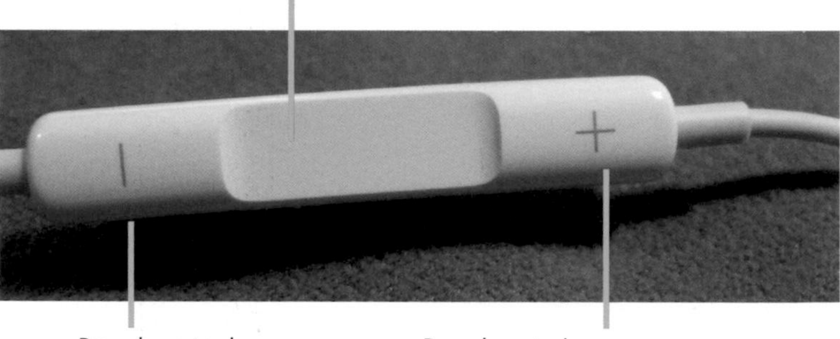

Press here to decrease volume

Press here to increase volume

Uses for the headphones – this is pretty obvious but consider

- Listening to music, podcasts, audio books
- Listening to the radio
- Watching movies
- Making phone calls
- Dictating VoiceMemos
- Giving Voice commands to your iPhone

Audio and Video Playback

As you would expect, the iPhone supports a number of audio and video formats. The iPhone supports audio in the form of AAC, Protected AAC, MP3, MP3 VBF, Audible (formats 2, 3, and 4), Apple Lossless, AIFF and WAV. In terms of video, the iPhone supports video at 640 x 480 pixels, 30 frames per second (FPS), .m4v, .mp4, .mov and MPEG-4 files.

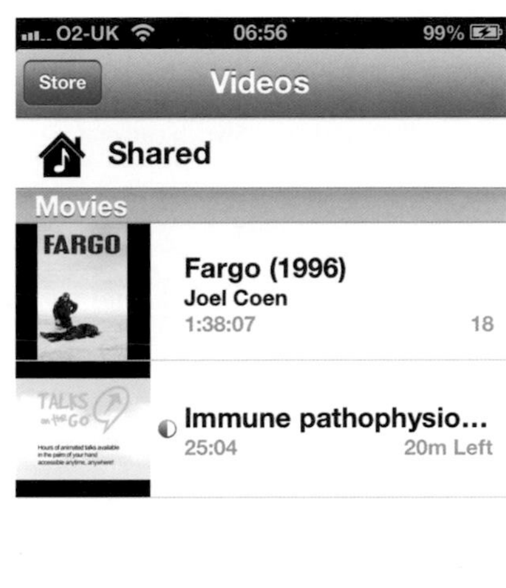

Audio files are played using the Music app in portrait or landscape mode. Video content, including YouTube, is played only in landscape mode.

Camera

You can take better night pictures if you use the Night Camera app.

The iPhone 5 has a main camera (back of phone) and a second camera on the front. The main camera is 8 megapixels (MP), and can shoot high resolution stills and HD video. The main camera also has a flash. The front VGA camera is used for FaceTime calls, and can takes photos and videos of you. This camera takes 1.2 MP photos and HD video (720p) up to 30 frames per second.

Both photos and videos can be geotagged, so you can see where in the world you were when the photo or video was shot.

Hot tip

Geotagging helps you determine where the photo was taken but you need to switch on Settings > Location Services.

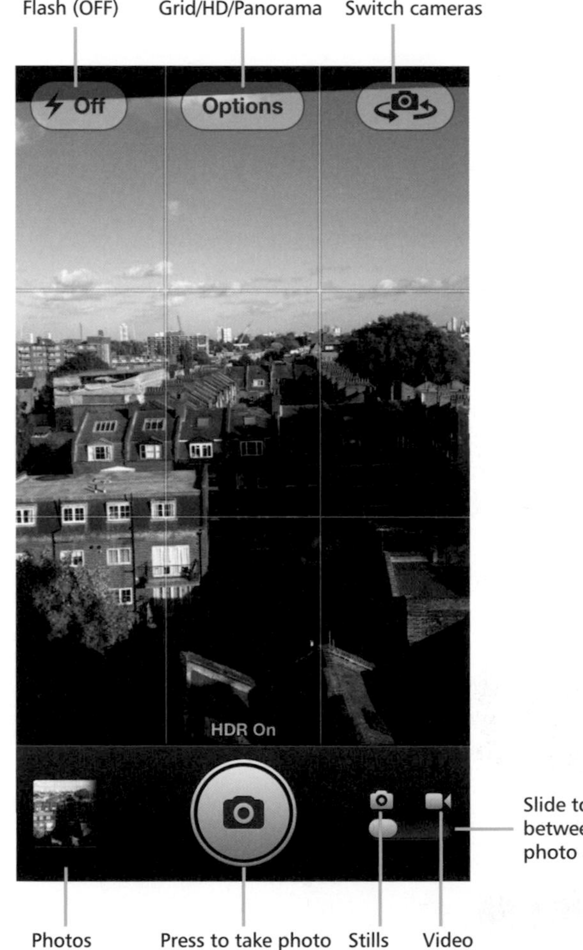

Shooting video

Slide the Stills/Video control to the right and you will see a Record button (red circle). Press to record video then press again to stop. The video will be stored and transferred to the computer when you next sync. Alternatively, you can email or MMS the video.

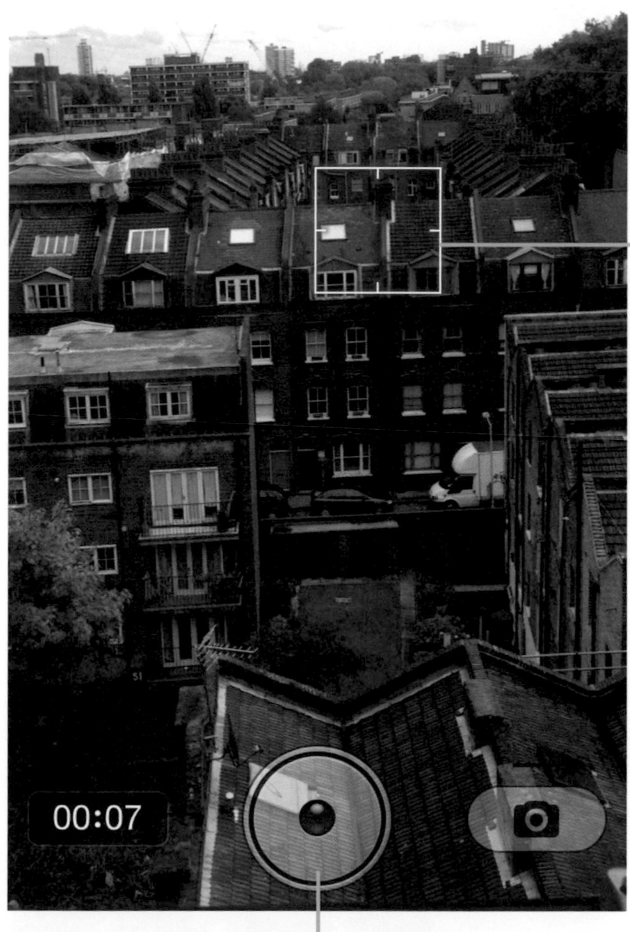

Autofocus

Press to take record video
Press again to stop recording

Customizing the iPhone

Applications

The iPhone comes with many apps preinstalled by Apple. These can be moved around, or even placed on a different screen, but you cannot delete them from the iPhone. These apps are the core features of the iPhone.

The App Store has thousands of apps which we will look at later. Many are free while others are available for purchase. With so many apps available for download the chances are that there will be an app for most things you might want to do.

Ringtones

Apple has supplied several but people will always want to have their own unique ringtone. You can buy these from the App Store or make your own using iTunes or GarageBand. You can assign a specific ringtone to someone in your Contacts list so you know it's them calling when the phone rings.

Backgrounds and wallpapers

Again, there are several to choose from but you can make your own (use one of your photos) or you can download from third party suppliers. Try browsing the Internet for wallpapers or use a specific app.

Accessorizing the iPhone

You can use a screen protector to prevent scratches on the screen. There are many iPhone cases available. These are mainly plastic but leather cases are available as well. Placing your iPhone in a case or cover helps prevent marks or scratches on the phone.

Headphones

If you want to use headphones other than those provided by Apple, that's fine. You may get better sound from your music but you will not have the inbuilt microphone, which is very useful when you make a phone call.

Lightning to 30-pin Adapter

Most of us have chargers round the house, or radio alarms and other iPhone/iPod music players that use the standard 30-pin dock connector. Apple has replaced this connector with the Lightning Connector which will make all your other 30-pin dock connector devices obsolete unless you buy the Apple Lightning to 30-pin Adapter. This should give a new lease of life to your existing devices that use the older 30-pin dock.

USB to Lightning charger cable

With extensive use the iPhone 5 battery may not last the whole day so you will probably need to carry around a spare charging cable. The USB to Lightning cable means you can plug it in to your PC or Mac at work and charge your iPhone during the day.

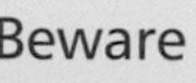

Bluetooth drains power on your iPhone. Try to switch it off if you don't need it.

User Settings

There are many settings you can adjust in order to set the iPhone up to work the way you want. These will be discussed in detail later but they are shown briefly here.

As well as the settings already on the iPhone, many apps will have panels for their settings. If an app is not working the way you want, have a look under the Settings Control Panel and scroll to the bottom to see if your app has installed a settings panel.

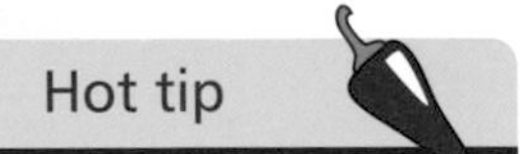

Many apps have their own settings. Go to Settings on the iPhone and scroll down to the bottom of the screen.

Wi-Fi

Keep this off if you want to conserve power. Switching it on will let you join wireless networks if they are open or if you have the password.

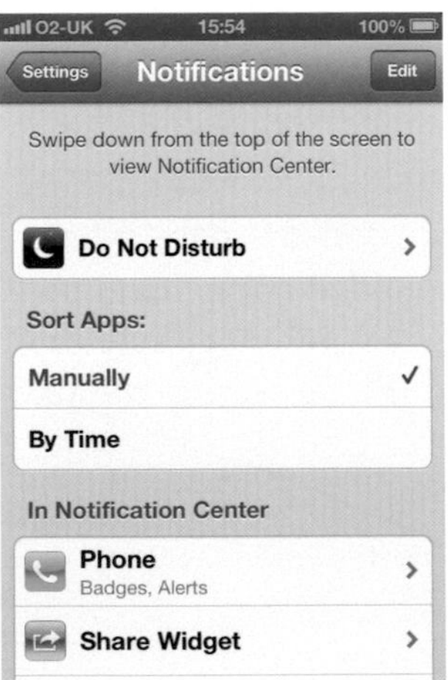

Notifications

You can allow applications, such as Skype and others, to notify you of messages even if the program is not running. This means that if you are using an app like Skype, but you are using another app when a friend sends you a message, a notification will appear on your screen to let you know you have received a message.

Sounds

You can place the phone on vibrate or have the ringtone on. You can assign different tones for different contacts.

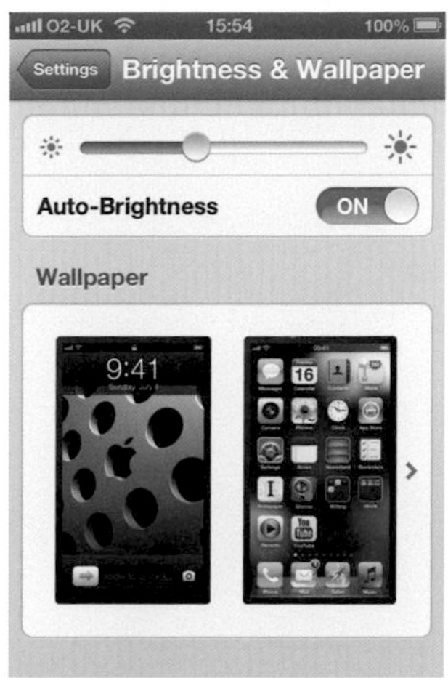

Brightness

The iPhone will adjust brightness automatically. If you always prefer it dimmer or brighter – switch automatic brightness off.

You can assign specific ringtones to selected contacts.

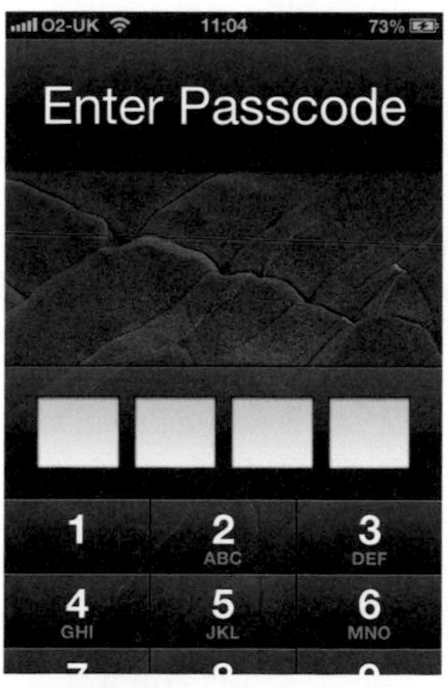

Wallpaper

Wallpaper is what you see when you press the Home Button when the iPhone is locked. Use you own images or download from third party suppliers.

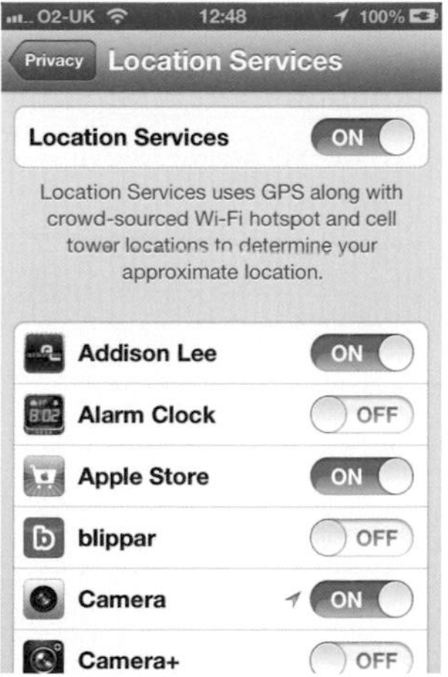

Location Services

You need to switch this on (Settings > Privacy > Location Services) in order to allow Maps and other apps to work out where you are in the world.

...cont'd

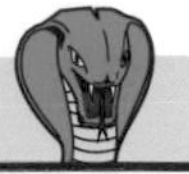

Beware

Your data on the iPhone is easily accessible if your iPhone is stolen. Use Passcode Lock and set to wipe phone after 10 failed attempts.

Passcode Lock

If you want to prevent people using your phone, add a passcode lock. This is a 4-digit password which will keep the iPhone contents free from prying eyes. You can also choose a complex passcode.

For added security you can switch on the *Wipe After 10 Failed Attempts* setting to prevent data theft.

International

Here you can choose the language and keyboard you wish to use.

You can activate multiple International languages if you use more than one. Activating the Korean keyboard is very useful if you want to change the font in the Notes app (*see* Chapter 6).

Hot tip

The iPhone has several settings that make it usable by people with vision problems.

Accessibility

For people who have difficulties with vision or sound, there are many tools on the iPhone that can help the user obtain full functionality from their iPhone.

These features are described in greater detail in Chapter 9.

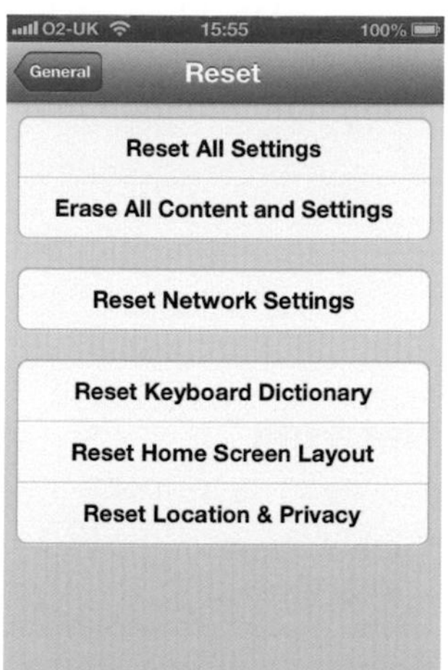

Reset

If all else fails, and your iPhone is causing problems, reset it back to factory conditions.

This is covered in greater detail in Chapter 11.

Here are the settings (preferences) for some of the apps installed on this iPhone. Not every app will install a settings panel but many do. It's worth checking Settings after you install an app to see if it has installed a settings file, since it may contain useful features to help you set it up exactly the way you want.

There are also settings options for:

Bluetooth

Keep this switched off when not needed (Bluetooth and Wi-Fi will drain your power faster). If you want to connect a Bluetooth headset or earpiece you will need to switch Bluetooth on and pair with your device.

Home Screen

You can go with the default Home Screen or choose your own.

Date and Time

This Control Panel adjusts the Date and Time.

Data Roaming

Most of us travel abroad for business or pleasure. We like to take our cell phones to keep in touch with friends, family and the office. Call charges are much higher from overseas, and if you want to receive data (email, browse the web, and other activities) you will need to switch on Data Roaming.

Beware

Data Roaming allows you to receive data when away from your home country, but is very expensive.

Switch on Data Roaming

1. Go to **Settings** > **General** > **Network**
2. Switch **Data Roaming** ON if required
3. Switch OFF when not needed

But beware – the cost of receiving data is very high and will be added to your phone bill. Your data package with your network supplier (e.g. AT&T, O2 etc.) will not cover the cost of downloading data using foreign networks!

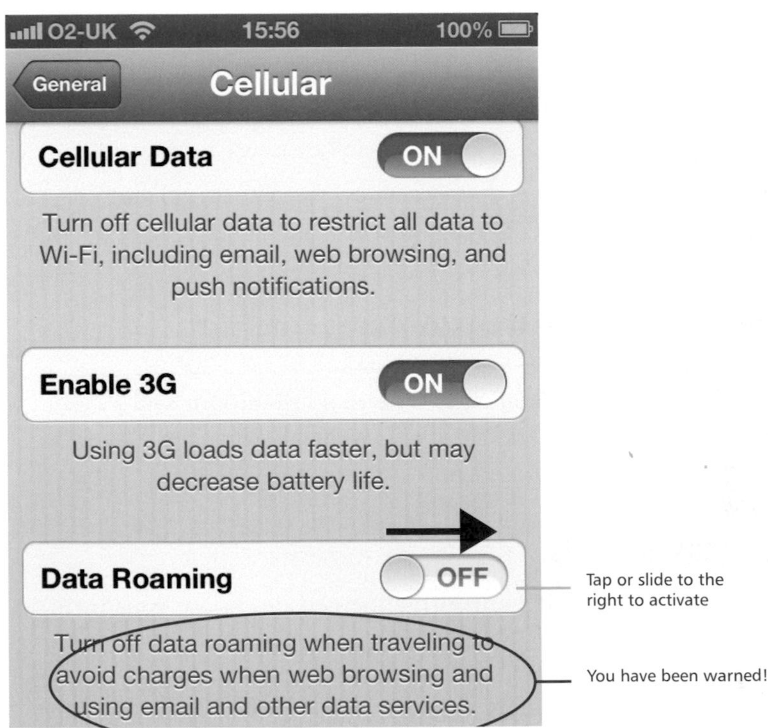

Tap or slide to the right to activate

You have been warned!

2 The Phone Functions

In this section we will look at how to use the phone functions, maintain contact lists, make calls using FaceTime, and keep these in sync with desktop computers. This chapter also explores Visual Voicemail, a revolutionary way to see your voicemail messages.

Assigning Ringtones

The iPhone has a number of polyphonic ringtones built in, or you can buy more from iTunes or even make your own. You can have the default tone for every caller or you can assign a specific tone for a contact.

To assign a ringtone

1. Select contact then click **Edit**
2. Under **Ringtone** press the right arrow
3. Choose the ringtone you wish to assign

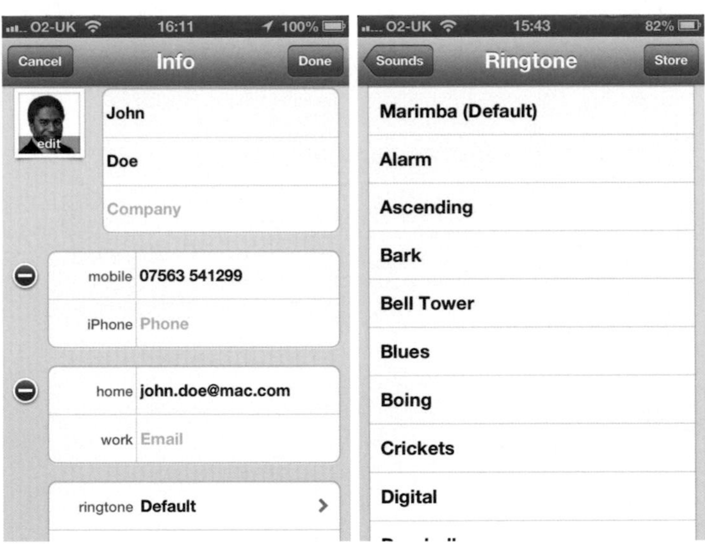

Hot tip

If you use a Mac, GarageBand is a great tool for creating custom ringtones. For instructions on using GarageBand to make ringtones see http://support.apple.com/kb/HT1358.

Obtaining new ringtones

You can buy these from the app store or make your own using GarageBand (Mac) or iTunes.

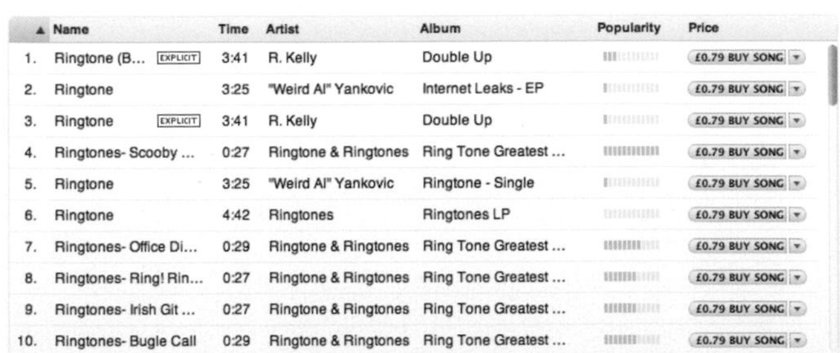

	Name		Time	Artist	Album	Popularity	Price
1.	Ringtone (B...	EXPLICIT	3:41	R. Kelly	Double Up		£0.79 BUY SONG
2.	Ringtone		3:25	"Weird Al" Yankovic	Internet Leaks - EP		£0.79 BUY SONG
3.	Ringtone	EXPLICIT	3:41	R. Kelly	Double Up		£0.79 BUY SONG
4.	Ringtones- Scooby ...		0:27	Ringtone & Ringtones	Ring Tone Greatest ...		£0.79 BUY SONG
5.	Ringtone		3:25	"Weird Al" Yankovic	Ringtone - Single		£0.79 BUY SONG
6.	Ringtone		4:42	Ringtones	Ringtones LP		£0.79 BUY SONG
7.	Ringtones- Office Di...		0:29	Ringtone & Ringtones	Ring Tone Greatest ...		£0.79 BUY SONG
8.	Ringtones- Ring! Rin...		0:27	Ringtone & Ringtones	Ring Tone Greatest ...		£0.79 BUY SONG
9.	Ringtones- Irish Git ...		0:27	Ringtone & Ringtones	Ring Tone Greatest ...		£0.79 BUY SONG
10.	Ringtones- Bugle Call		0:29	Ringtone & Ringtones	Ring Tone Greatest ...		£0.79 BUY SONG

Making Calls Using Keypad

Select the keypad icon. This brings up a standard keypad on the touch screen. Dial the number.

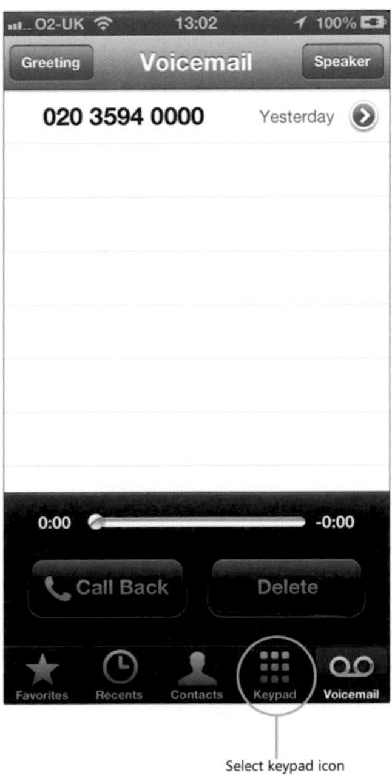

Make FaceTime Video Calls

To use FaceTime

- The caller and recipient must both use iPhone 4 or later
- Alternatively, you can use a FaceTime-enabled Mac
- FaceTime calls can be made using Wi-Fi or Cellular

The FaceTime settings

1. Go to **Settings > FaceTime > ON**
2. Select contact you wish to call
3. Tap **FaceTime**
4. Make FaceTime call
5. Recipient must tap **Accept**

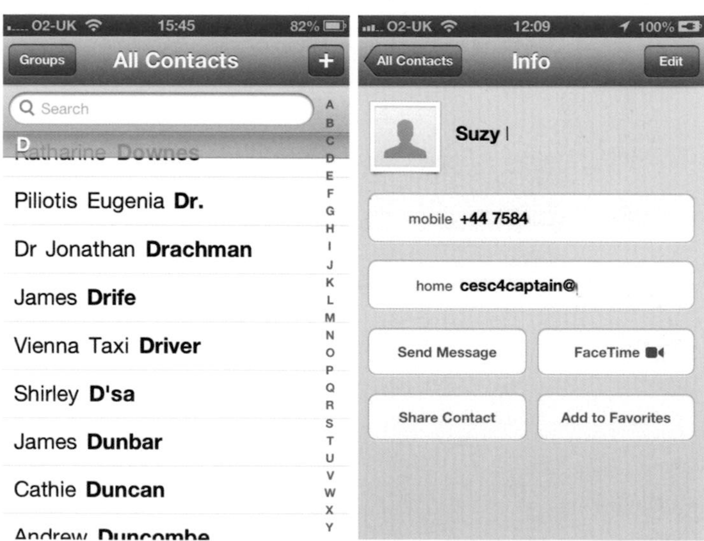

If you have already had a FaceTime video call with someone you can go to Recents and make another FaceTime call.

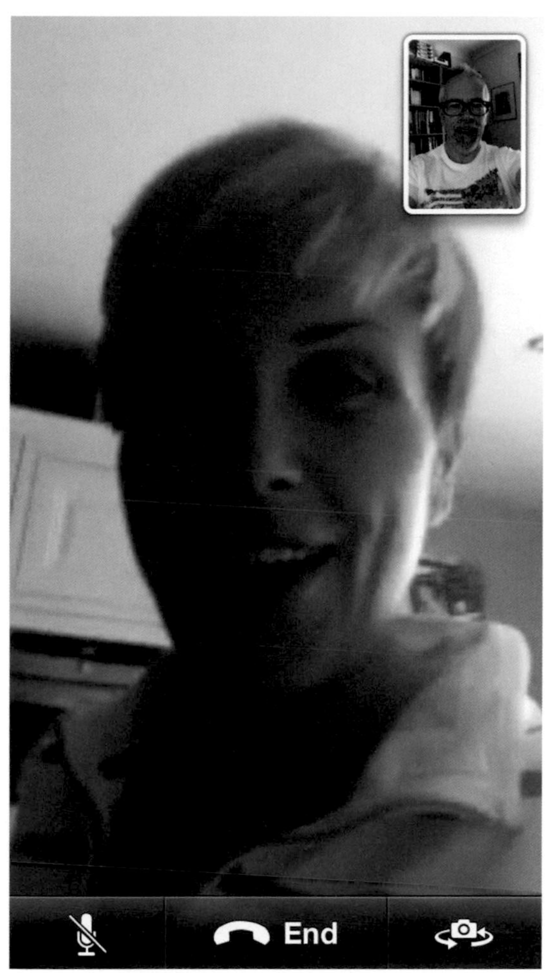

Actions during a FaceTime call

Mute the call	Tap [mute icon]. You are able to see and hear the caller, and the caller can see you but not hear you
Switch cameras (from front to main camera)	Tap [switch camera icon]
Use another app during a FaceTime call	Press the Home Button
End FaceTime call	Tap [End button]

Using the Contacts List

1. Tap the **Contacts** icon on the **Home Screen**
2. Flick up or down until you find the contact you wish to call
3. Select the action you wish to take, e.g. send text message, phone the contact

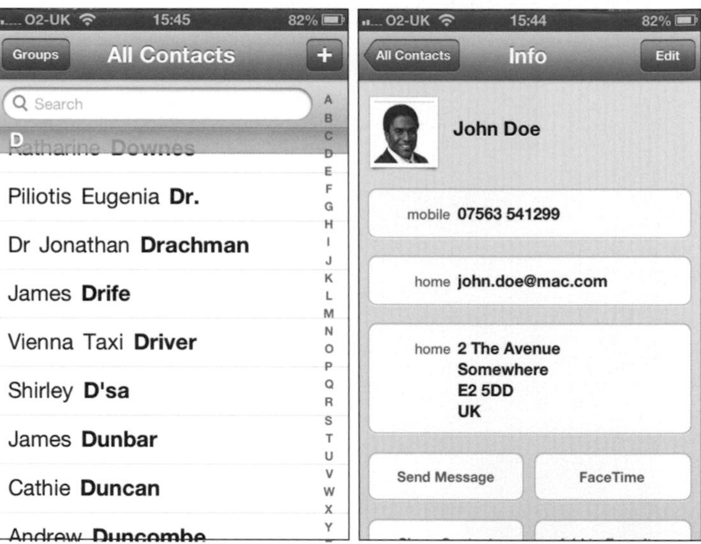

Add photo to contact

If you want to assign a photo to a contact, find the photo you want to use (or take one of the person) and tap **Assign to Contact**. This means that you get a more personalized phone call, instead of just seeing a name or a number on the screen.

Using the Favorites List

People you call regularly can be added to your favorites list. This is the first icon (from the left) when you open the phone application.

To add someone to your favorites list

1. Open **Contacts**
2. Select the contact you wish to add
3. Tap **Add to Favorites**

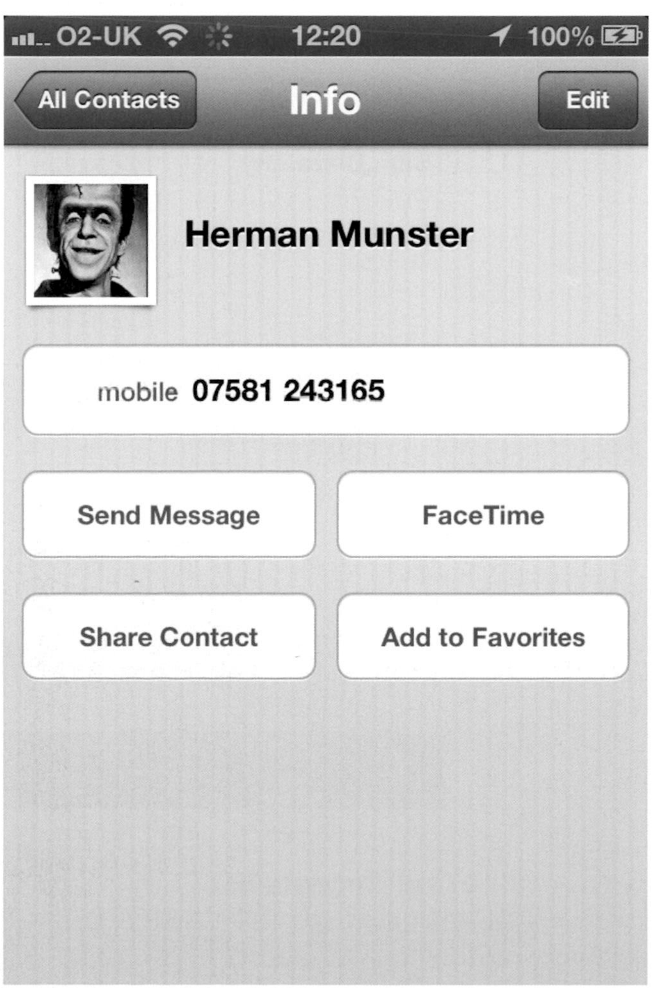

Add the contacts you call most to your Favorites List.

You can rearrange the Favorites list order by tapping Edit then moving your contacts up or down until you have them in the order you want.

Recents List

Recent calls you have made or missed are listed under Recents.

Missed calls

- These are in the **Missed** list and are listed in red
- **All** shows the calls made, received and missed
- Calls made are shown by the icon
- Calls received are shown without an icon

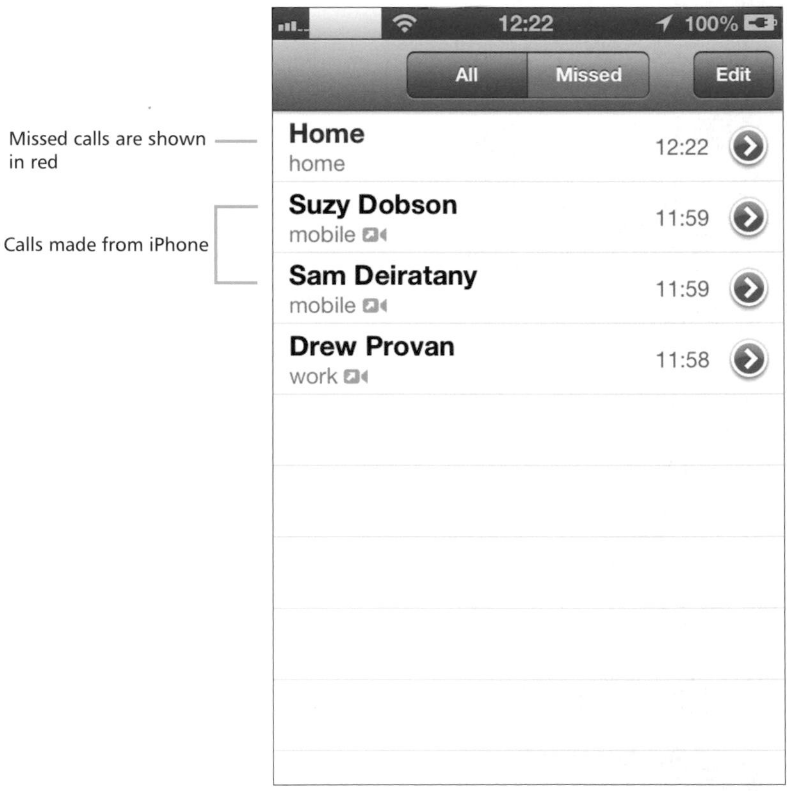

To return a call using Recents list

From the names shown in the Recents list, simply tap the name of the person you wish to call.

Answering Calls

When you receive a call the iPhone will either ring or vibrate, depending on your iPhone settings. If the iPhone is locked, you will see the name of the caller on the screen and you will need to slide the **Answer** button to the right. If the iPhone is unlocked when the call comes in, you will be given the option to **Answer** or **Decline** (and send to voicemail).

Slide up for more options

When you receive an incoming call, you can answer by sliding the green button to the right.

If you want to divert the caller to voicemail, slide up from the bottom right and you will see various options including *Reply with Message* and *Remind Me Later*.

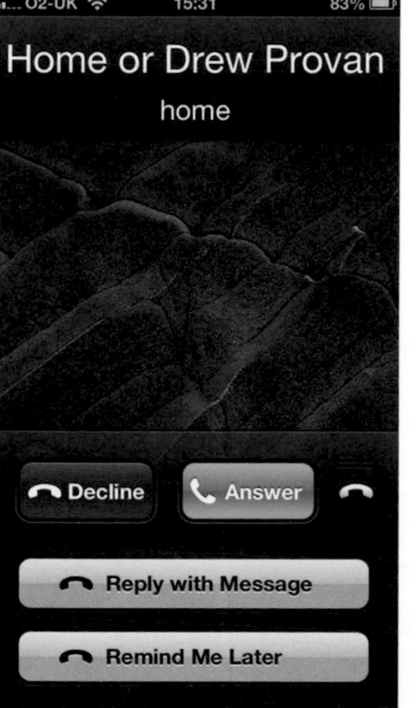

After sliding up from the bottom right you can see the various options available.

Hot tip

If you don't want to speak to a caller, hit the Sleep/Wake (On/Off) button and they will be directed to voicemail. The caller won't know you've done this, luckily.

Do Not Disturb

There are times when you do not want to see or hear Notifications from apps, or receive phone calls. For example, during the night you may want to divert all calls to voicemail rather than be woken up by phone calls.

1. Open **Settings** > **Do Not Disturb**

2. Slide the slider to **ON** if you want to switch on Do Not Disturb

Allow some callers to get through

You may want to allow friends and family, or those in your favorites list to get through and not be diverted to voicemail.

1. Open **Settings** > **Notifications** > **Do Not Disturb**

2. Choose the scheduled time (if you wish to schedule)

3. **Allow Calls From** > choose **Everyone, No One, Favorites**, or specific groups

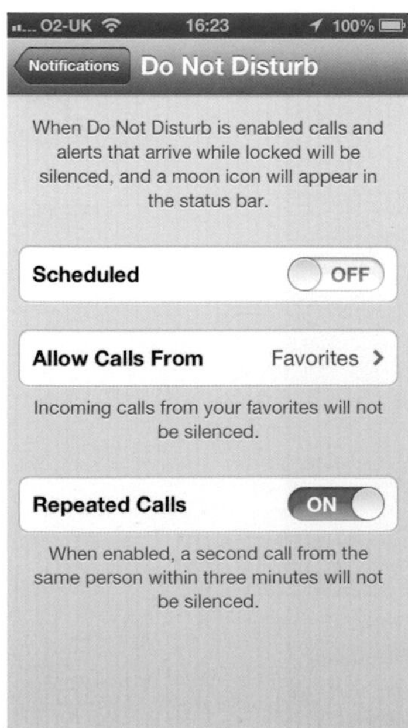

Missed Calls

It happens to all of us from time to time: the boss calls and somehow you managed to miss it. If your iPhone was locked when he called, you can see at a glance that he has called.

You can find out exactly when he called by looking at the missed calls list.

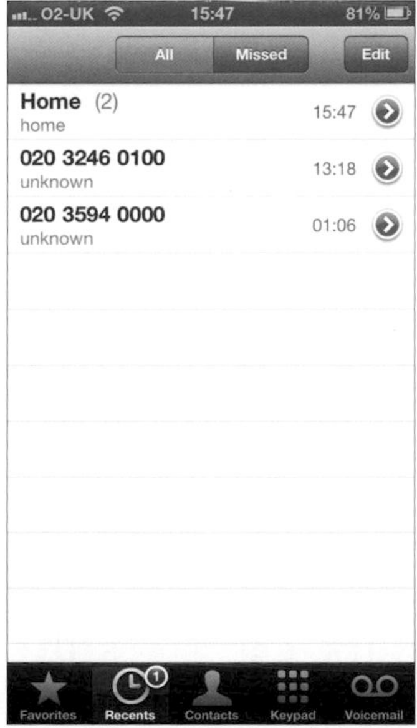

Make the Most of Contacts

The Contacts application on the iPhone lets you call someone, send them an SMS or MMS, email them, and assign them specific ringtones.

Add someone to Contacts

- If someone calls and they are not in your Contacts list why not add them to your list?
- Click the arrow to the right of their number

Try to enter as much contact information as possible, since this gives you more options for contacting them.

Here is a missed call (you can see it was missed at 13.18).

To add that person to your Contacts, tap **Create New Contact**, add their First and Last names, and then hit **Save**.

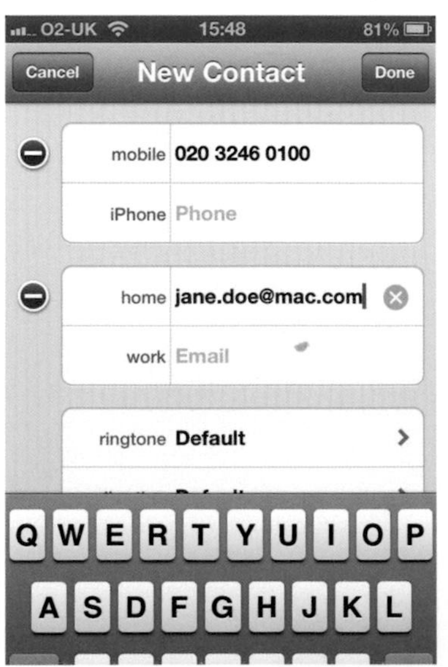

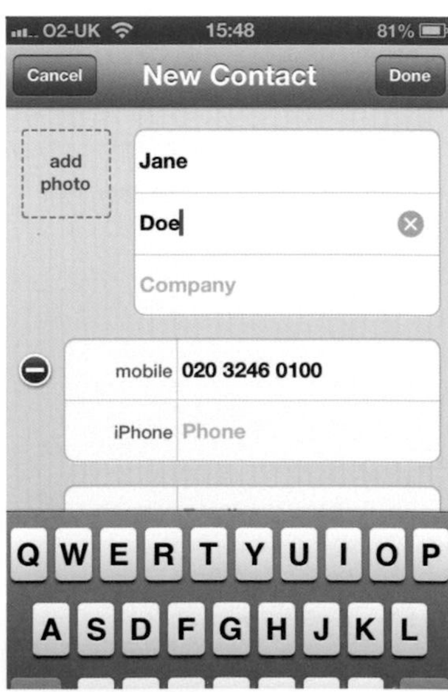

Adding Contacts

- Tap the **Contacts** app to open and tap the **+** symbol
- Tap the **First Last** name field
- The cursor will be in the First box – add their first name
- Tap the **Last** box and add their second name
- Tap **Company** if you want to add their company
- Tap **Save**
- This will take you back
- Tap the arrow **>** next to add new phone to add a cell or other phone number
- Work your way through the rest of the fields
- When you are finished hit **Done**

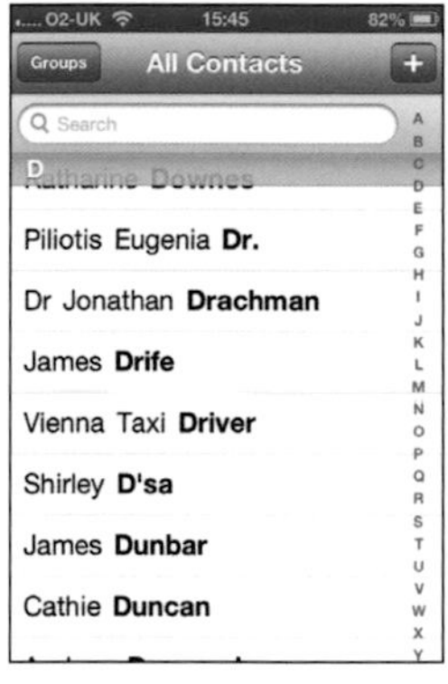

Deleting Contacts

This is much easier:

1. **Tap** the contact you wish to remove
2. Once their details are loaded tap **Edit** at the top right
3. Scroll down to the bottom of the screen and tap **Delete Contact**
4. That's it!

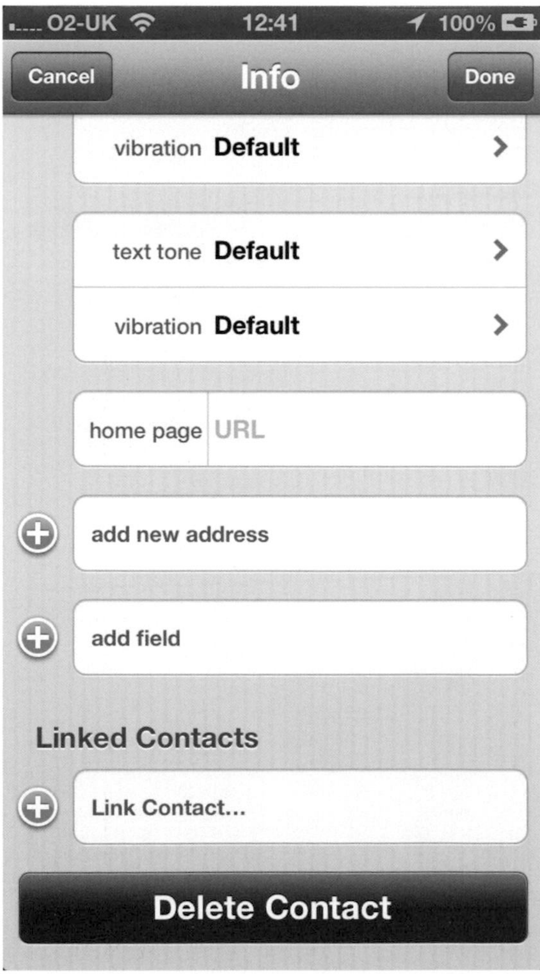

Importing Data from a PC

Most of us prefer to manage and edit our contacts using a computer, rather than the iPhone, because we have a real keyboard and it's easier using the computer. PC users will probably have their contacts in Outlook or Outlook Express. All this contact information can be synchronized with the iPhone each time it is plugged in to the PC.

1. Connect the iPhone to the PC
2. Make sure iTunes is open
3. Go to the **Info** tab
4. Make sure the **Sync contacts from** shows Outlook
5. The **All** contacts radio button should be filled
6. If you keep your contacts grouped, select the **groups** you wish to sync with the iPhone
7. Click **Apply** and the contacts will be synced between the PC and the iPhone (two way)
8. This will happen each time you connect the iPhone to the PC

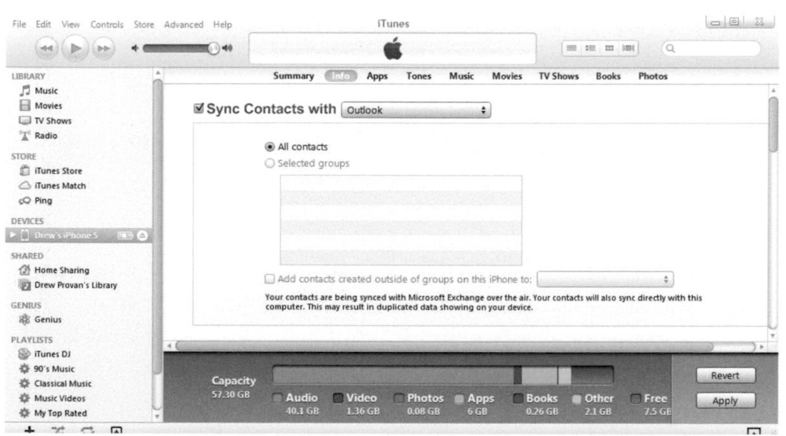

Importing Data from a Mac

This is similar to the PC method except the Mac uses Address Book to store its contact data, rather than Outlook.

Direct sync with the Mac

1. Connect iPhone to Mac
2. On iTunes click the **Info** tab
3. Ensure **Sync Address Book Contacts** is checked
4. If you want to sync only specific **groups**, check the ones you want to sync
5. Click **Apply**

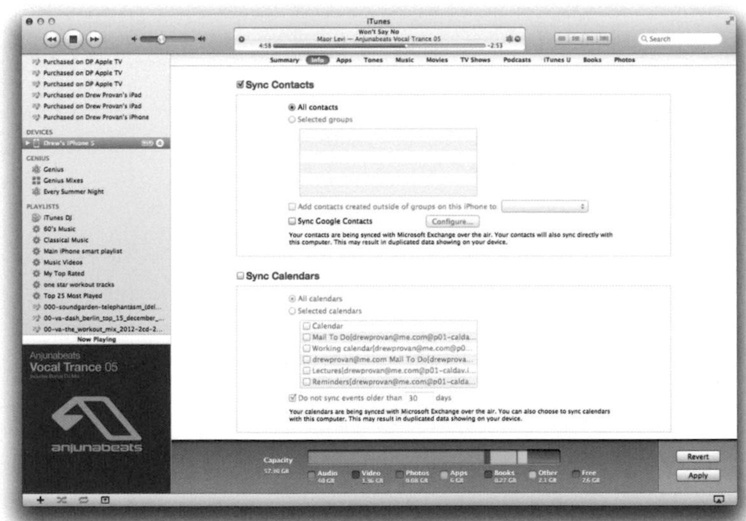

Now your contacts will be synchronized each time you plug the iPhone into the Mac. You can also sync Contacts, Calendars, and other items wirelessly using iCloud (you will need an iCloud account). If you use the iCloud option do not check any of the items in the iTunes pane (above).

Cloud Syncing with iCloud

iCloud is a cloud-based data storage service provided by Apple. You can let your Mac or PC upload your calendar, contacts, notes, music, apps and even full backups to the iCloud server. This communicates wirelessly with your iPhone, keeping all these functions totally in sync.

iCloud Control Panel

In the Apple System Preferences, and in PCs in the Control Panel window, you will find the iCloud control panel. If it's not there you can download it from Apple.

Configure your iCloud account

- Double click the **control panel**
- Enter your **username** and **password**
- Select what to sync wirelessly, and the frequency of syncing
- That's it, the whole sync process will take place without you having to do anything more

iCloud System Preferences on the Mac

And the Control Panel on the PC. Here you can set up exactly which items you want to sync using iCloud.

Hot tip 

With iCloud syncing, all changes to the iPhone Contacts or Calendars are automatically sent to the cloud and transferred to your desktop computers (and vice versa, with changes on the desktop being sent to the iPhone).

Hot tip 

Find My iPhone is a great tool and I would strongly recommend taking advantage of it.

Make Calls Using Headphones

You don't have to hold the iPhone to your ear each time you want to make a call. It's often more convenient to use the headphones. This means you can keep the phone on the desk and make notes during the call.

The headphones are very sophisticated, the right cord contains a white rectangular button which is useful when listening to music, but they are also great for making calls.

How to use the headphones

The is the middle of the controller

Beware

You can use third party headphones with the iPhone but it is likely you will lose some functionality.

Make a phone call	Dial as normal and speak normally. You will hear the caller via the headphones and they will hear your voice, which is picked up by the inbuilt microphone
Answer a call	Click the middle of the control button once
Decline a call	Press the middle of the controller and hold for ~two seconds (you will hear two low beeps to confirm)
End call	Press the middle of the controller once
If already on a call and you wish to switch to an incoming call and put current call on hold	Press the middle button once to talk to Caller 2 (and press again to bring Caller 1 back)
Switch to incoming call and end the current call	Press and hold the middle of the controller for ~two seconds (you will hear two low beeps to confirm)
Use Voice Control to dial the number	Press and hold the middle button

Hide or Show Your Caller ID

Sometimes you do not want the person you are calling to know your iPhone phone number. You can easily hide your number so it does not display on their screen.

1. Go to **Settings** > **Phone** > **Show My Caller ID**

2. Tap Show My Caller ID **ON** or **OFF** depending on whether or not you want it to show

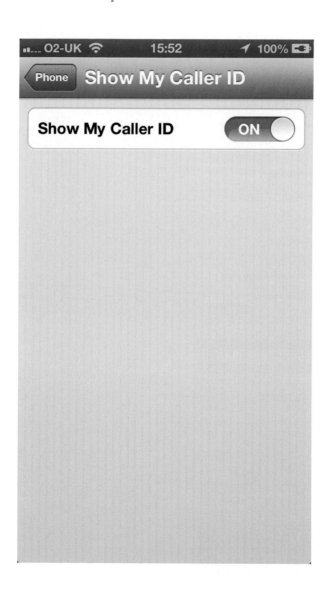

Call Forwarding

Sometimes you need to forward calls from your iPhone to another phone, for example, if you are somewhere with no cell phone coverage. This is pretty straightforward.

Setting up call forwarding

- Go to **Settings** > **Phone** > **Call Forwarding**
- Slide the **Call Forwarding** slider to the right (**ON**)
- You will be asked for the number you wish to use
- When you no longer need to have your calls forwarded, go back and switch it off

Hot tip

Activate call forwarding if you cannot access the iPhone. You could forward to a landline or your PA.

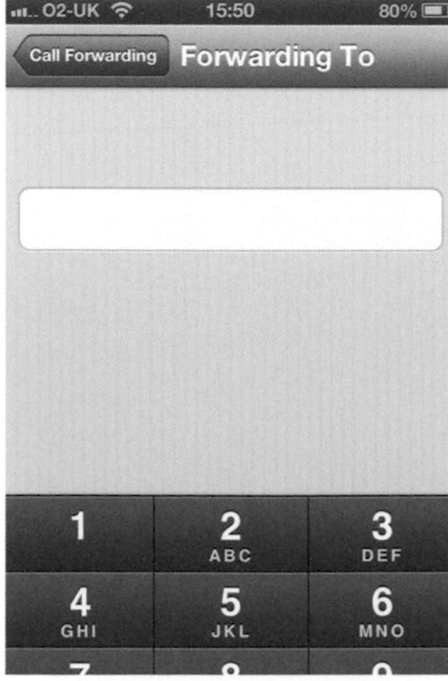

Conference Calls

This allows you to talk to more than one person at a time and is much like making conference calls using a landline.

Make a conference call

1. Make a call
2. Tap the **Add Call** icon on the screen
3. The first call is put on hold
4. Tap **Merge Calls**
5. Now everyone can hear each other
6. Repeat until up to five people are on the same call

Visual Voicemail

Hot tip

Visual Voicemail makes it very easy to listen to specific voicemail messages.

This is a fantastic way to retrieve voicemail. No longer do you have to listen to irrelevant messages in order to hear the one you want. With Visual Voicemail you can tap the message you want to hear, and you can listen to that message and that message only.

To retrieve Visual Voicemail

- Tap the **phone** icon at the bottom of the screen
- Tap the **Voicemail** icon at the far right
- View the voicemail messages
- **Tap** the one you want to hear
- To listen again, tap the **Play** icon
- If you want to listen to an earlier part of the message, **drag the progress slider to the left**
- You can call the caller back by tapping **Call Back**
- You can tap the arrow to the right of the message and add the caller to your Contacts list, or add them to the favorites list

Beware

Sometimes you cannot access Visual Voicemail (poor network signal). To retrieve your voicemails tap and hold "1" on the keypad.

What happens if Visual Voicemail is not available?

This sometimes happens but it's easy to get your voicemail:

- Tap **Phone** > **Keyboard**
- Press and hold the **1** key
- Retrieve your messages

Press and drag slider to LEFT to hear earlier section of voicemail

Customizing Your Greeting

When people get through to your voicemail they will hear a standard greeting, courtesy of your phone provider. It's very easy to make your own personalized greeting.

Create a greeting

1. Select **Phone** from the Home Screen
2. Tap **Voicemail**
3. Tap **Greeting** at the top left of the screen
4. Choose **Custom**
5. Tap **Record** to record your outgoing message then **Stop**
6. Make sure the **Custom** option is checked if you wish to use the message you have just recorded

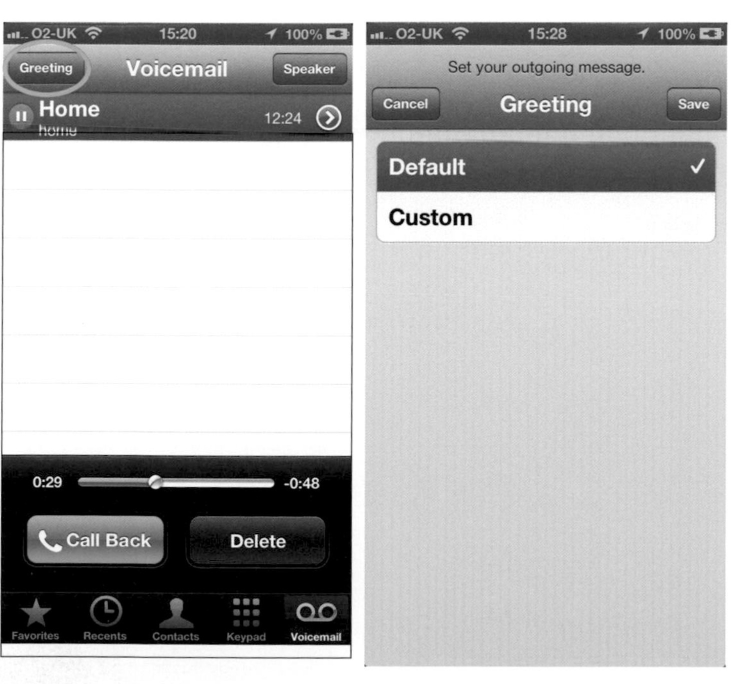

Call Waiting

What is the value of call waiting? If call waiting is switched off, and someone phones you while you are on a call, they will be put straight through to voicemail. However, if call waiting is activated, they will know your line is busy and can wait until you are off the call. Or you can answer their call and put the first caller on hold.

1. Go to **Settings** > **Phone**
2. Tap **Call Waiting >**
3. Slide the **OFF** button to the **ON** position

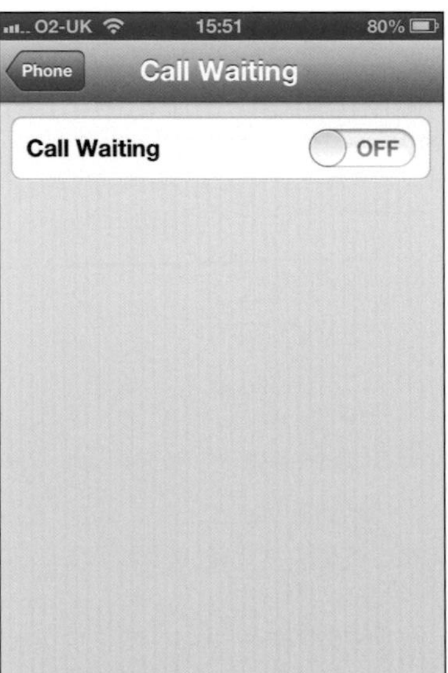

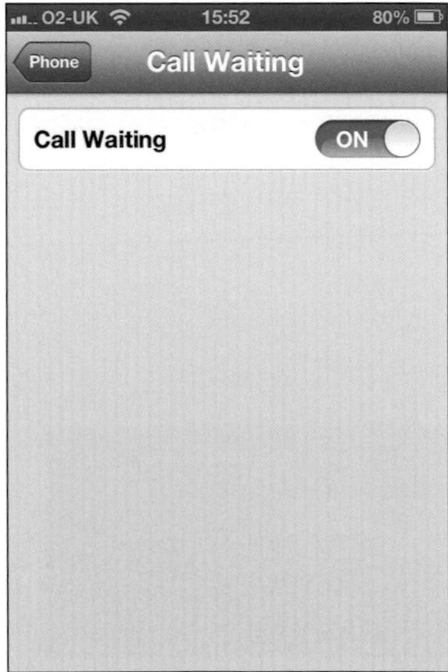

iPhone Usage Data

How many SMS messages do you have left this month? Or talk minutes? There are times when you need to monitor your usage, since exceeding your limits on your contracted allowance will cost you extra.

How can you check how much you have used?

The iPhone has Usage data under **Settings** > **General** > **Usage**. The information here is very limited and it does not tell you what you have used, or have left, in this month's cycle.

Third party applications

There are a number of apps that can track your monthly usage. These include *Optus Mobile Usage* for the US and *Allowance* for the UK. Other countries will have their own specific apps.

If you exceed your monthly allowance on the iPhone you will be charged extra.

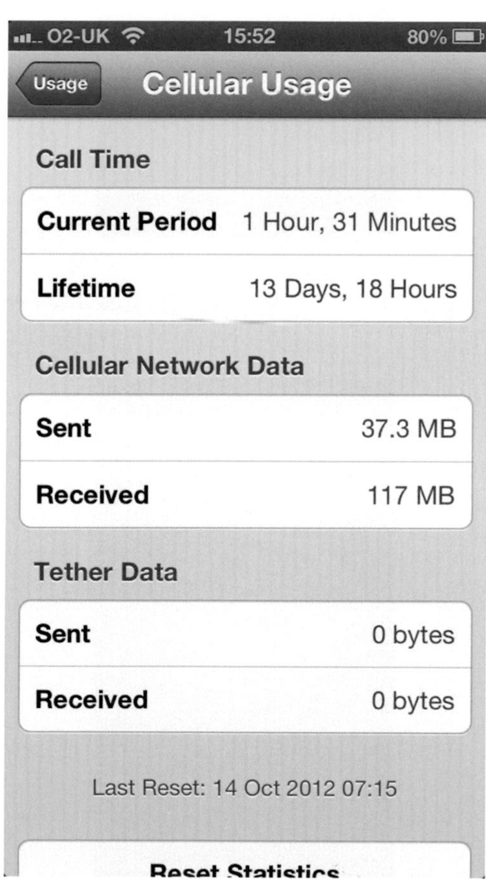

Third Party Apps for Usage

There are many apps for monitoring cellular and Wi-Fi data usage. One of these is Data Usage Monitor. Once you tell the app the billing data, it works out your usage for the month which will prevent you exceeding your data allowance. (If you are on unlimited data there's no need to worry!)

There are some great third party apps that help you monitor your monthly phone, text and data usage.

The app also comes with a useful built-in speed tester.

3 Messaging

Sending text and multimedia messages is no longer a chore. The iPhone carries out these functions effortlessly.

Text Messaging

Sending text messages on the iPhone 5 has become even more slick than with previous iPhones. You can send messages as SMS (simple message system), MMS (multimedia message system – basically text with pictures), and iMessage.

SMS

1. Tap the **Messages** icon on the Home Screen

2. Tap the **new** message icon at the top right of the screen

3. Enter a **recipient name** or a phone number at the top

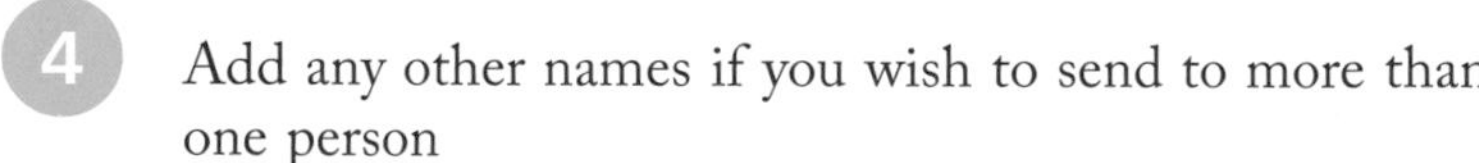

4. Add any other names if you wish to send to more than one person

5. Go to the **text box** at the bottom and enter your message

You can send SMS, MMS and iMessages to multiple recipients.

6. Hit **Send**

7 The progress bar will show you the status of the message

8 Once sent, your message will appear in a green speech bubble (blue if iMessage)

9 Once the recipient replies, you will see their message below yours in a white speech bubble

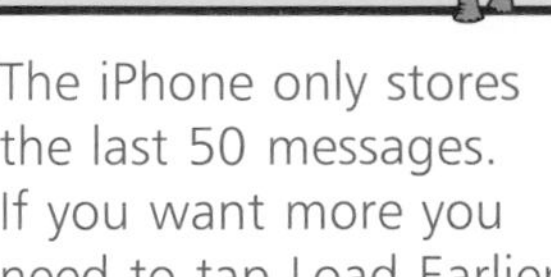

The iPhone only stores the last 50 messages. If you want more you need to tap Load Earlier Messages.

iMessage

You can send iMessages using cellular or Wi-Fi to other people with iOS devices (or Macs). Simply send your text in the usual way. You will know it's an iMessage rather than SMS because your message will be in a blue speech bubble. You can also check the status of your text message (delivered or read) by checking below your message.

You can tell this message is an iMessage – you see iMessage at the top, plus my text is in a blue speech bubble. You can also see that my message was successfully delivered and the person I texted is writing me a reply (the **...** ellipsis in the speech bubble on the left is the reply he is composing).

Hot tip

To see how many characters you have used go to Settings > Messages > Character Count > ON. 160 characters is the limit for one SMS.

If SMS Message Fails

Sometimes things go wrong, maybe you entered a wrong digit, and the message does not get sent. You have the option of retrying. You can also check the contact details and amend the number there.

1. Tap on the red exclamation mark

2. Tap on **Try Again**

Send Texts to Multiple Recipients

The Messages app allows you to send texts to more than one person. You can also send texts to groups of individuals.

Send SMS to multiple recipients

1. Type the **name** of the first recipient
2. A shaded block surrounds their name
3. Tap the **To:** field again and add a second name
4. Repeat this until all recipients are added

Tap after each entry to add other names

Text Message Sounds

Some people like silent texts, others prefer to feel a vibration, but many people like to hear their text messages arrive on the iPhone.

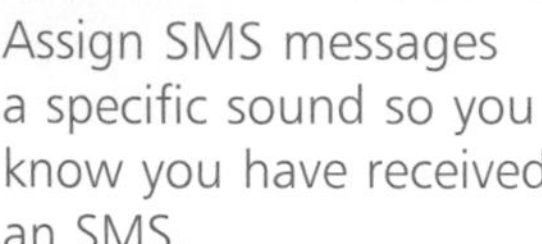

Assign SMS messages a specific sound so you know you have received an SMS.

This is easy to set up

1. Tap **Settings**
2. Go to **Settings** > **Sounds**
3. Tap **New Text Message**
4. Select the **sound** you want from the list
5. Or you can check **None**

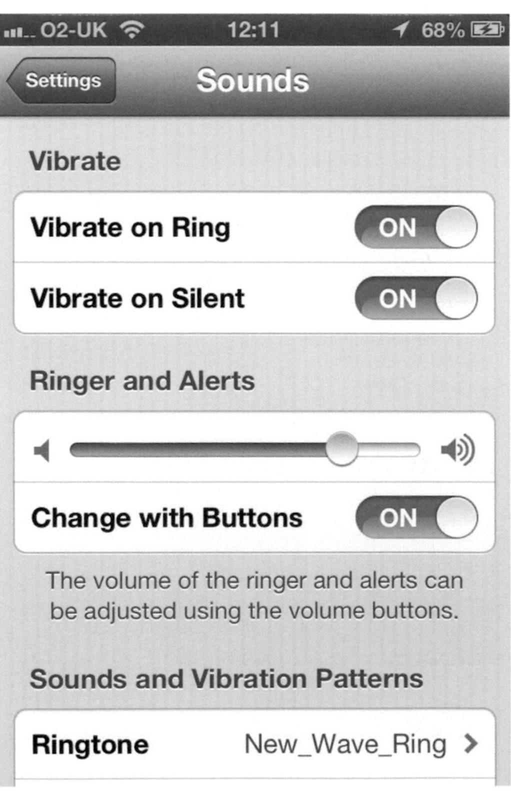

Removing Text Conversations

For privacy, most people remove their text message conversations. You can delete the entire conversation – each and every entry – or you can delete parts of the conversation. It is difficult to save your conversations, but there is a workaround.

Deleting the entire conversation

1. Open up the text message
2. Tap **Edit**
3. **Click the red icon** with the white bar through the center (this deletes the conversation)
4. Alternatively, you can avoid opening the message by simply **sliding your finger across from left to right**, a Delete icon will appear – press **Delete**

Deleting parts of a conversation

1. Open a text with multiple entries
2. Click **Edit**
3. **Tap the speech bubbles** you wish to delete (a red circle with a white check inside will appear)
4. Tap **Delete** at the bottom of the screen

Saving a conversation

1. With the text message conversation window open press the **Home Button** and the **On/Off** button together
2. This will take a snapshot which is saved to your photos
3. You can download to your computer later

Sending MMS Messages

The iPhone can send more than just plain boring text messages. MMS means Multimedia Message Service, which is basically a means of sending images, including video, to a recipient, rather than a simple SMS message. Each MMS counts as two SMS messages, so be careful how many you send.

To send an MMS

1. Tap **Messages** and tap **New**
2. Enter the **name** of the recipient
3. **Click the camera icon** (to the left of the text box) and Take Photo or Video or Choose Existing
4. You will then see your photo albums
5. **Choose the picture or video** you want to send
6. The picture will appear in the message box
7. Type your text message to accompany the picture or video
8. Hit **Send**

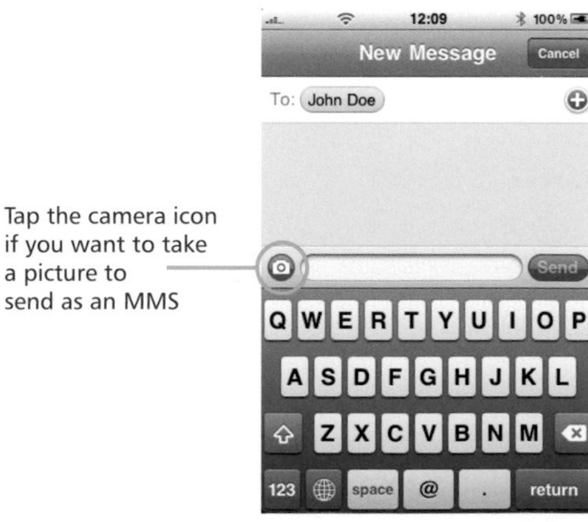

Tap the camera icon if you want to take a picture to send as an MMS

Choose recipient

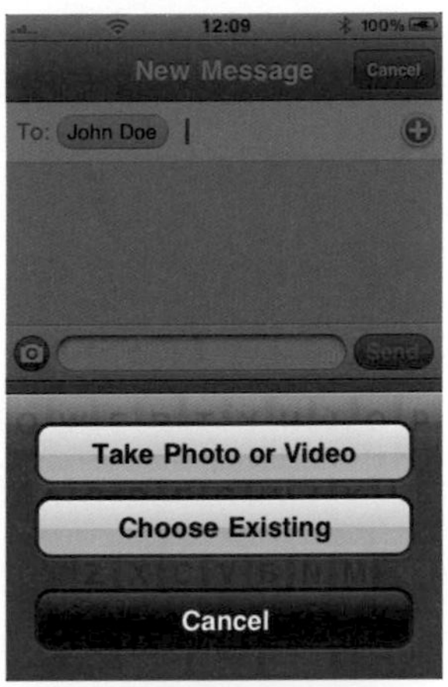

Take photo/video or use existing

Tap image

Confirm by pressing Choose

Picture in text box

Add text and send

Other Messaging Clients

On the iPhone there are several apps that let you message friends and colleagues. Examples include Skype, WhatsApp, Viber, and others.

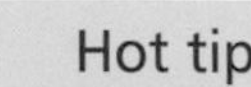

Skype lets you chat to friends and call them for free.

Skype

Viber

Using Skype

1. **Get yourself a Skype account** using your computer (*www.skype.com*)
2. **Download the free iPhone Skype app** from the App Store
3. Open the app and log in using your registered **Username** and **Password**
4. Your **Contacts List** will be displayed. You can choose to see only those online (makes the list shorter)
5. **Tap** the contact
6. You choose to **Call** or **Chat**

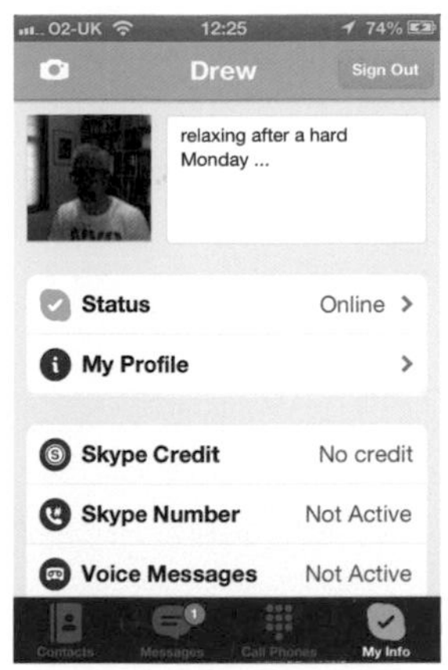

My profile page

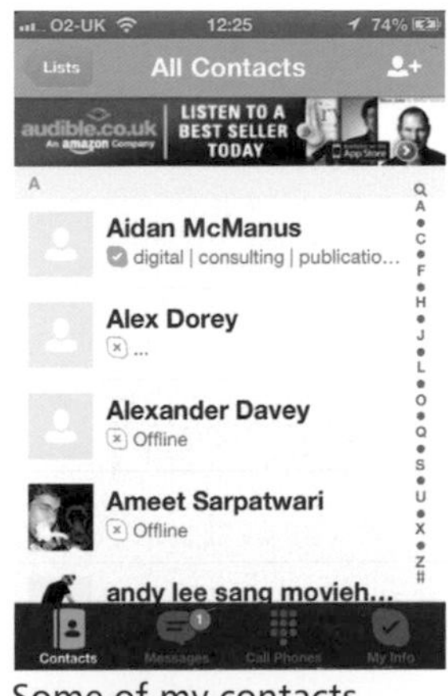

Some of my contacts

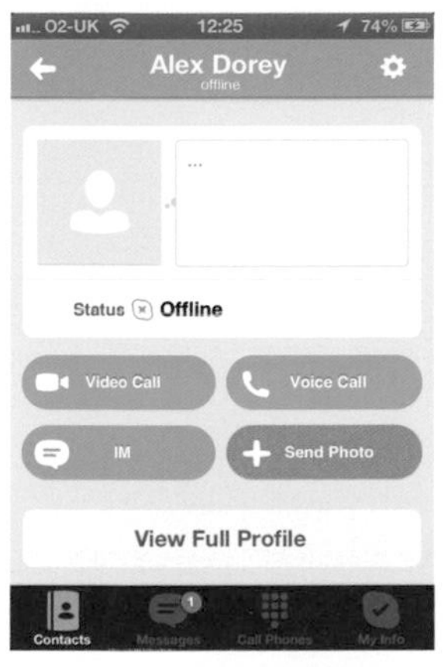

Choose to Call or Chat

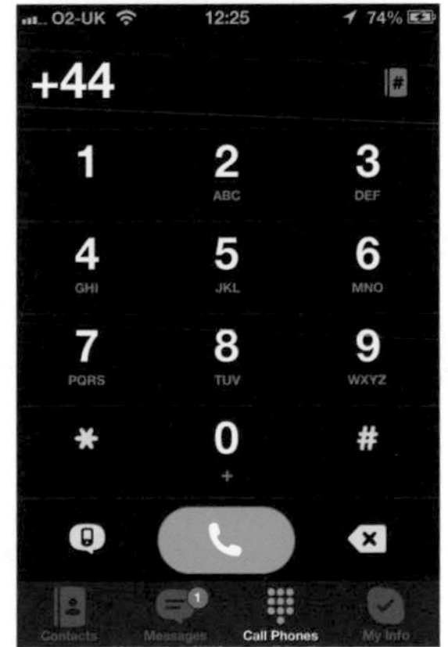

Press Call and this appears

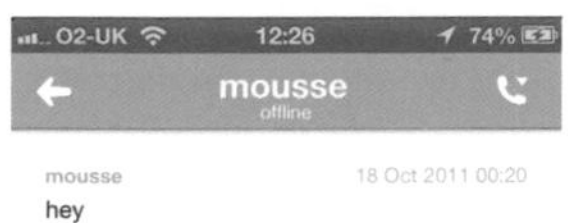

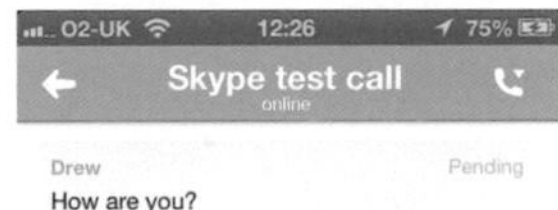

Start chatting. Enter text ... then hit Send
(I was chatting to to the Skype Test Call rather than a real contact, but it is more fun talking to real people!)

Managing Text Messages

Forwarding a text message

You can easily forward a text message to another person.

1. Open the message and tap **Edit**
2. Tap the text that you want to forward
3. Tap **Forward** and enter a recipient name

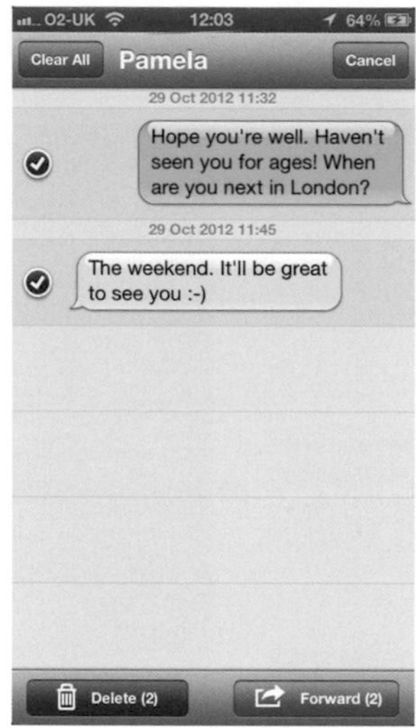

Deleting a text message

1. Open Messages to show your list of text messages
2. Swipe the text message left to right then tap **Delete**

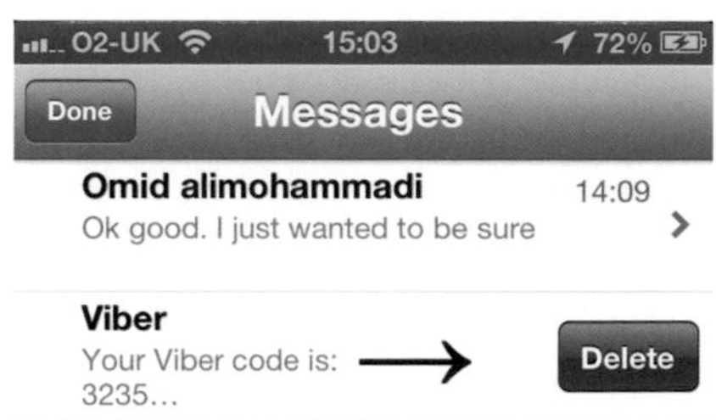

Editing text messages

You can selectively delete parts of a text message thread:

1. Open the message and tap **Edit**
2. Tap the text that you want to delete
3. Tap delete

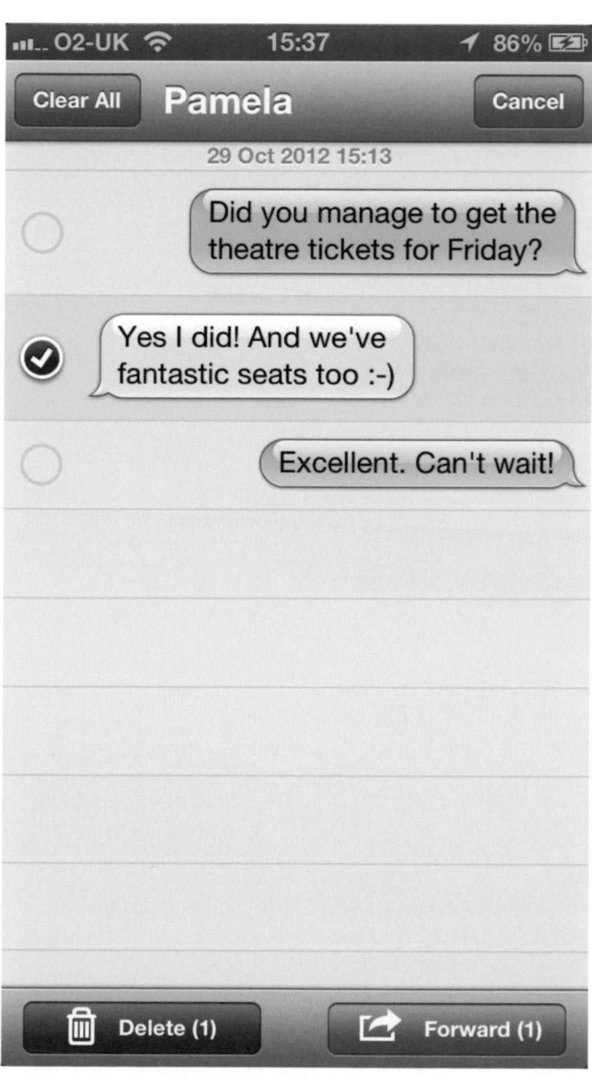

Live Links

When you send a text message, an email, or use a social networking app where text is inserted, you can add phone numbers, web URLs and email addresses. The recipient can then click on these to return the call, visit a website, or send an email.

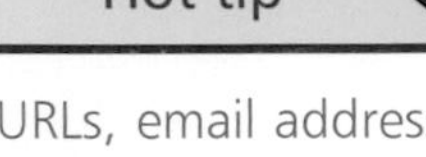

URLs, email addresses and phone numbers in messages, web pages and emails are live and can be tapped to call the number, view other web pages or send emails.

SMS with telephone number

Tap the phone number to call the number. You can tell it's a live link because the numbers are blue and the phone number is underlined

SMS with email address

Clicking here will bring up a new blank email so you can send an email to this address

Live links in emails

If you send an email to someone and include a website, email address or URL these are also clickable.

Clicking here opens Safari and takes you to the URL in the email

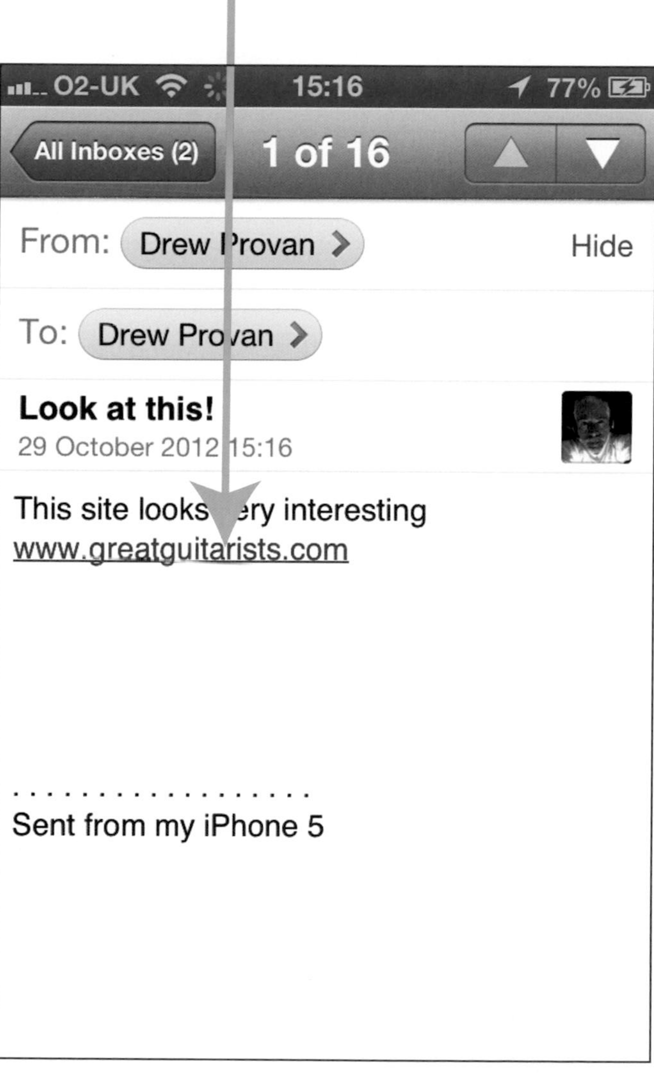

Live Links in Safari

Live links to phone numbers and email addresses don't end with Mail. You can use phone numbers in Safari. If you see a number you want to dial on a web page, put your finger on the number and keep your finger there until a box pops up showing you the various options.

You can:

- Call the number
- Send a text message
- Create a new contact
- Add to an existing contact

1. Put your finger on the number and keep it there

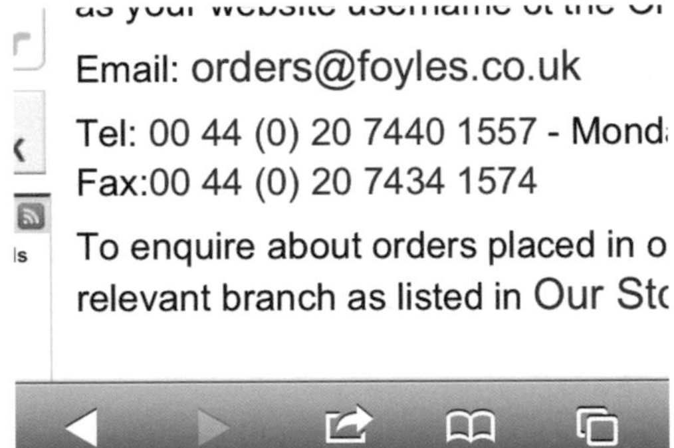

To call a number on a web page simply tap the phone number and you will be shown several options.

2. You will see the various options

4 Audio & Video

The iPhone is a workhorse but is also a fun device, able to play audio and video just like an iPod. Here we will explore how to get content onto the iPhone and how to use Voice Control to tell your iPhone what you want to hear.

The Music App

Tap the Music app icon to open it

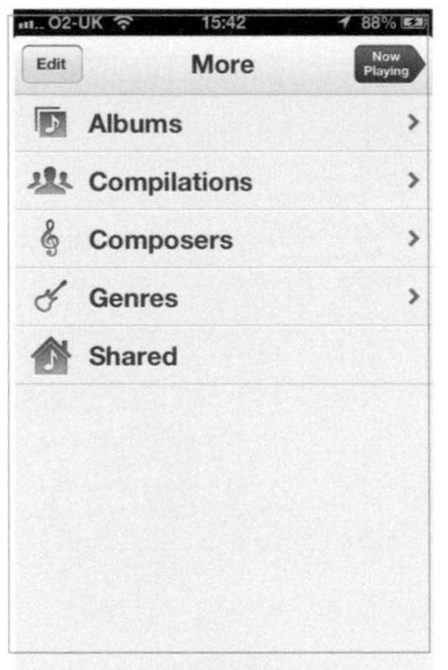

Under the More tab you can view by Album, Composers, Genres, and Shared

You can view the Music audio by Artist, Playlist, Songs, Videos or More ...

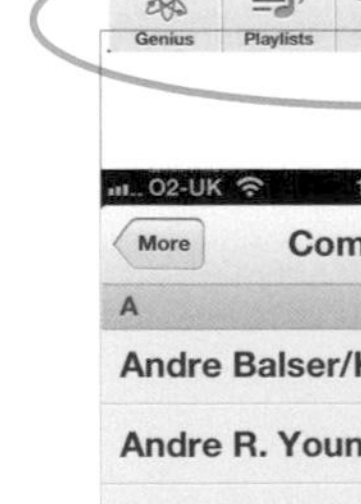

This view shows the Music content by Composer

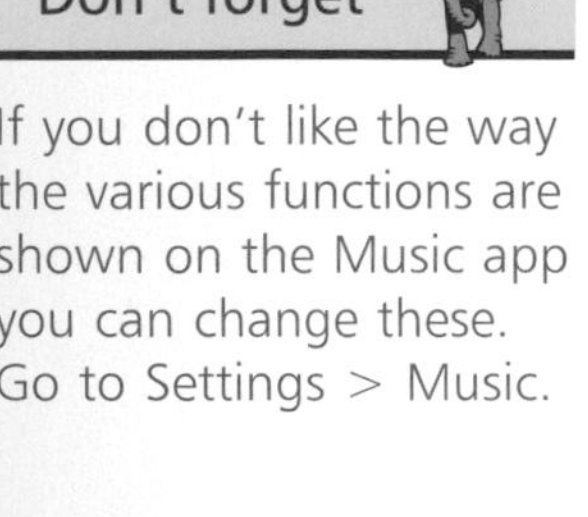

Don't forget

If you don't like the way the various functions are shown on the Music app you can change these. Go to Settings > Music.

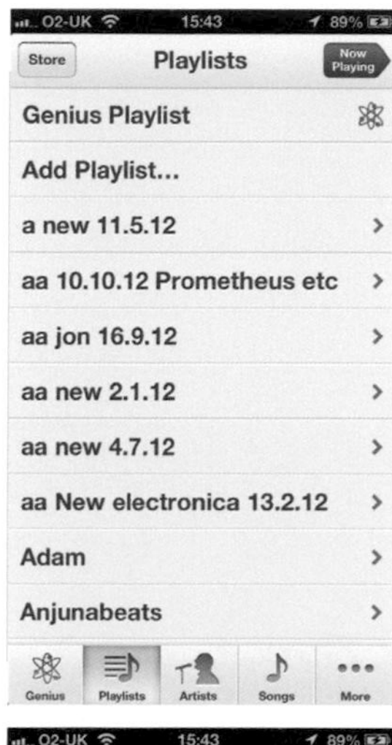

This view shows the Music content by Playlists

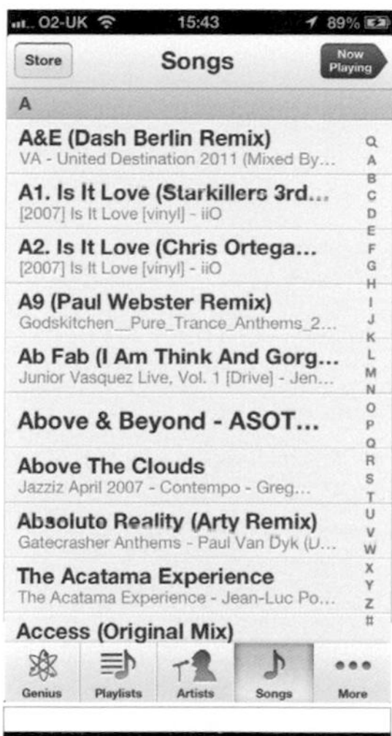

This view shows the Music content by Songs

Here we can see the Genius Smooth Jazz Mix

Play Audio on the Music App

1. Tap **Music** icon on the dock
2. Tap **Artists** if you want to search this way, or choose **Playlists** or **Songs**
3. **Tap** the name of the artist
4. **Choose** the album you want to hear
5. You can always browse using **Cover Flow** if you can't decide what to play
6. **Tap** the first track (top of the screen) to play the tracks in order

Hold your iPhone in landscape mode to activate Cover Flow.

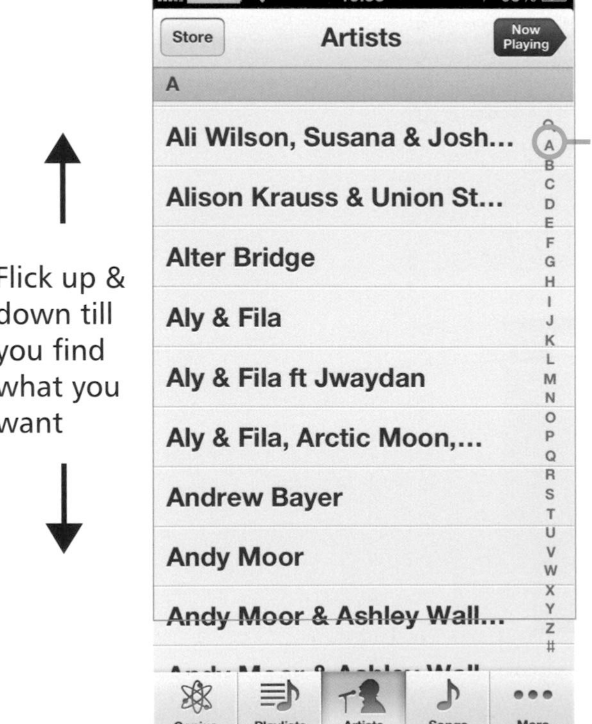

Flick up & down till you find what you want

Or tap the letter of the artist you want to play

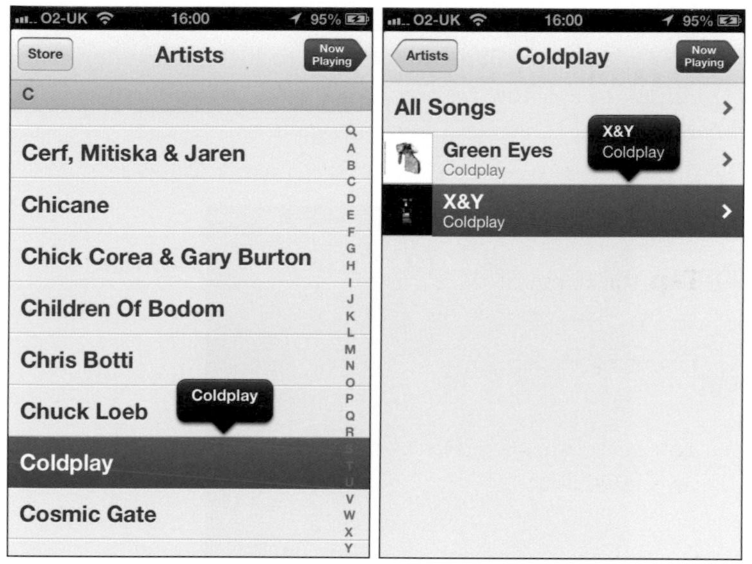

Tap *Coldplay*. You then move to the Albums view. **Tap** *X&Y*.

You can then see the tracks. **Tap** *Speed Of Sound* (first track). The speaker icon shows you which track is currently playing.

Music App Controls

Repeat, Genius, Shuffle and Scrubber Bar

This is useful for setting albums to repeat, to listen in random order (Shuffle), to see how far through a track you are and rewind (Scrubber bar), and to create a Genius playlist.

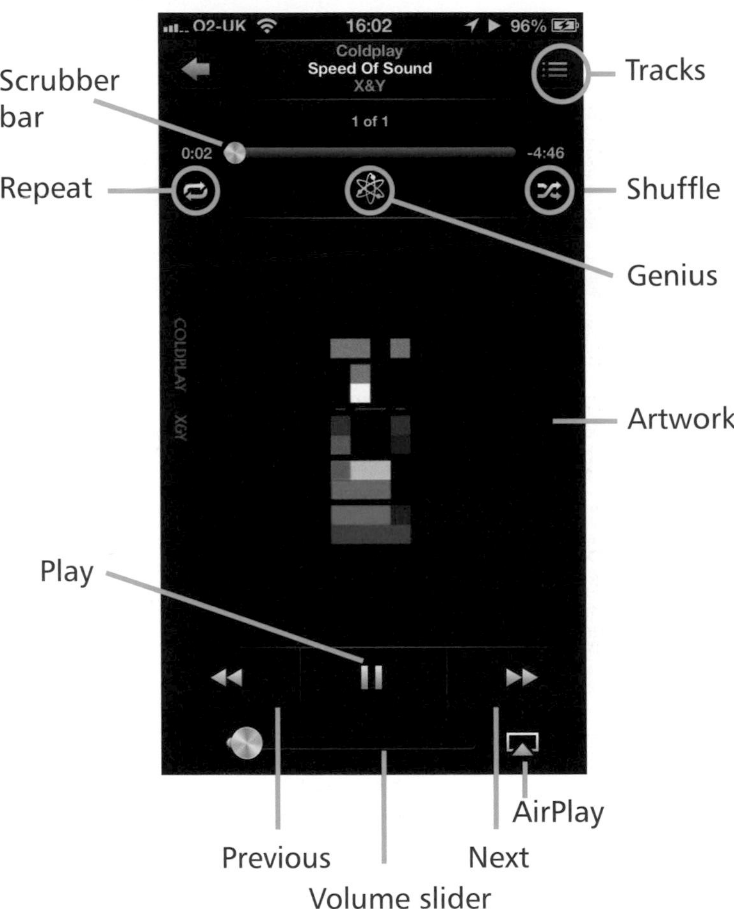

Shuffle

Tap the Shuffle icon (blue when on, white when off).

Scrubber bar

To see how long the track is, and how far through you are, tap the cover of the album.

Repeat

You can repeat a song or album by tapping the Repeat icon. This is white if *off*, blue if *on*. You can set the audio to repeat once, twice, or endlessly.

Shuffle

You can listen to your audio in random order by tapping the Shuffle icon. Like Repeat, when Shuffle is on the icon turns blue. If you want to switch Shuffle off, tap the icon again.

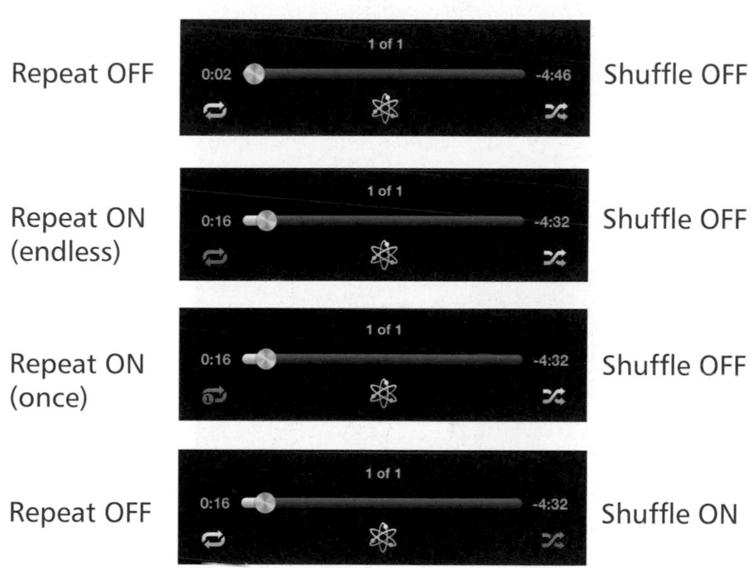

The figure above shows the various combinations for Repeat and Shuffle. In the third example, Repeat is set to *once* – shown by the number 1. If you tap again, it will show the number 2.

Don't forget Cover Flow

The Music app on the iPhone shows Cover Flow just like iTunes!

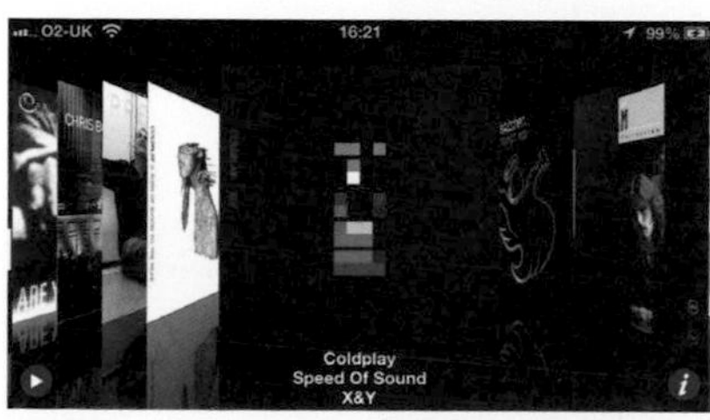

Turn the iPhone to landscape mode in Album, Song and other modes and you see Cover Flow in action

Flick through the Albums till you find what you want

Hot tip

Controls that are active (e.g. Repeat) are shown in blue. To switch them off, tap once and they should return to white icons.

View the Audio Tracks

Sometimes you want to see what tracks are available while you are listening to audio.

While viewing the album artwork screen:

1. **Tap the small bullet list** icon at the top right of the screen
2. The album cover flips to show audio tracks available
3. To get back to the main screen again, **tap the Album Artwork icon** at the top right

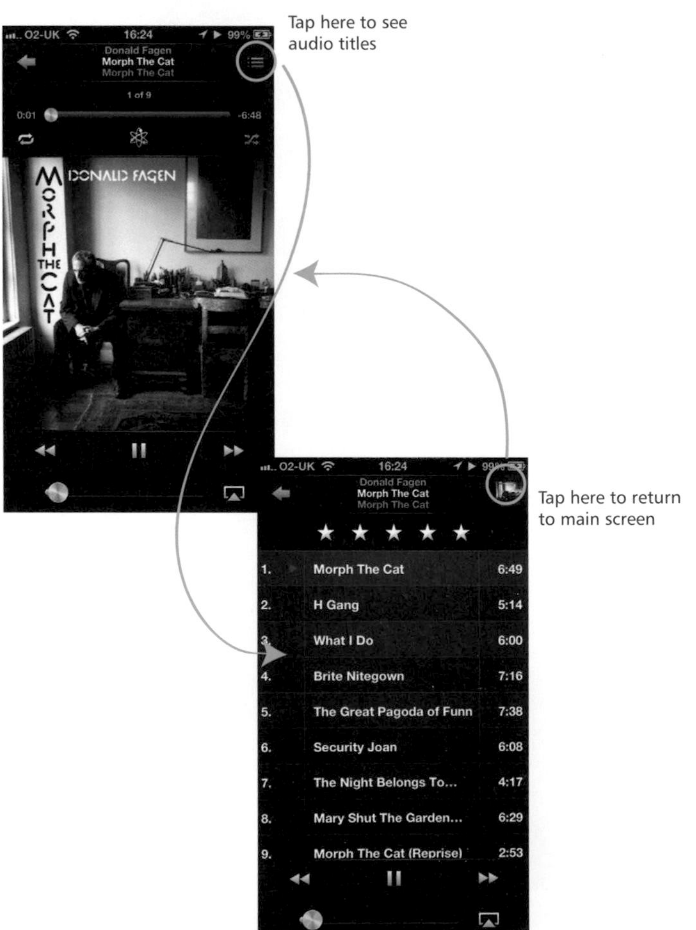

Adjusting the Volume

There are several ways of increasing or decreasing the audio volume.

Headphones

Use the **+** and **–** on the headset.

Volume control switch on iPhone

Use the physical volume control on the iPhone.

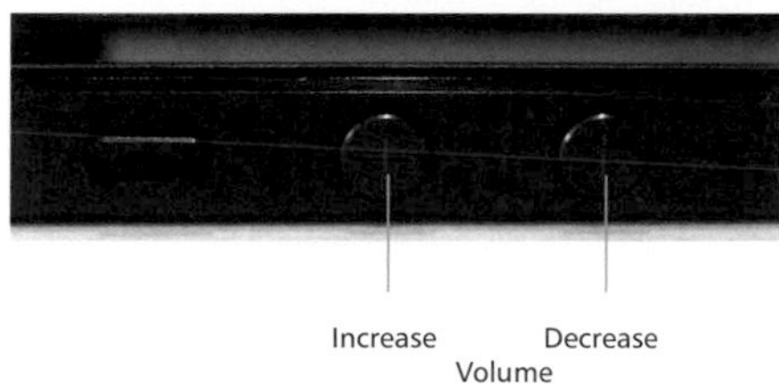

From the Music app screen

Move the circle right (increase volume) or left (to decrease).

Control the Music app from within any app

You don't need to quit an app just to see the Music app controls – just double click the home button and swipe to the right, then to the right again to show the volume (and AirPlay controls if you are near an Apple TV).

Even when you are using another app, you can still access your Music app controls by clicking the Home Button twice.

Search for Audio

Sometimes you can't see the music or artist you are looking for. Hit the search tool at the top right of the Music app screen and type the name of the artist, album, song, podcast, or whatever you are looking for.

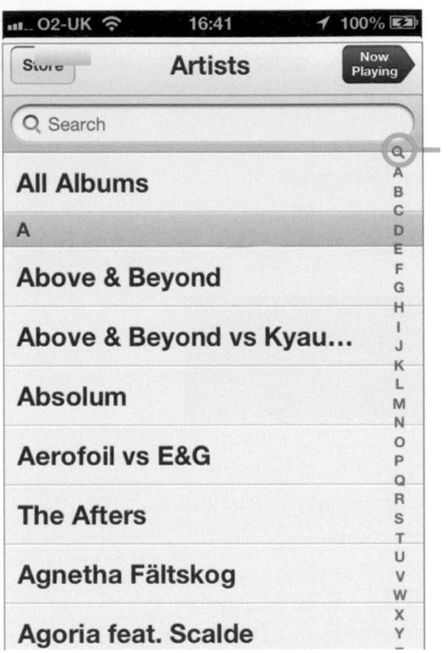

Tap the Search tool

Hot tip

You can search for audio or video in your Music app within the Music app itself, or you can use Spotlight.

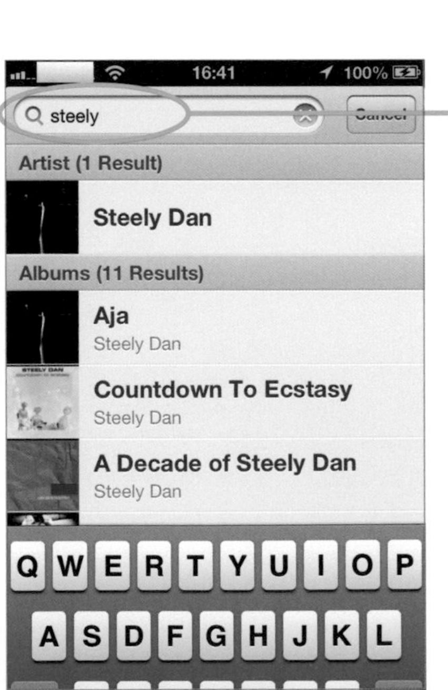

Enter your search terms here

Playlists

Playlists and Smart Playlists are very useful, especially if the music on your Mac or PC will not physically fit onto the iPhone. Making playlists, and choosing to sync specific playlists, helps you decide what music to sync to the iPhone.

In iTunes

1. Choose **File** > **New Playlist**
2. **Name** the playlist
3. From the Music window, **select and drag** the songs you want to add to the new playlist
4. **Drag** the audio files to the playlist
5. When the iPhone is plugged into the Mac or PC, go to the Music pane and **check** the playlists you want to sync to the iPhone

This does *not* move the original files – but it provides *links* to the originals.

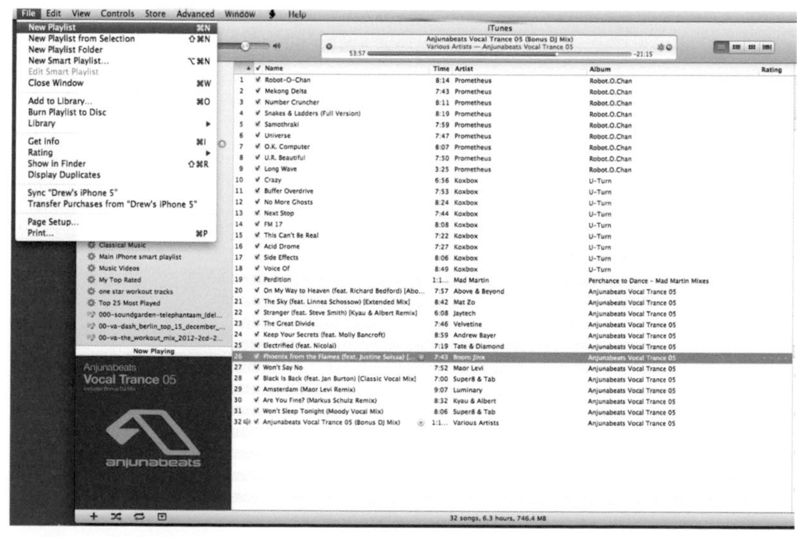

Beware

Chances are your music, video, photos etc. will not all fit on the iPhone. You need to create smart playlists that sync selected music, video and photos to the iPhone.

Sync Specific Playlists

To sync specific playlists with the iPhone you need to choose the playlists to sync, from the settings in the iTunes window, when your iPhone is plugged into the Mac or PC.

1. Plug the iPhone into the computer
2. Click **iPhone** in the iTunes window
3. Select the **Music** pane
4. Make sure sync is set up for **selected** music, artists and genres
5. **Choose** which playlists to sync
6. To avoid hearing the same music over and over, change the playlists you sync every now and again

Ensure "Selected Playlists" is checked
Check each playlist you wish to sync
Sync Music
3802 songs
Playlists
Artists
Genres
Albums

Smart Playlists

There is an easier way to get music onto your iPhone. Instead of making playlists, and choosing which songs to add to the iPhone, you can design Smart Playlists. These are playlists which are predefined to contain specific items of music or other audio.

Make a Smart Playlist

1. From iTunes choose **File** > **New Smart Playlist**
2. A setup window with Smart Playlist rules will open
3. **Choose a rule**, such as Album rating = 5 ★
4. In the **Rating** column of iTunes, rate the music you want to add to the Smart Playlist
5. To remove music from the playlist, adjust the rating so it is no longer 5 ★

Hot tip

Use the star rating system to create smart playlists.

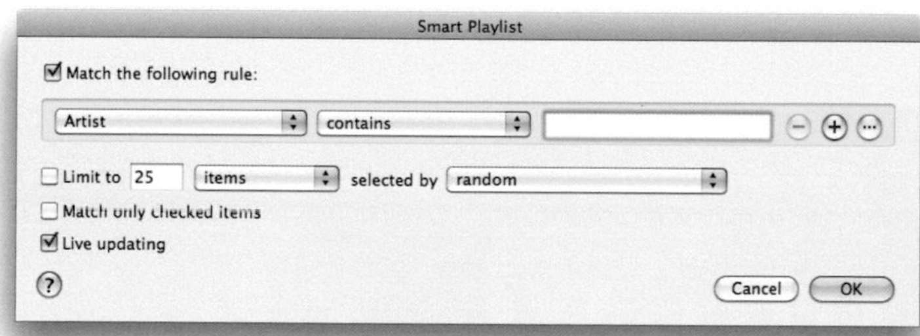

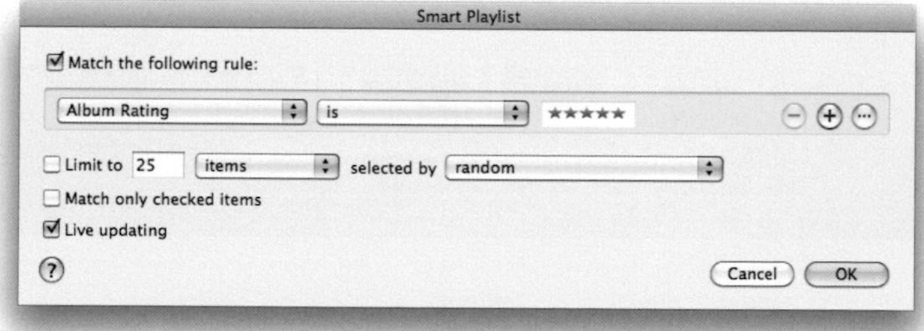

Don't forget to name the Smart Playlist!

Watching Video

The iPhone is a great video player. Video now has its own app (it used to be within the Music app).

1. Tap **Videos**
2. **Scroll** through the available videos
3. **Tap** the video you wish to watch
4. The playback screen will automatically rotate to landscape
5. **Adjust** volume, rewind, change language and other features using the controls which are shown below
6. If you want to stop, simply press the **Play/Pause** button and it will save your place

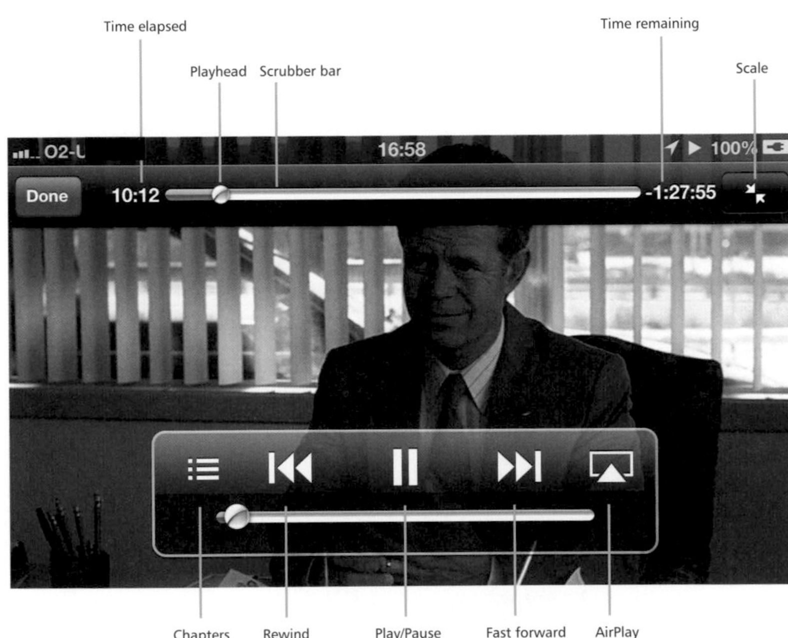

Sharing Video

Your iPhone 5 may have limited space but you can still watch any movie on your Mac or PC provided you have set up Home Sharing.

1. Open the Videos app and tap **Shared** (top of screen)

2. Your Mac or PC videos will load (PC or Mac must be on, iTunes must be running and **Home Sharing** set to ON)

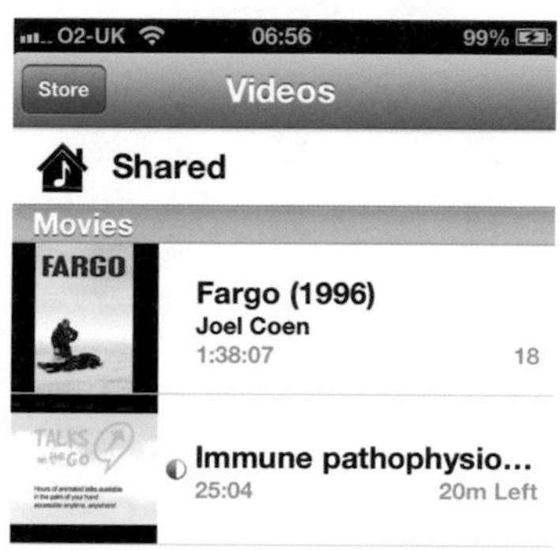

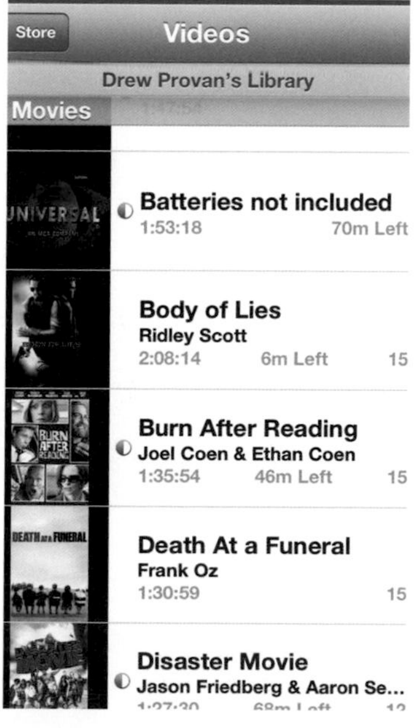

Other Video Icons

Next to the videos you will see small circles which may be wholly filled, partly filled or absent. This tells you how much of each video you have previously viewed. If you stopped watching a video half way through, the circle will be half white and half blue.

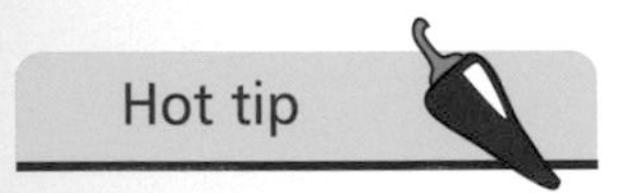

Hot tip

The icons next to the video title show you whether a video is unviewed, partially viewed or completely viewed.

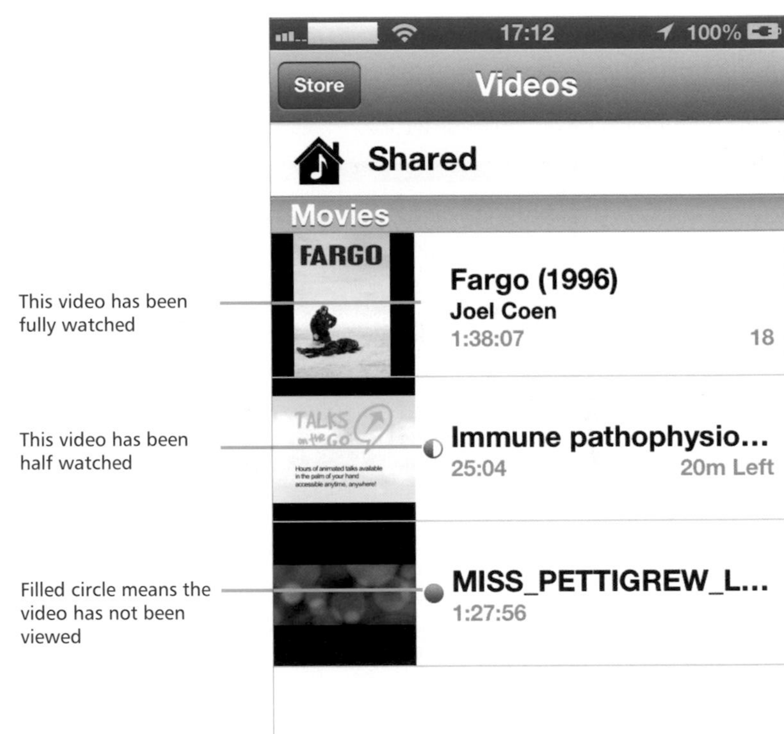

Where to Obtain Videos

You have a few ways of getting videos on your iPhone:

- Home movies, either using a camcorder or the iPhone itself
- Convert your purchased DVDs to iPhone format
- Buy or rent movies from the iTunes store

iTunes store

Select the video you wish to purchase or rent. Once downloaded it will be added to the Movies window in iTunes. When you sync your iPhone choose the movies you wish to sync.

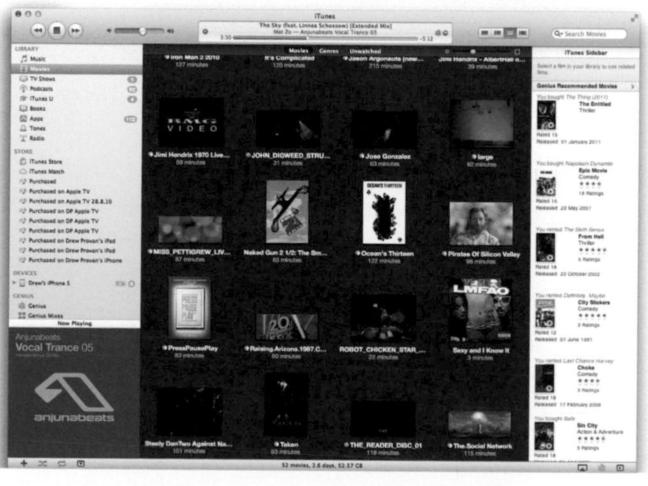

Convert Your DVDs

There are several programs available for Mac and PC that will convert purchased DVDs into an iPhone-friendly format.

Handbrake

This is an open source application for Mac. Simply put your commercial DVD in the Mac optical disk drive, open Handbrake and choose the format for the save. There is an iPhone-specific video format available.

Once converted, the video should be dropped onto the Movies tab of iTunes. In the iPhone Video tab make sure this video is checked so that the next time you sync the iPhone the video will be copied to the iPhone.

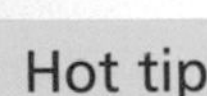

Hot tip

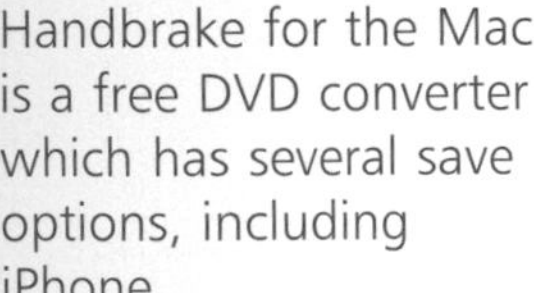

Handbrake for the Mac is a free DVD converter which has several save options, including iPhone.

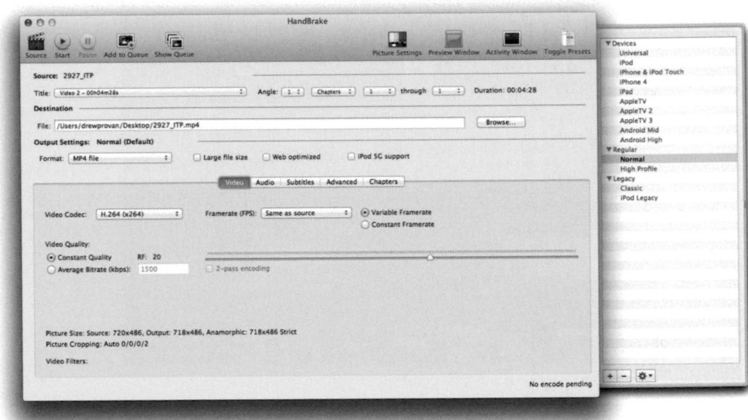

PC software for converting DVDs

There are many different programs for the PC, including Roxio Crunch.

Is it legal?

For a variety of reasons some DVDs may not convert properly, possibly through copy protection. In general, the copying of commercial DVDs, even for your own iPhone use, is not necessarily legal.

Podcasts

The iPhone is also great for listening to audiobooks and podcasts.

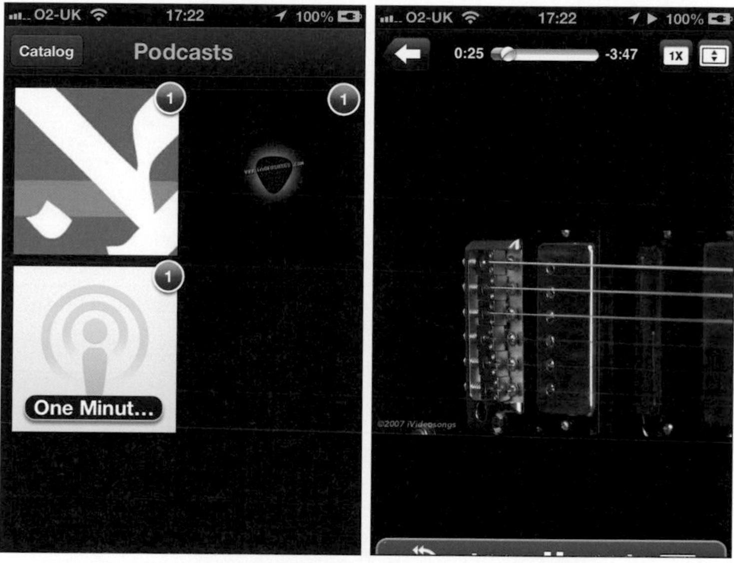

Open the Podcasts app to see the podcasts and tap the one you want to hear or see (if it is a video podcast like the one above).

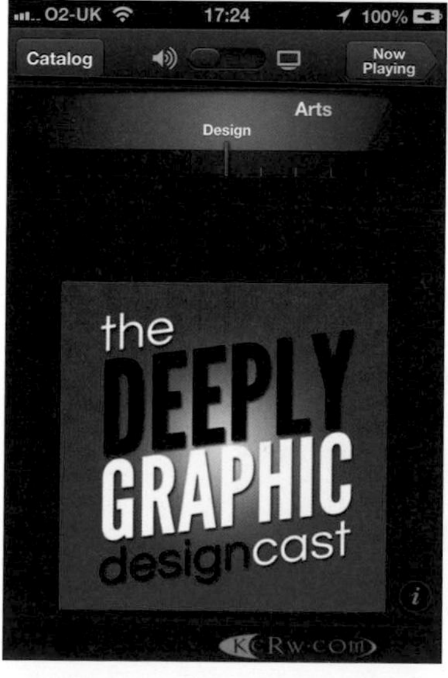

Tapping Top Stations will take you through the top podcasts by category.

Creating Your Own Playlists

Using the Music app you can create your own playlists.

To set up your own playlist

1. Go to **Music** > **Playlists**
2. Tap **Add Playlist...**
3. Name it
4. Tap the **+** icon to add songs
5. If you want to remove or edit the playlist, open the playlist and tap **Edit**

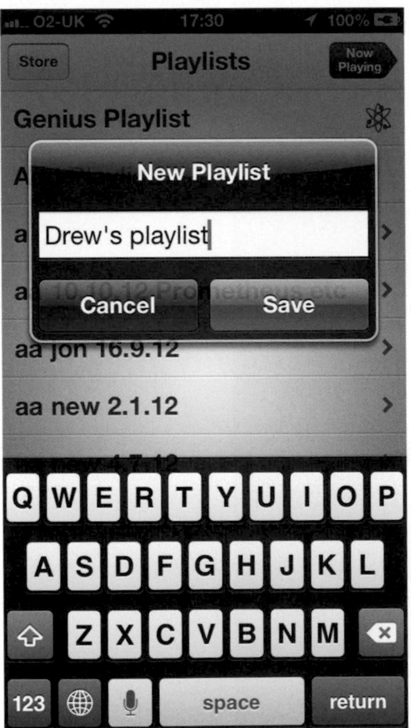

Add your tracks to the On-The-Go playlist. Edit later when you want a different selection.

Genius Recommendations

Genius is available within iTunes, on iPods and the iPhone. Genius works out what you listen to and can help make playlists based on song types. It works out what music fits well with other music.

For example, let's say you are listening to something jazzy, which you like. Genius can help make a playlist from your music based on the jazz track you are listening to.

Here's how:

1. Open **Music** and select **Playlists**
2. Tap **Genius Playlist**
3. **Choose the song** you want to use as the basis of your Genius playlist
4. If you get bored with this list of songs simply **Refresh**

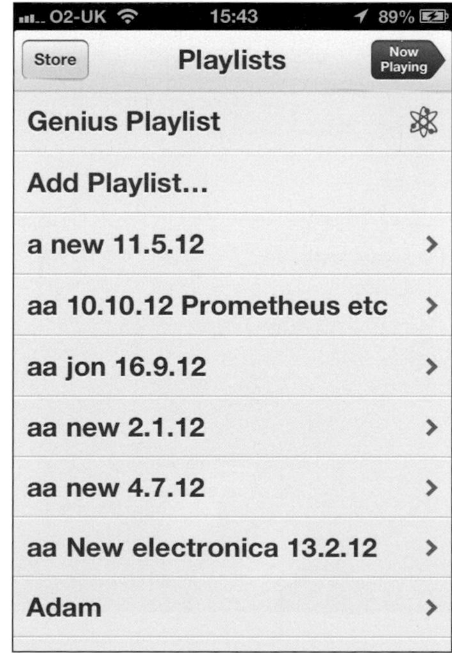

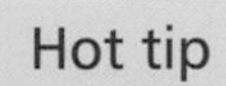

If you cannot decide what to listen to, click Genius and let the iPhone decide for you.

Play Music Using Siri

Siri voice recognition can find your music and play it.

1. **Press and hold the Home Button** until Siri opens
2. Say **Play ...** (*whatever song you want to play*)
3. Siri will find the song and start playing it

5 Photos & Video

The iPhone has a built-in camera, and is able to shoot movies as well as still images. In addition, you can even edit your movies directly on the iPhone.

iPhone Camera

The camera in the iPhone can be used for taking still photographs and video.

Tap to Focus

The iPhone camera can adjust the focus and the exposure — by tapping the screen when taking a picture or shooting video.

Beware

Night shots, or scenes with reduced light, often produce poor quality images on the iPhone.

Geotagging

The iPhone camera will provide geotagging data, including your geographical coordinates, provided you have switched Location Services on (**Settings** > **General** > **Location Services**).

The camera has a resolution of 8 megapixels which is more than enough to take good pictures and video. The poorest results are seen when the lighting is low. Night shots are particularly bad. For best shots make sure there is lots of light around. The iPhone 5 also has a camera flash for the main camera.

Location of camera lens

You will find this on the back of the iPhone at the top left corner. Take care not to scratch the lens, and clean the lens only with the cloth provided.

Main camera lens
Keep it clean!

Still Images Using Main Camera

1. Tap the **camera** icon to load the app
2. The shutter will open to show the image
3. Take care to keep still (place your elbows against your sides to steady your arms)
4. Touch the camera icon towards the bottom of the screen
5. The picture will be visible for a second or two before being dropped into the folder called **Camera Roll**, which you can find by launching the Photos application
6. Take care not to place your finger over the lens

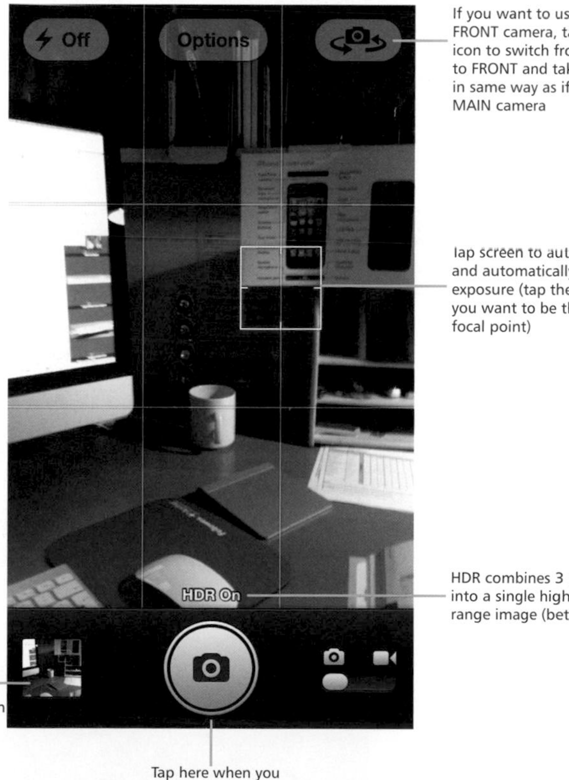

If you want to use the FRONT camera, tap this icon to switch from MAIN to FRONT and take picture in same way as if using MAIN camera

Tap screen to autofocus and automatically adjust exposure (tap the area you want to be the main focal point)

HDR combines 3 photos into a single high dynamic range image (better)

The photo will be added to the Camera Roll — tap here to open

Tap here when you are ready to take the photo

Where Are My Pictures?

- Photos and video taken using the camera end up in an album called Camera Roll
- Other pictures you have copied to the iPhone, by checking specific albums for syncing, are shown below the Camera Roll
- Find the photos you want by tapping the library and selecting the image
- You can email and view pictures in your libraries on the iPhone but you cannot delete them (although you *can* delete pictures from the camera roll – these are pictures you have taken using the iPhone camera)
- To remove photos from albums you need to use iTunes

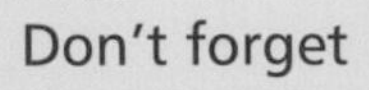

Don't forget

Camera Roll contains the images taken with the iPhone. The other albums listed are those synced from your PC or Mac to the iPhone.

Pictures taken with the camera are in this album

Pictures synced from your computer are here

Taking Videos

1. **Tap the camera icon** to load the app. The shutter will open to show the image
2. **Push the Camera/Video slider** to the right to put the camera into video mode
3. **Touch the camera icon** at the bottom of the screen. To record in High Definition, tap screen and **tap HDR**
4. The Record icon flashes red on and off during filming
5. When you have finished, tap the camera icon at the bottom. Your video will be in the Camera Roll Album

The video will be added to the Camera Roll — tap here to open
Tap to take video Tap again to stop — red light flashes on and off during filming
Slider is pushed to right for Video

Hot tip

Videos are located in the Camera Roll album.

Editing the Video

You can edit the video you have taken on a Mac, PC or directly on the iPhone itself.

1. Tap the **Photos** application
2. Tap **Camera Roll** and locate your video
3. **Tap the video** to open it – the image can be viewed in portrait or landscape, but landscape is easier for trimming
4. **Touch the screen** and the trimming timeline will be shown at the top of the screen
5. Decide what (if anything) you want to trim and drag the sliders on the left and right until you have marked the areas you wish to trim
6. Tap the yellow **trim** icon at the top right of the screen and the unwanted video will be removed

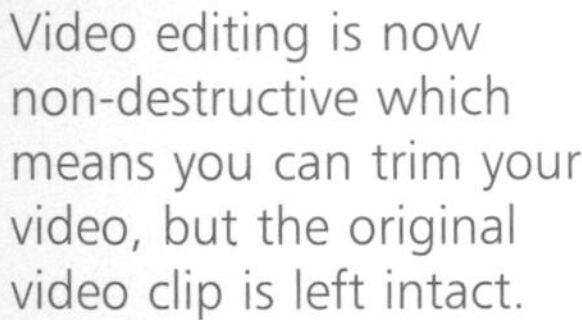

Hot tip

Video editing is now non-destructive which means you can trim your video, but the original video clip is left intact.

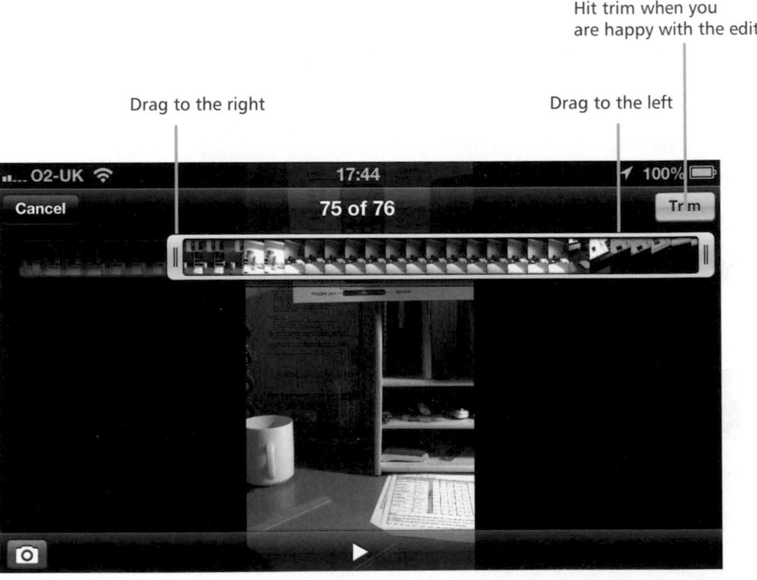
Hit trim when you are happy with the edit
Drag to the right
Drag to the left
O2-UK
17:44
100%
Cancel
75 of 76
Trim

Sharing Photos & Video

Email or MMS

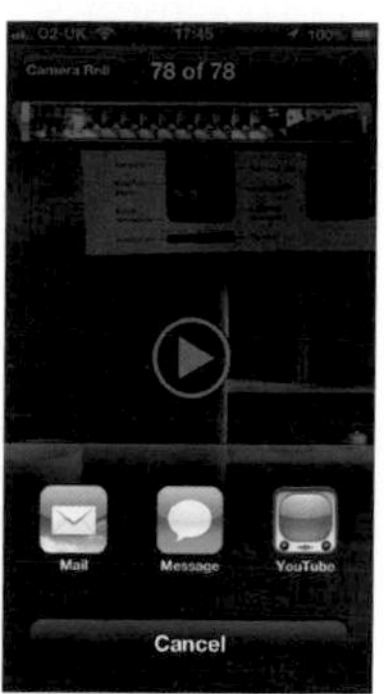

1. Go to **Photos** > **Camera Roll** and locate the photo or video

2. **Tap the icon** on the bottom left and decide whether you want to email or send the photo using MMS

3. Alternatively you can **post** to YouTube

4. You can also **assign** a photo to one of your contacts or use the image as a **wallpaper**. Just tap the relevant icon

Don't forget

As well as editing and watching the video on the iPhone, you can send your video clips to YouTube, Mail, Photo Stream, Twitter, Facebook, Assign to Contact, Print, Copy, or Use as Wallpaper.

YouTube and iMessage sharing

1. **Locate the photo or video** you wish to upload and tap the **Sharing** icon (bottom left)

2. Choose **YouTube** or **Message**

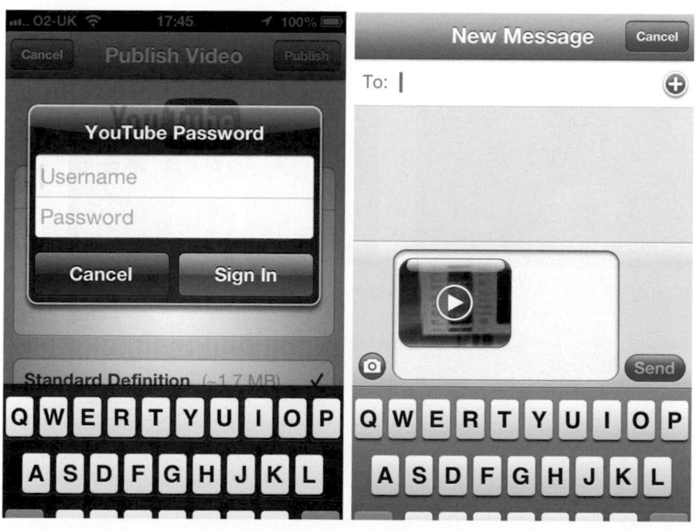

Panoramic Photos

You can now take panoramic shots where you pan across a scene and the iPhone stitches the images together to give a very wide photo which would be impossible to take using the standard camera settings.

1. Open Camera and tap **Options**. Choose **Panorama**

2. Once you tap the photo icon (bottom of screen) you need to **pan from left to right keeping the arrow on the center line** for best results

3. Once the arrow reaches the right side, the software will generate the panoramic image which will be saved to your Camera Roll

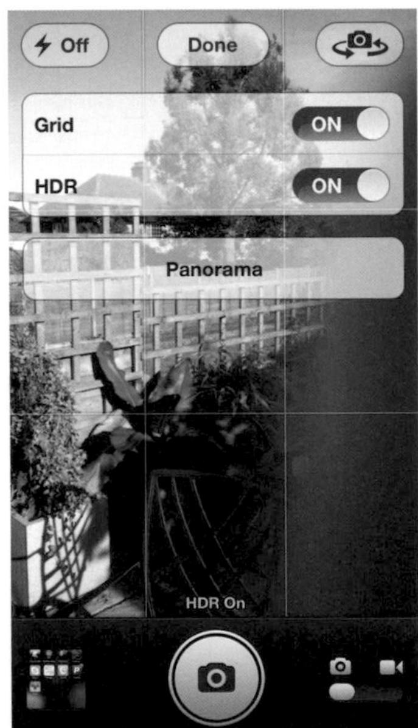

Tap Panorama and follow the on-screen instructions

Final panoramic photo generated by the Camera app

6 The Standard Apps

Each iPhone comes preinstalled with a core set of applications, which make the iPhone so versatile and useful. In this section we explore each of these apps in turn and show how to get best use out of them.

Calendar

For people who want to get organized, people in business, education and many other sectors, the core applications are: Calendar, Mail, Contacts, Phone and Notes.

These apps integrate well with each other on the iPhone and also the PC and Mac.

Setting up Calendar

Before you start entering data into Calendar, there are one or two settings you should check:

1. Go to **Settings** > **Mail, Contacts, Calendars**
2. Tap **Mail, Contacts, Calendars** to open
3. Scroll down the page until you find **Calendars**
4. Switch **New Invitation Alerts** to ON
5. Choose what to **Sync** (Do you want all events or just those for the past two weeks, month, three months, or six months?)
6. Make sure **Time Zone Support** is correct or times on your calendar will be incorrect
7. **Set your default calendar** – when you make new appointments using Calendar this is where the appointments will be added (You can add to another calendar quite easily, though.)
8. That's it. Now you can start getting appointments into your Calendar using: iPhone, Apple Calendar or Microsoft Outlook on the PC
9. We'll discuss each method in turn, and also look at how to keep your desktop computer and iPhone Calendar in sync at all times

Beware

Make sure your Time Zone is set correctly or all your appointments will be incorrect.

Calendar Views

1. Tap the **Calendar** icon to open the application 

2. You will see the **Month View** – if it opens in **Day** or **List**, tap **Month**

3. This shows an overview of the month

4. A black dot means you have an appointment on that day, but it does not tell you how long the appointment is or what it is. But look at the bottom of the screen and you will see what the day's appointments are

5. If you need a detailed view of your appointments, check out the Day view

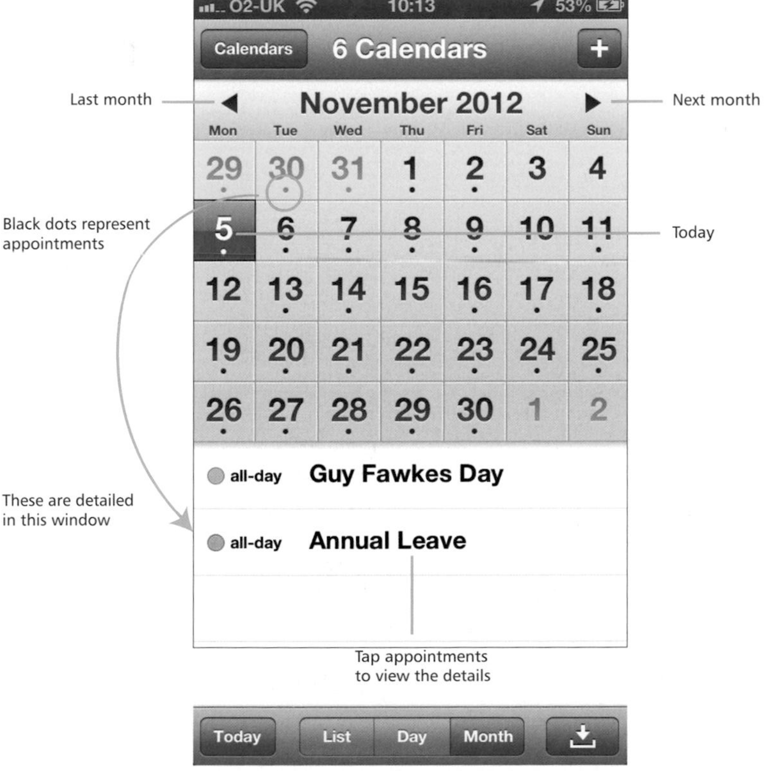

Day View

This provides a more detailed view of your day, showing the times on the left margin, and all your appointments are shown in the colors chosen by you.

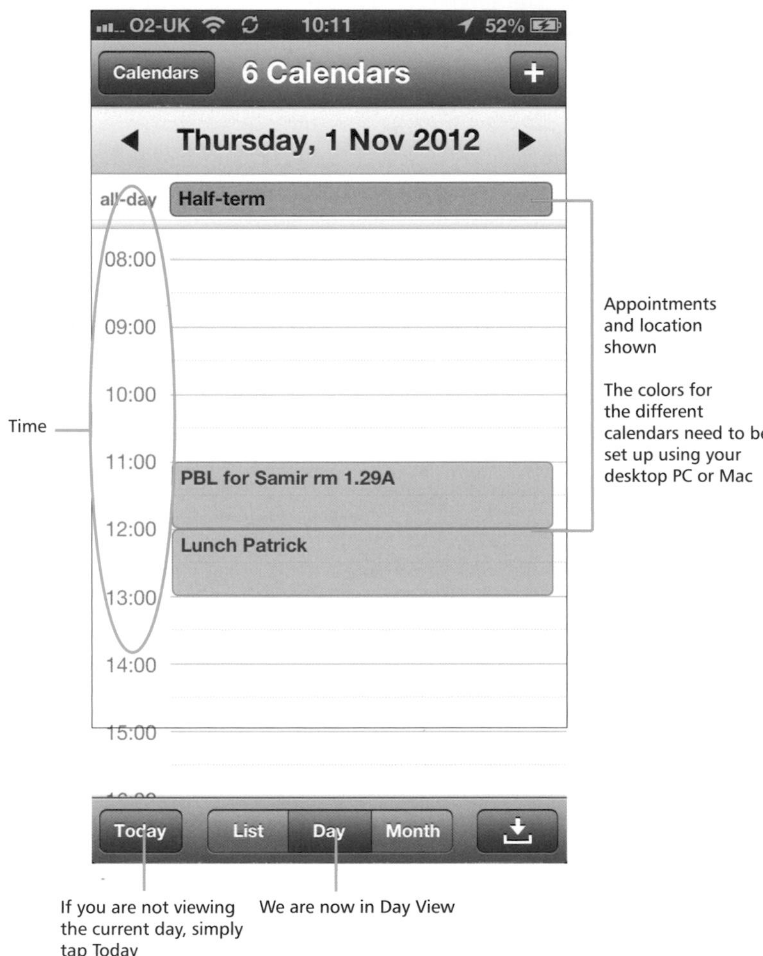

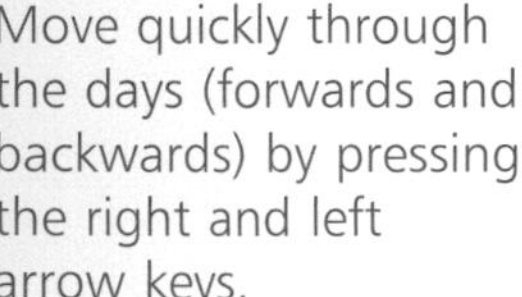

Move quickly through the days (forwards and backwards) by pressing the right and left arrow keys.

How to move quickly through the days in Day View

List View

Sometimes you want to see all your appointments as a list, rather than browsing through several months' worth of appointments using the other views.

Simply tap List and you will see every appointment, with the earliest at the top and the latest at the bottom.

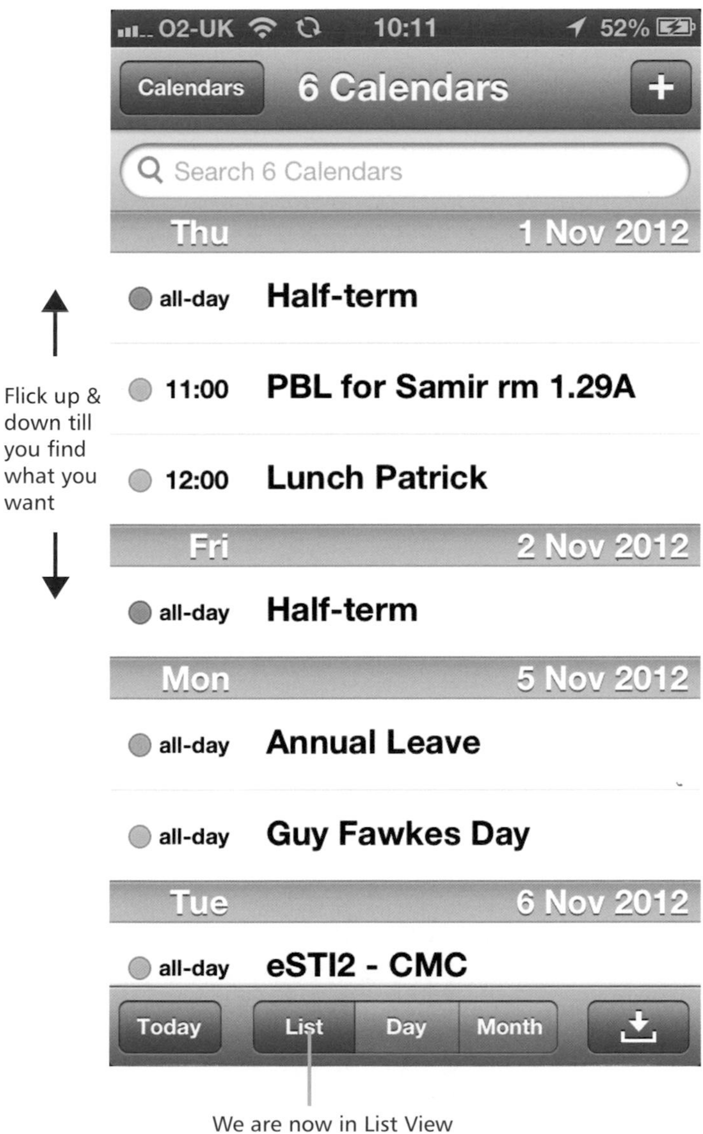

Searching Calendar

It's very easy to find appointments using the Search function within Calendar. You can also use Spotlight Search to find appointments.

1. Tap **Calendar** to open
2. Tap **List view**
3. Tap the **search box** for an item, e.g. Lecture. After you enter a few letters the appointments containing those letters will appear below
4. Tap the appointment found to see the details

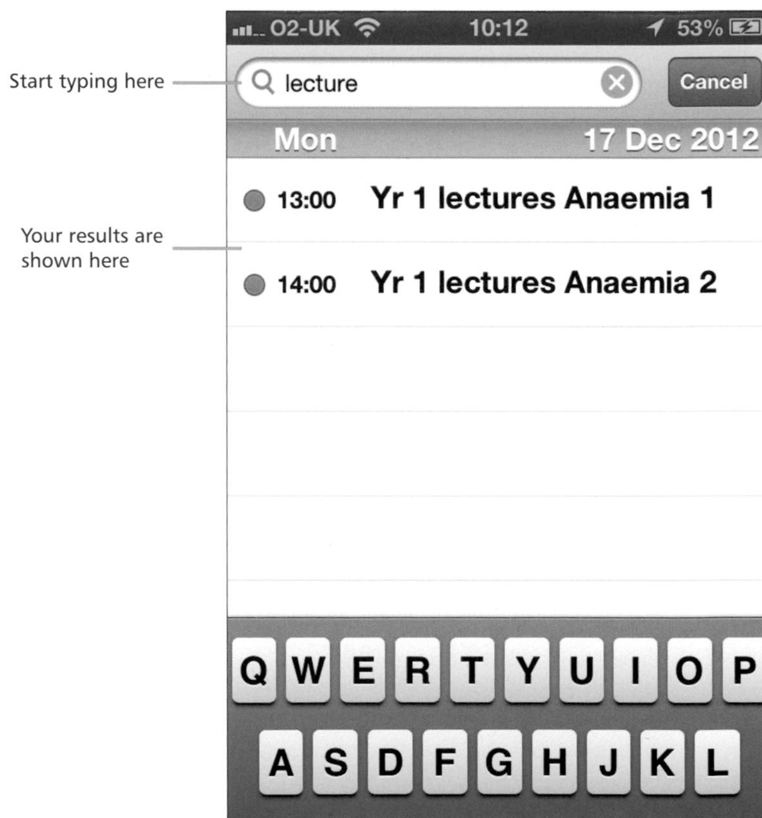

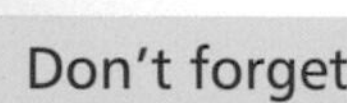

Don't forget

You can search your calendar using the inbuilt search tool or use Spotlight.

Spotlight Search

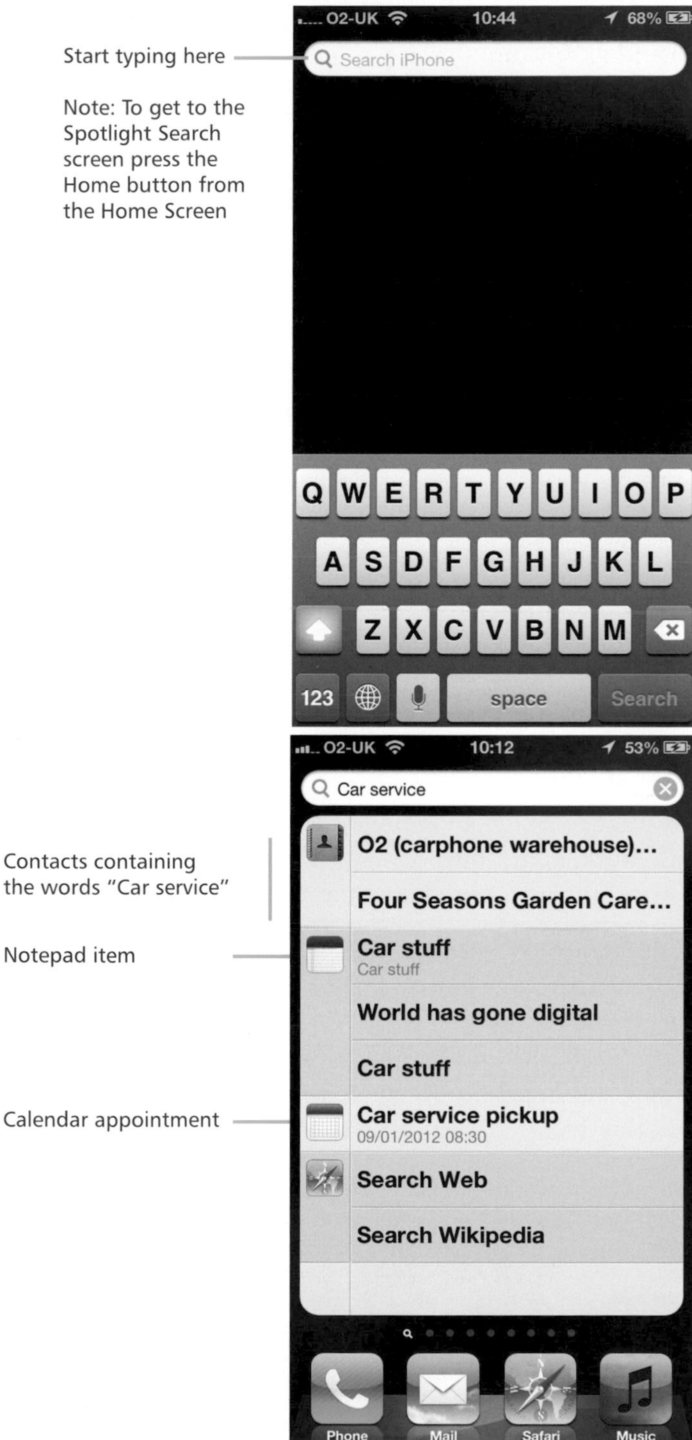

Adding Appointments

Add appointments using iPhone

This is very straightforward.

1. Tap **Calendar** to open
2. You can either go to the day of the appointment you wish to add, or you can simply tap the **+** icon at the top right of the screen
3. Enter **Title**, **Location**, then hit **Done**
4. Enter **start** and **end** time. If the date is not correct, choose the correct date
5. If it **repeats** (e.g. birthdays, anniversaries, etc) enter the frequency
6. If you want an **alert** to appear on the screen, tap the appropriate time for the alert

Multiple calendars

You might want to assign an appointment to a specific calendar, for example work, home, birthdays, vacation, etc. When you make the appointment you will be shown the Calendar tab.

You must decide which calendar the appointment belongs to *now* because, once chosen, you cannot change your mind and alter it on the iPhone. If you do want to switch an event to another calendar you will need to do this in Outlook. This is an odd feature of the Calendar app, and hopefully Apple will sort this. (Correct at the time of printing.)

Choose the correct calendar for the appointment by tapping here

Set up new appointment:

Enter details for **Title** and **Location**, tap **Starts/Ends** and enter start and end time for the appointment.

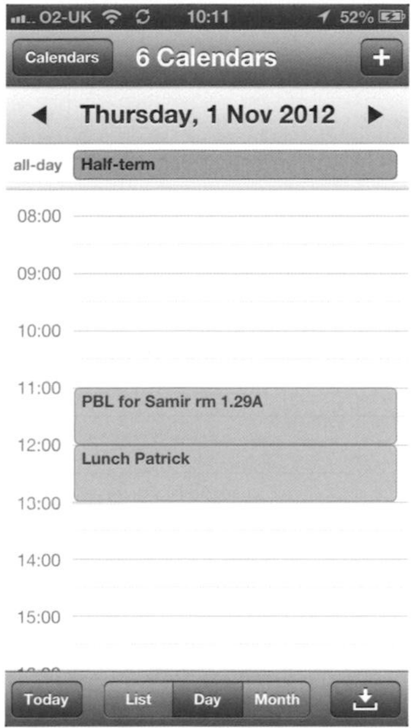

Tap the "+" to add

Enter appointment and location

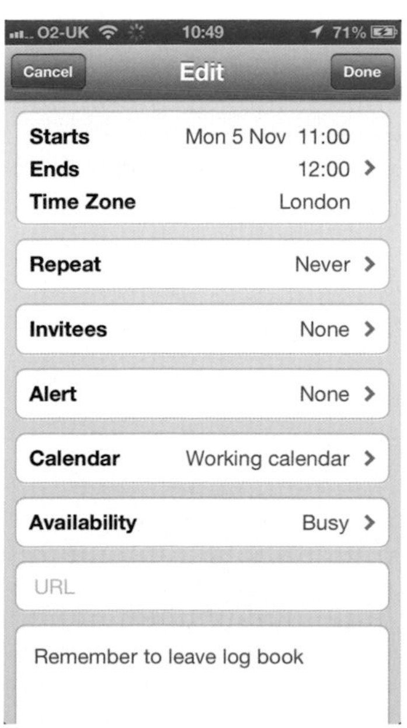

Tap "Starts/Ends"

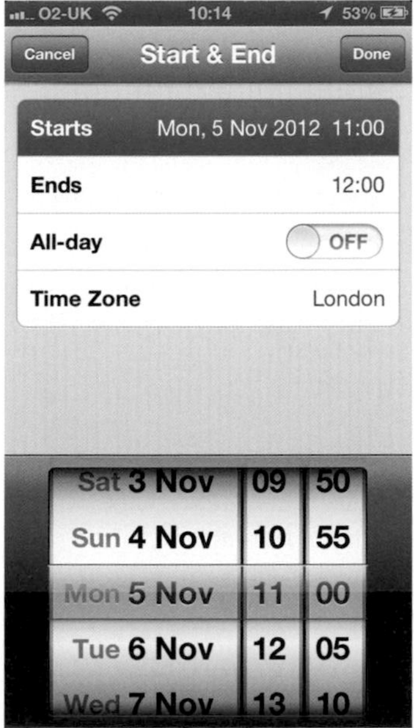

Set Start and End time

...cont'd

Next, decide whether you want alerts, the appointment to repeat and which Calendar you wish to contain the appointment.

Set up your repeat items, such as birthdays and anniversaries.

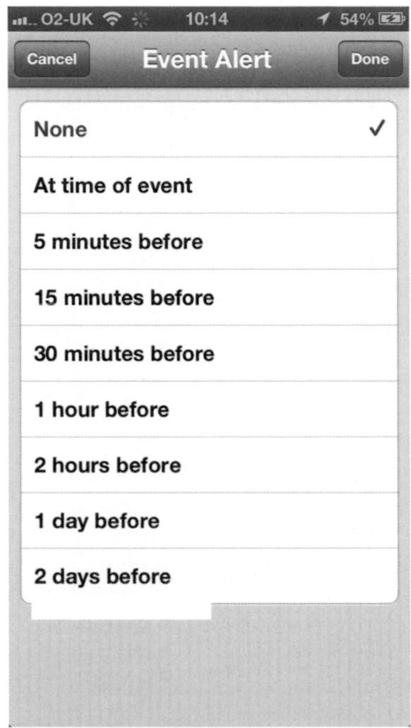

Set up the alert

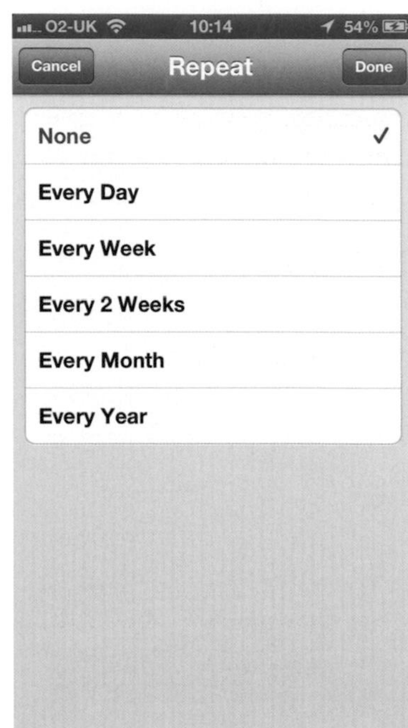

Decide on repeat frequency

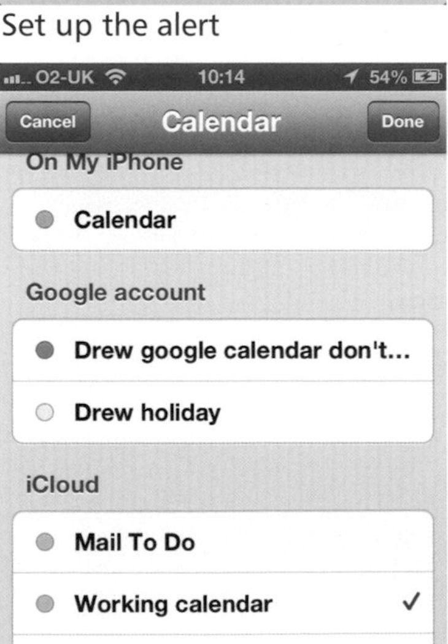

If you have multiple calendars, choose the one you wish the appointment to be associated with

Setting up Multiple Calendars

Why do you need multiple calendars? Well, you might want to keep work and home separate. You could put all your holidays, dental appointments and other personal items into the Home calendar and keep all your business appointments separate.

Many people share their calendars with, for example, their secretaries. You can publish Outlook and Apple Calendar calendars online but you don't necessarily want your work colleagues to view all your personal calendar items.

On the Mac

1. Open **Calendar**
2. Click the **+** symbol (bottom left)
3. Give your new Calendar a **name**
4. Right click the name of the new calendar and **choose the color**
5. If you only want to see the appointments associated with a specific calendar uncheck those you do *not* want to see

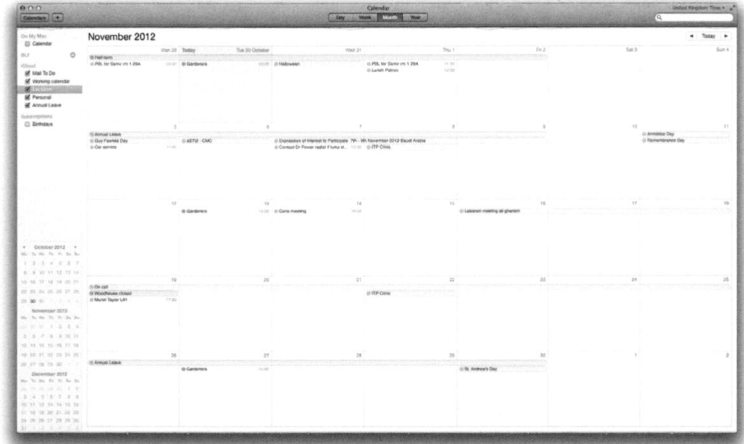

Hot tip

Keep your work and personal calendar information separate by creating separate calendars.

Add Appointment to Calendar

1. Double click anywhere on the **calendar**
2. Double click the **New Event** box and it will open
3. Give the event a **title** and enter the **location**
4. Check the **All Day** box if it's an all-day event, otherwise leave unchecked
5. Enter **Date** and **Time** of start and end
6. Decide which calendar to associate with the appointment (from the drop-down list)
7. If you want an **alarm** (text, email, open a file, run a script) set it here
8. If you are inviting others to the meeting, use the **Add Invitees** option and enter their email addresses
9. If you want to add **attachments** or make **notes**, add these then hit **Done**

Add Appointment to Outlook

1. Open **Outlook** and **double click** somewhere on the calendar
2. An untitled appointment will open
3. Give it a **Subject** and **Location**
4. Add **Start time** and **End time**
5. Check or uncheck **All Day** box
6. Enter **Notes** and set up **alarm**
7. To associate with a specific calendar, drag the appointment to that calendar name in the left column
8. **Save and close**

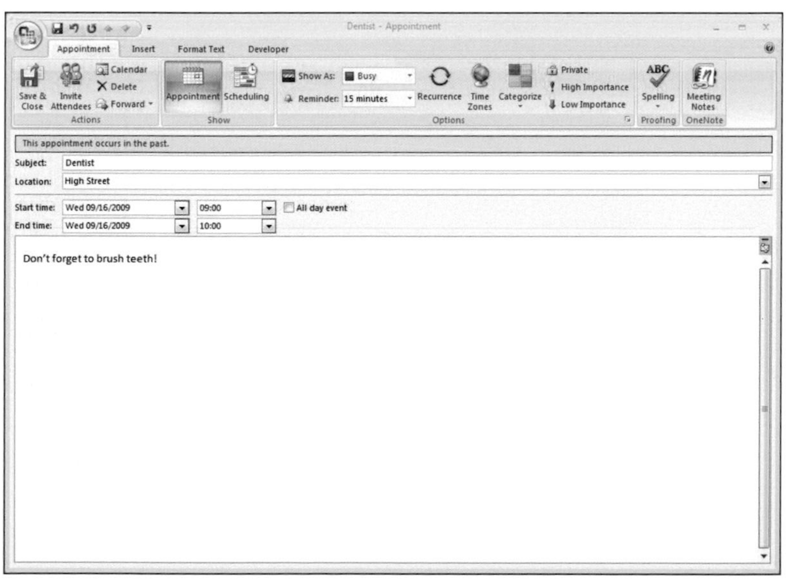

Outlook Multiple Calendars

Calendar overlays multiple calendars very easily but with Outlook there is a tweak you have to use, otherwise you end up with all your separate calendars side by side which makes them very difficult to read.

Hot tip 

Microsoft Outlook shows separate calendars side by side. You need to merge them into one using the Overlay function.

View in Overlay Mode

1. Make sure all your separate calendars in **Outlook** are checked (left column). If you have three calendars you will see all three side by side

2. Click the **View in Overlay Mode** and they will all merge!

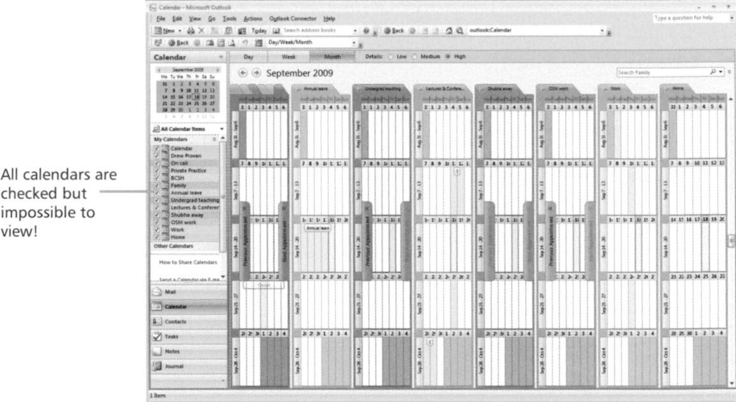

All calendars are checked but impossible to view!

Click the arrow here to view in Overlay Mode

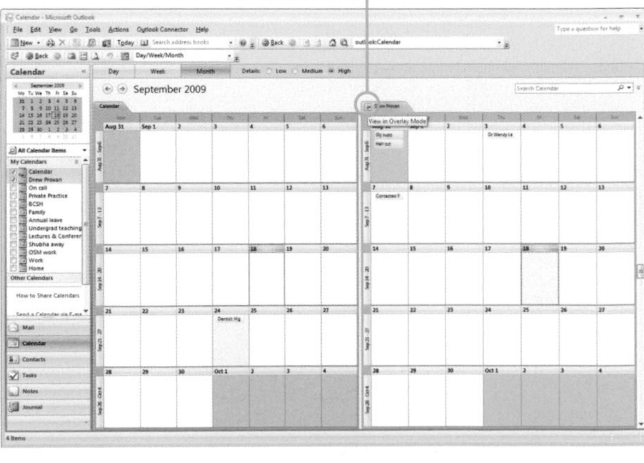

This gives you an overlaid calendar with all your appointments:

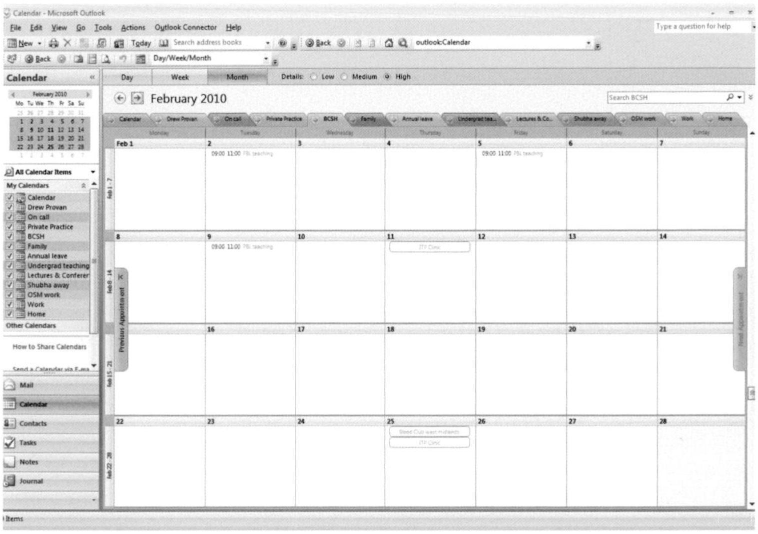

Changing the calendar associated with an appointment?

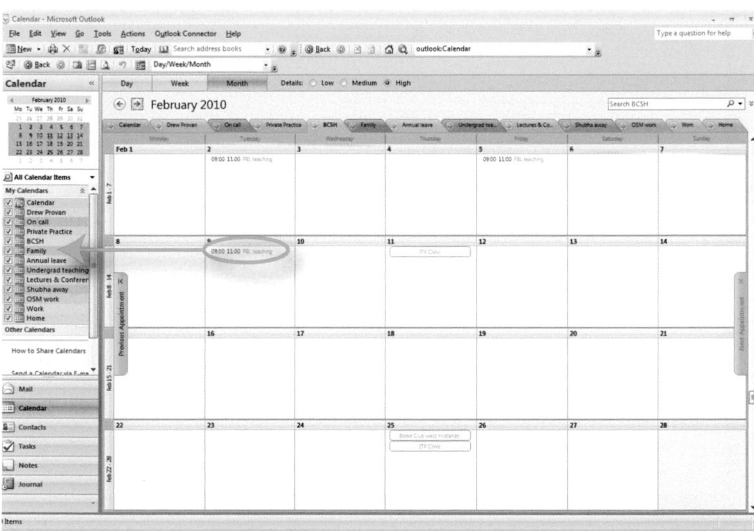

Drag & drop the appointment onto the calendar it should be associated with

Sync Calendar with PC and Mac

Mac

There are two main ways to sync your calendar information:

- By direct USB connection with the Mac – iTunes will automatically perform a sync unless you have switched this feature off
- Using cloud computing, e.g. iCloud – this will wirelessly sync all your data (Contacts, Calendars but not Notes)

Hot tip

Calendar data can be synced using a USB connection with your desktop computer, or wirelessly using iCloud.

iCloud syncing

1. In the **iCloud** control panel **select Calendar sync**
2. Edit the **settings** to suit your requirements
3. These are shown opposite

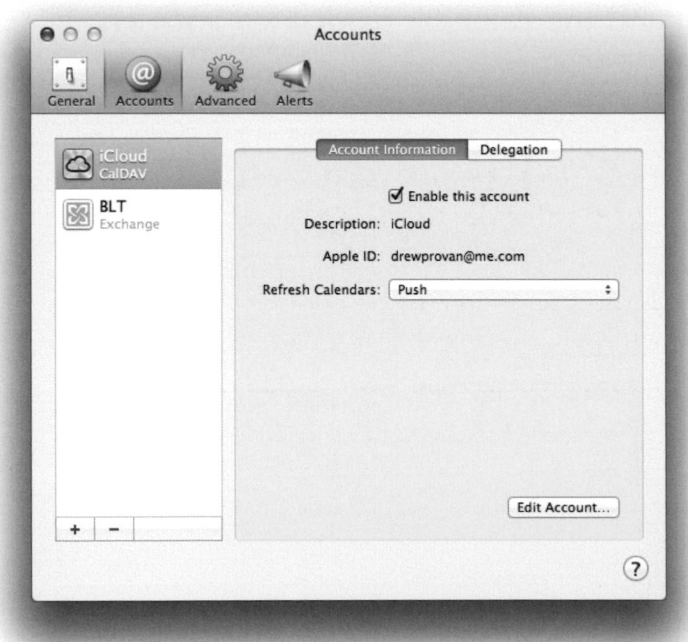

...cont'd

Wireless sync on the PC

1. Go to **Control Panels** > **iCloud**
2. Check the box for **Outlook sync**

USB sync on the PC

1. Under the **Info** panel in iTunes, check the button for **Sync calendars with Outlook**
2. Each time you connect the iPhone to the PC, using USB, automatic syncing will take place

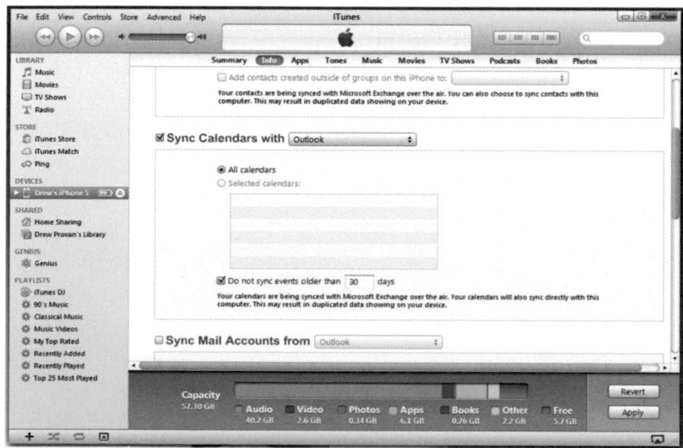

Notes Application

All good PDAs have some kind of note-taking software and the iPhone is no exception. The Notes application can be found on the Home page, but you can move it to wherever you want it. The notes you make can be synced with your desktop computer and we will look at this later.

To make a note

1. Tap the **Notepad** icon to open the application
2. Tap the **+** symbol to make a new note
3. Tap **Done** when you're finished
4. You will return to the screen showing all your notes
5. You can navigate back and forth through your notes, email them and trash them

Tap the "+" to make new note

Tap any note to open, read and edit

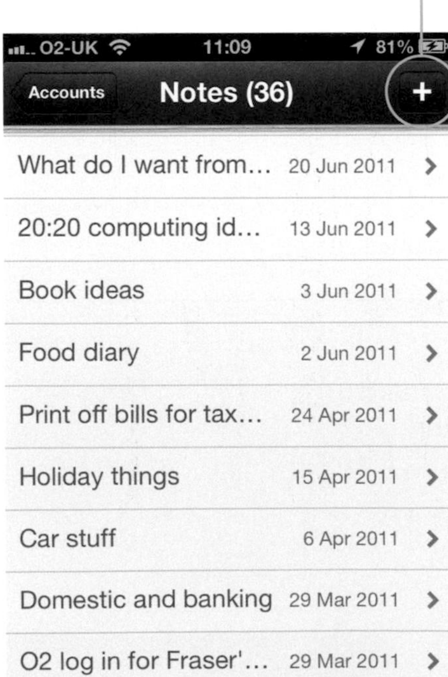

Notes controls

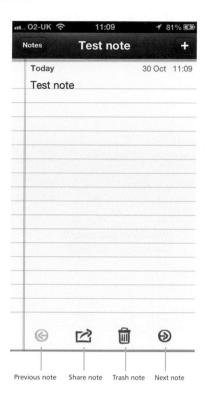

If you don't like the default font in Notes, change it in Settings.

Don't like the default font?

The default iPhone Notes font is Marker Felt (the Test note above uses this font) which many people don't like much. If you don't like it, change it.

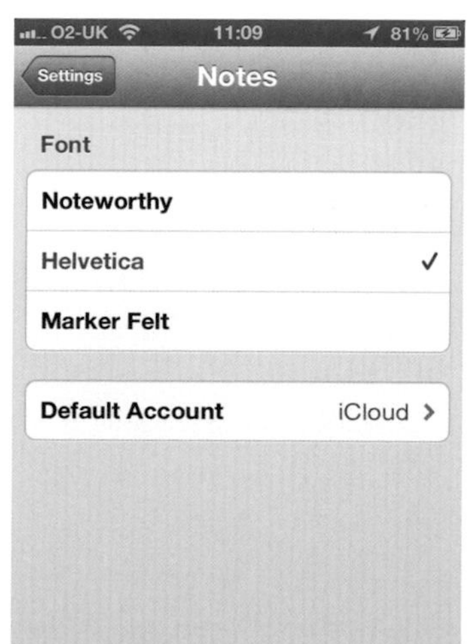

Change the font

1. Go to **Settings** > **Notes**
2. Choose the font you prefer

Sync Notes with Computer

On the Mac

Notes used to be embedded within the Mail app before Mountain Lion (OS X 10.8) but now Notes is a separate app. To ensure your Notes on the Mac and iPhone 5 stay in sync you will need to configure iCloud to sync your Notes. If you don't have an iCloud account you will need to set one up.

On the iPhone 5

1. Go to **Settings > iCloud**
2. Make sure Notes is set to **ON**

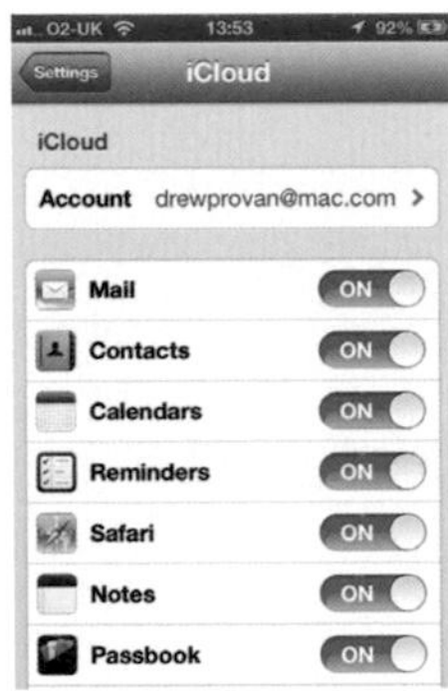

On the Mac side

1. Open the **iCloud** System Preference
2. Make sure Notes is checked for syncing

On the PC

Similar to Mac, you can sync Notes using iCloud or you can connect your iPhone to your PC using the Lightning cable and configure iTunes to sync your Notes.

1. Plug the iPhone into the PC
2. When **iTunes** opens, select the **iPhone** tab in the left column
3. Under the **Info** tab select the **Notes** pane
4. Make sure **Notes** are set to sync with Outlook

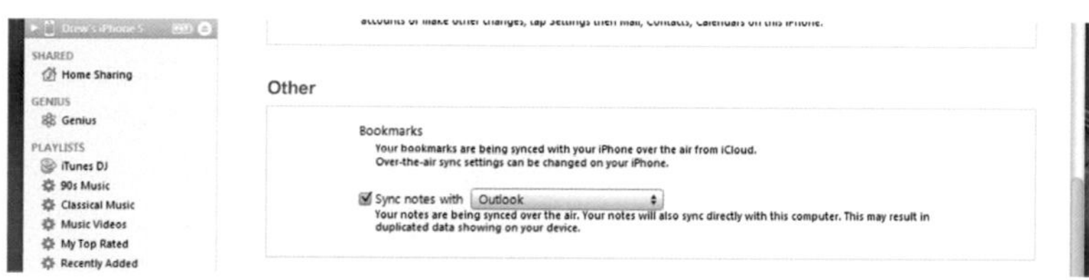

5. Syncing will occur each time you plug the iPhone into the PC
6. If you want to stop syncing your notes, **uncheck** the tab

Wireless route using iCloud

Maps Application

Maps is a great application – it can help you find where you are now, where you want to go, help you plan the route, tell you which direction you are facing and where all the traffic is.

Hot tip

The satellite view takes longer to load. For speedy viewing of maps, use the standard "Map" view.

Hot tip

To see which way you are facing, tap the search icon (bottom right) until it shows a white beam.

Don't forget

Maps will only work if Location Services is switched on.

Open Maps: You are here!

Tap blue circle to see which way you are facing

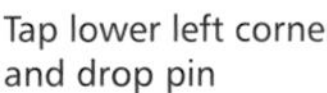

Tap lower left corner and drop pin

Pin shows your location in satellite view

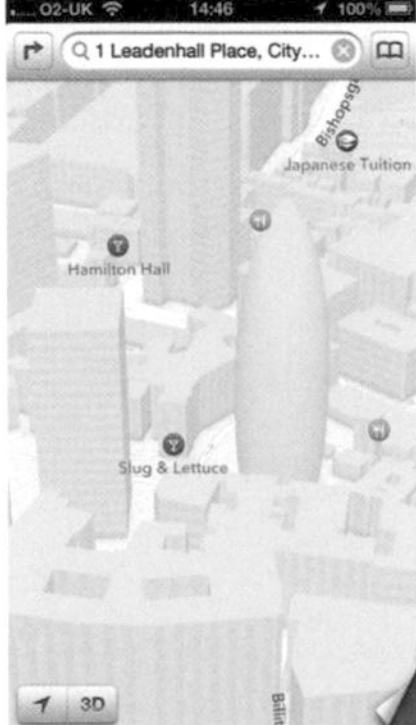

Standard 3D view

Satellite 3D view

Finding a route

Tap the Directions button and enter your start and end points.

Maps will calculate a route. It will also tell you how long it will take by car, public transport and by foot.

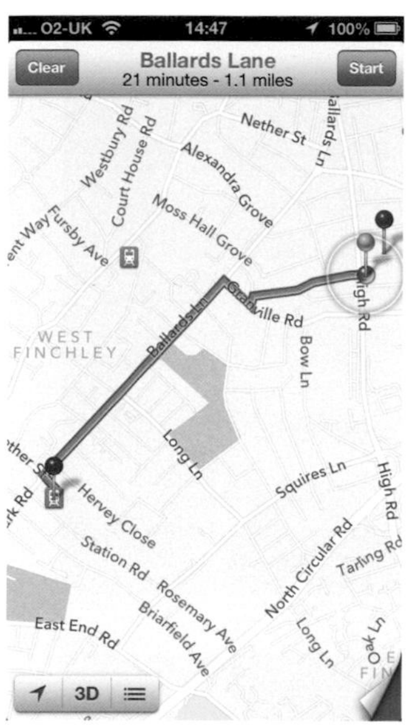

Here I have selected a simple route and chosen to go on foot. The Maps app tells me how long it is (in miles) and how long the journey should take. I could stay on this view but I prefer the turn-by-turn directions view (shown below).

The turn-by-turn options leads you in small steps, making it very easy to navigate on foot, in the car, or using public transport.

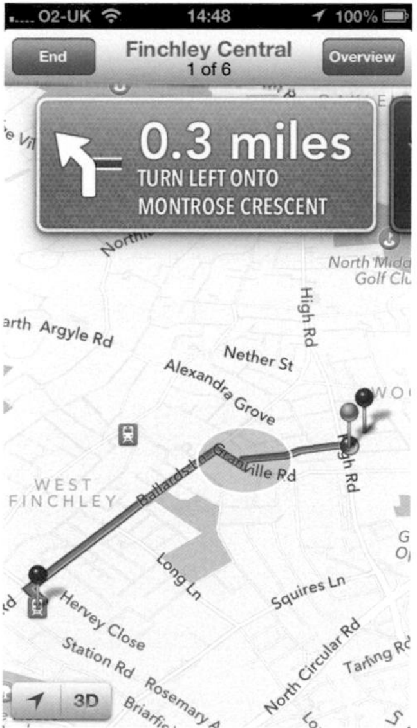

Hot tip

The Google Maps app is a good alternative that can be downloaded to your iPhone 5. It includes voice-guided, turn-by-turn navigation, live traffic conditions and information on public transport. Google claims to constantly keep the "map of the world" updated!

Weather Application

This app tells you what the weather forecast is for the next six days. You can program the app to show the weather in multiple places. You can also choose between Centrigrade or Fahrenheit.

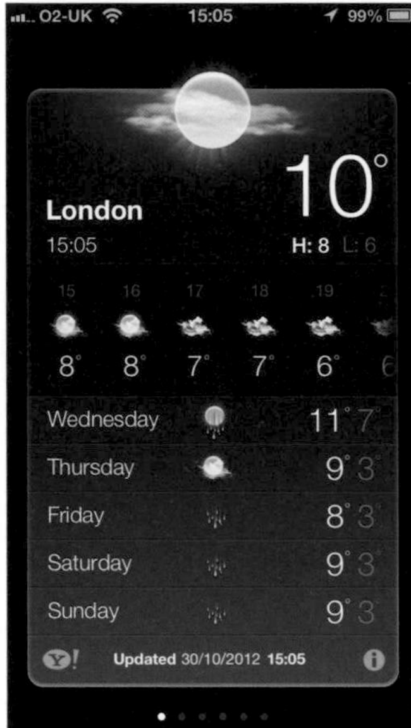

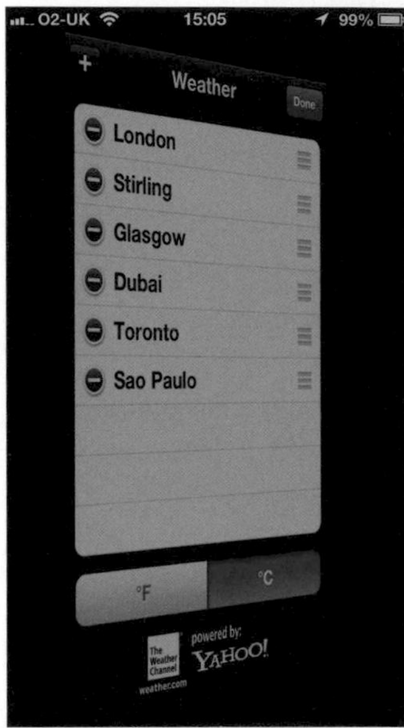

Tap the "i" and the screen will flip round

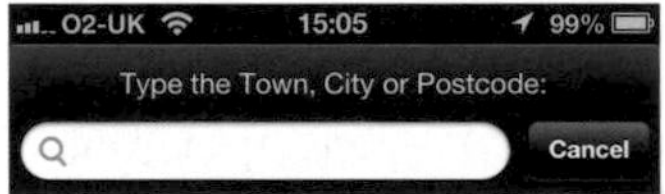

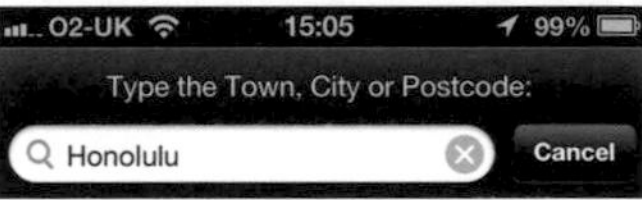

Honolulu, HI

Honolulu, NC

Tap the Search box and enter the name of a location. When you find what you want tap it then tap the lower right corner to flip the screen back

Stocks & Passbook

The Stocks app makes it easy to see how your stocks and shares are doing, both numerically and graphically.

What's happening on the FTSE 100?

Passbook stores your boarding passes and other coupons. You need to purchase additional software using the App Store to make Passbook fully functional.

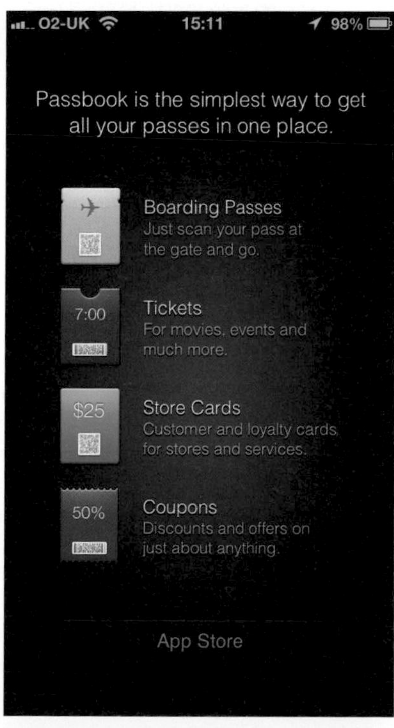

iBooks

This is a “standard” app but won’t be on your iPhone by default. You need to go and grab a copy from the app store (free). You will need to have an iTunes account, even to download free books.

The app is very similar to the iPad version, albeit with a smaller screen.

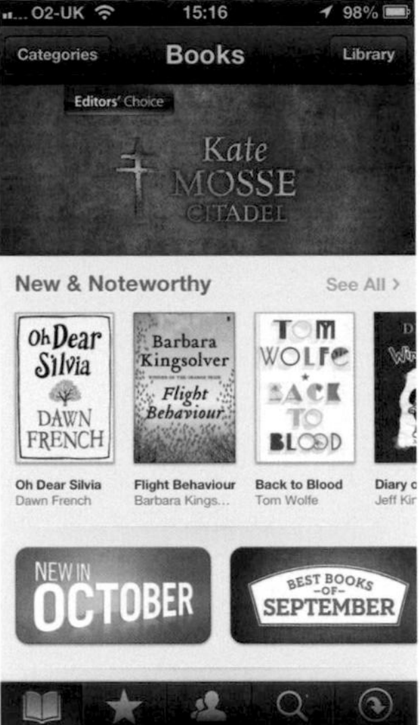

Tap Store and you can browse, buy and download books

iBooks has 2 main views: Store, which is like iTunes, where you can browse through the various categories of books and download to your iPhone. You will need an iTunes account.

If you tap Library, you will see the books you have downloaded. If you have any PDFs in the library you will see these if you tap PDFs.

Library view — Books

Library view — PDF files

Nike+ iPod App

This app works with the Nike gadget that fits in your sneakers. When you run, it sends data to your iPhone which is then uploaded to the Nike website when you sync your iPhones using iTunes. If you enjoy running you will find this app indispensable!

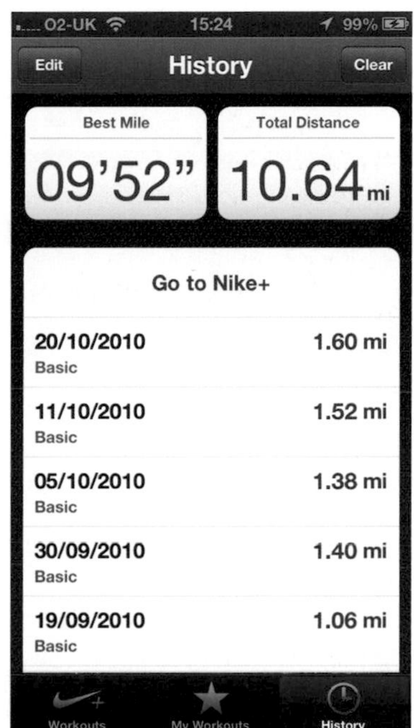

Select the workout, do the run, and view your past runs

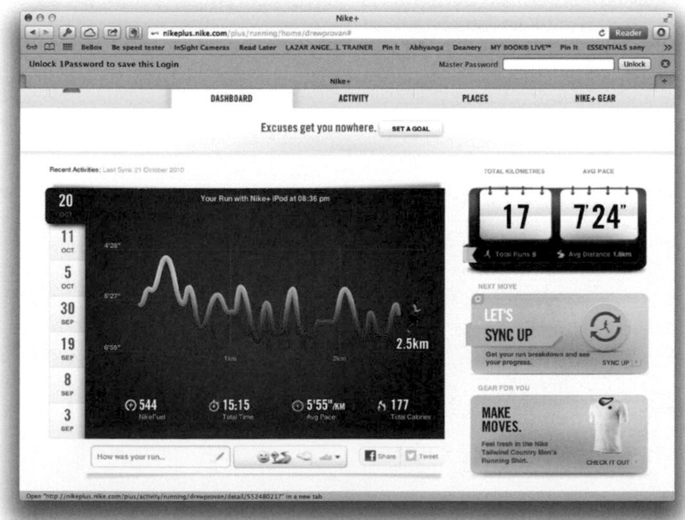

Here is the Nike+ Dashboard showing my runs

Calculator

As expected, this is a fully-functioning calculator. You can view a standard calculator if you view in portrait mode. However, if you rotate the screen to landscape, the calculator changes to a scientific calculator.

To access the scientific calculator, turn the iPhone to landscape.

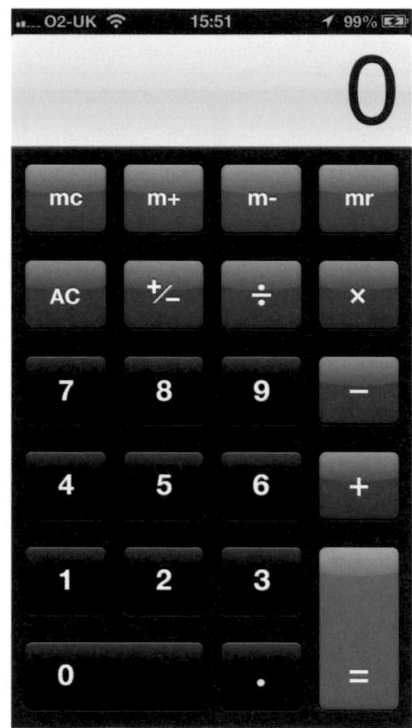

Rotate through 90° to see the scientific calculator:

Clock

This app functions as a clock, alarm, stop watch and timer. You can see what time it is in any city in the world by adding these to your clock screen.

Current time in 4 cities

Tap edit to add or delete locations. Drag up and down

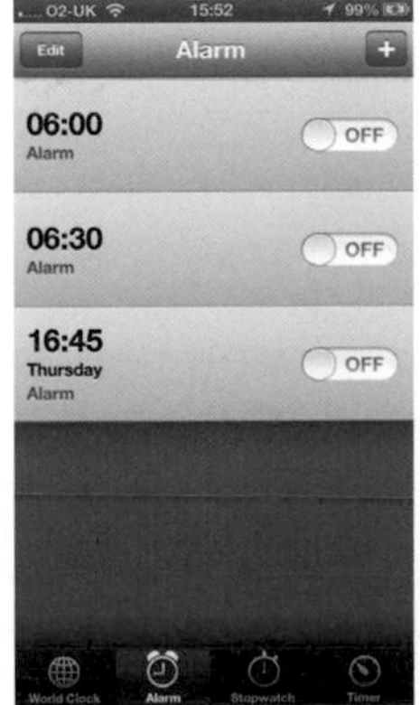

Alarm clock function

Stopwatch

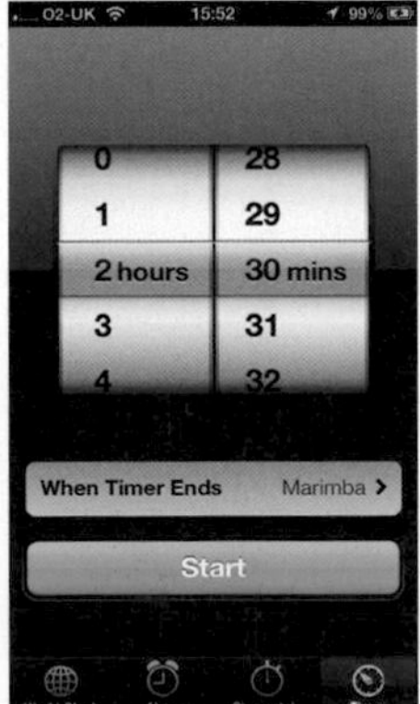

Timer function

Compass

The compass needs to be calibrated before you use it – wave the iPhone in a figure of eight. The needle points to north and you can find your current location by tapping the lower left icon.

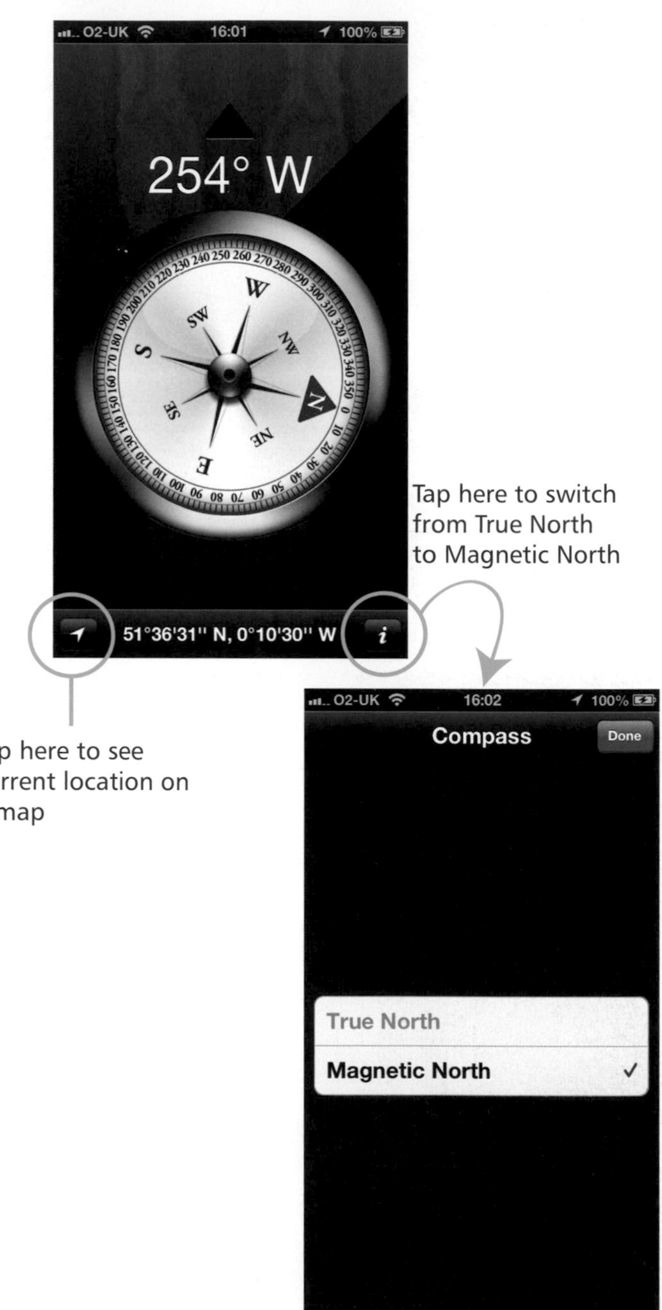

iTunes Store Application

This is the iPhone version of the iTunes store on the Mac or PC. You can buy audio and video content for your iPhone.

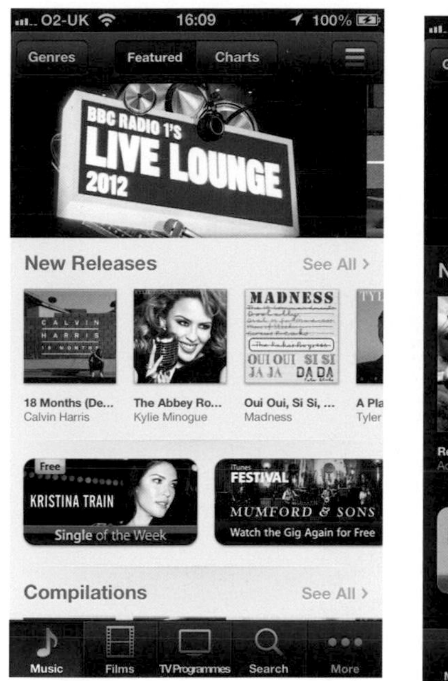

Purchase music

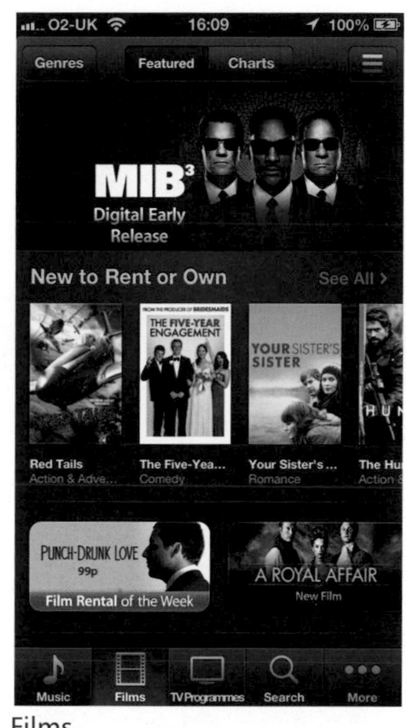

Films

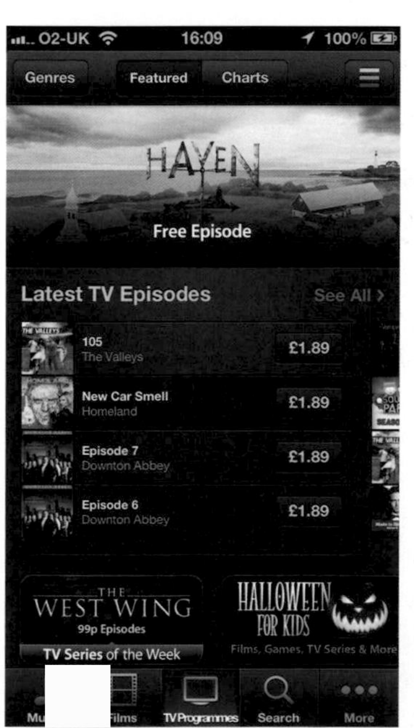

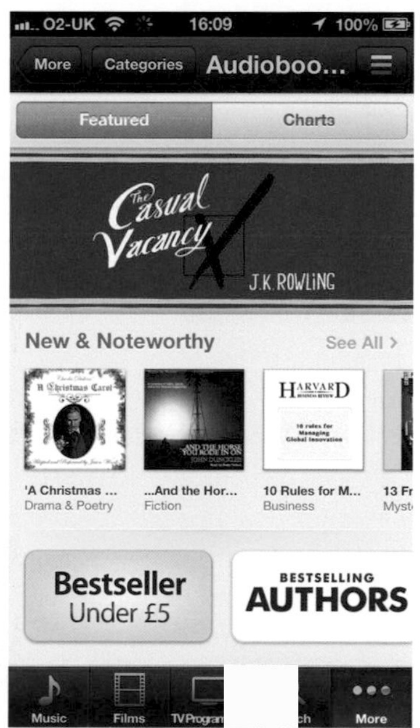

TV programmes and audiobooks

Reminders

iOS 6 includes Reminders, a simple to-do list app that can store and sync Reminders with your Mac (using the Reminders app on the Mac) or PC (syncs with Tasks in Outlook).

Using Reminders

1. Tap Reminders to open the app
2. **Tap the +** to add a new Reminder (or just tap on a line)
3. The keyboard will appear. Type the name of your reminder
4. Tap the **right arrow** if you want to add more details

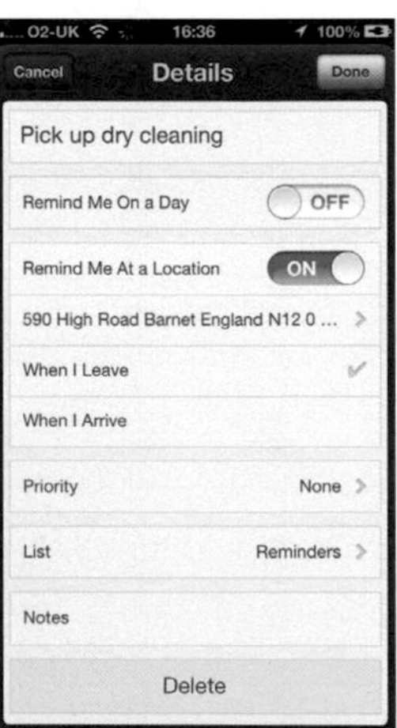

Location-based Reminders

You can ask Reminders to alert you when you are leaving or arriving at a location. For example, you might want to pick up your dry cleaning when you are near that location. By entering the zip code, Reminders will know where you are and if you are near the dry cleaners it will remind you to pick up your dry cleaning.

Siri

Siri is the voice recognition assistant that can make appointments, find items on your iPhone, open apps, get directions to locations, open Passbook, post to Facebook, send tweets and more.

To use Siri

1. **Hold the Home Button** down until Siri appears

2. Speak your instructions clearly, e.g. *Call John, directions to nearest garage, what is the weather like tomorrow, open Safari*

3. Siri will show you what it thinks you said, and will carry out the operation

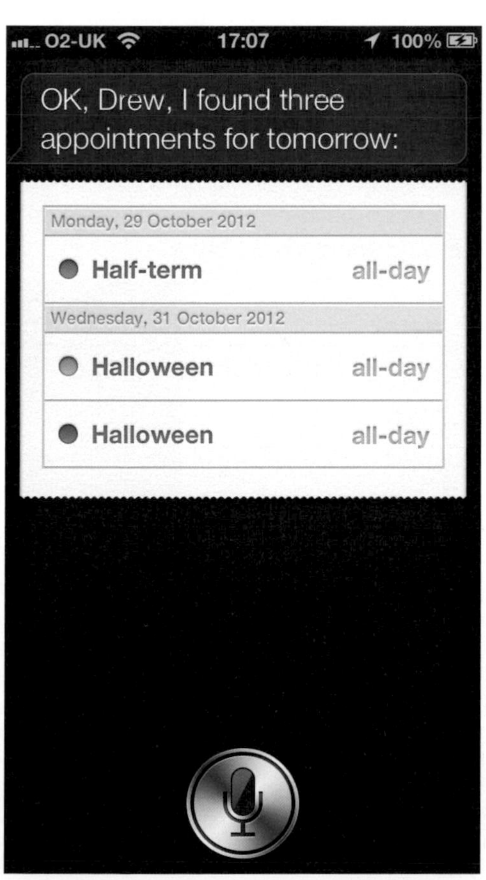

Voice Memos

The iPhone is a great voice recorder. You can make voice notes for yourself then email them to colleagues or yourself to listen to later.

1. Tap **Voice Memos** to open
2. Tap the **Record** icon (it changes to a Pause icon). You will see the time elapsed
3. Pause recording by hitting the **Pause** button
4. If you need to take a call, or use another app, you will see **Recording Paused** on a red bar at the top of the screen. To return to Voice Memos, tap the red bar at the top of the screen
5. When finished, tap the **Stop** button
6. You will then be taken to a screen showing all your voice memos
7. Listen to them on the speaker, using headphones, email them or send them via MMS
8. You can **Trim** the memos if there is unwanted material you wish to remove

Time elapsed

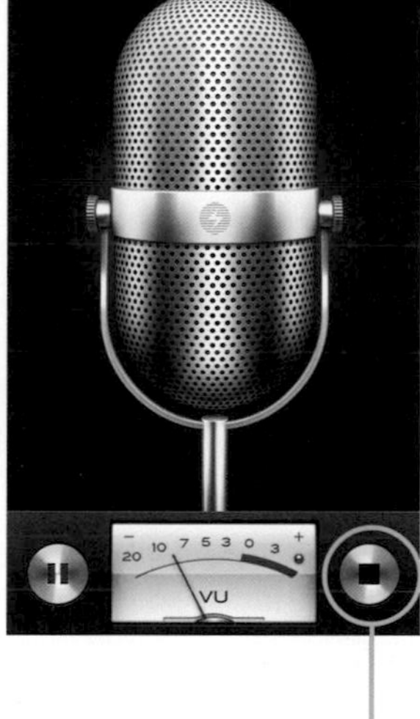

Tap here to Record
Tap again to Pause

Tap here to go
to Voice Memos

Tap here to Stop

Tap home button during recording.
You will then see the Home Page.
To return to the Voice Memo recording
tap the red area

Listen to the recording, or
send it by Email or MMS.
Below the Voice Memo
is being emailed

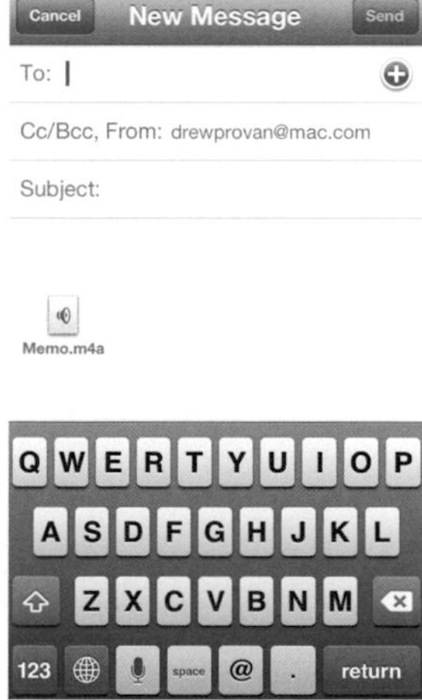

Photos

This was covered, in part, in Chapter 5.

Tap Photos to view albums

Tap the album to view it

Move through using arrows
or flick with your finger

You can email, send by MMS,
assign to contact or use as wallpaper.

Or you can press the play button
and watch a presentation of
all the photos in that album

7 Web Browsing

Browsing the web on the iPhone is very easy using Apple's inbuilt browser, Safari. We will look at how to use Safari, save and organize bookmarks and use live links within web pages.

Network Connections

Your iPhone can download data, such as emails and web pages, using a number of different types of connection. Some types of connection are faster than others. In general, Wi-Fi and Bluetooth should be kept off if you are not using them because they use a considerable amount of power.

Wi-Fi and Bluetooth drain battery power. Switch off when not required.

GPRS

This is a slow network! But often better than nothing.

EDGE

This is a relatively slow connection but is fine for email.

3G and 4G

These are faster connections than EDGE. 4G is pretty close to Wi-Fi speed.

Wi-Fi connection

Joining a wireless connection will give you fairly fast download speeds. There are many free Wi-Fi hotspots. You can use home Wi-Fi once you enter the password.

Bluetooth

This is a short-range wireless connection, generally used for communication using a Bluetooth headset.

What do the various icons mean?

Look at the top of the iPhone and you will see various icons relating to cellular and other networks.

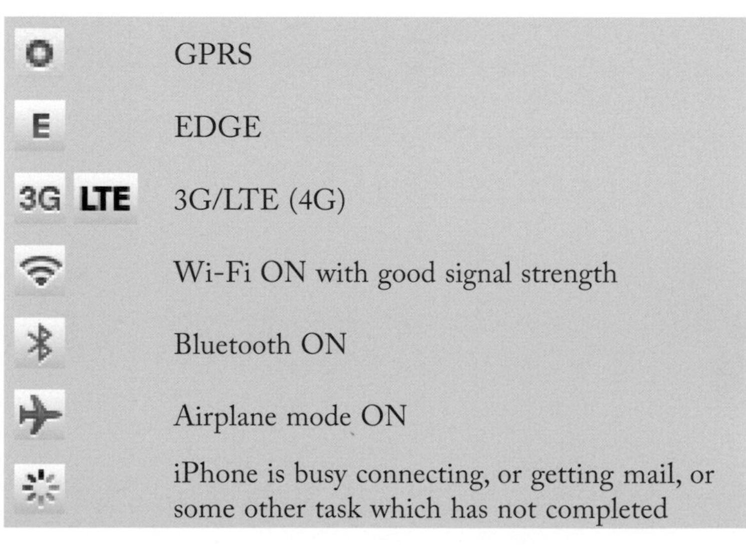

Icon	Meaning
O	GPRS
E	EDGE
3G LTE	3G/LTE (4G)
	Wi-Fi ON with good signal strength
	Bluetooth ON
	Airplane mode ON
	iPhone is busy connecting, or getting mail, or some other task which has not completed

Configuring Networks

Wi-Fi

1. Go to **Settings** > **Wi-Fi**
2. Tap **Wi-Fi**
3. Tap **ON** if it is off
4. Choose a **network** from those listed and enter the password
5. Tap **Ask to Join Networks** if you want to be prompted each time a new network is found. It's generally easier to leave this OFF
6. If you want to forget the network (e.g. maybe you have used one in a hotel), tap the name of the network you have joined, and tap **Forget this Network**

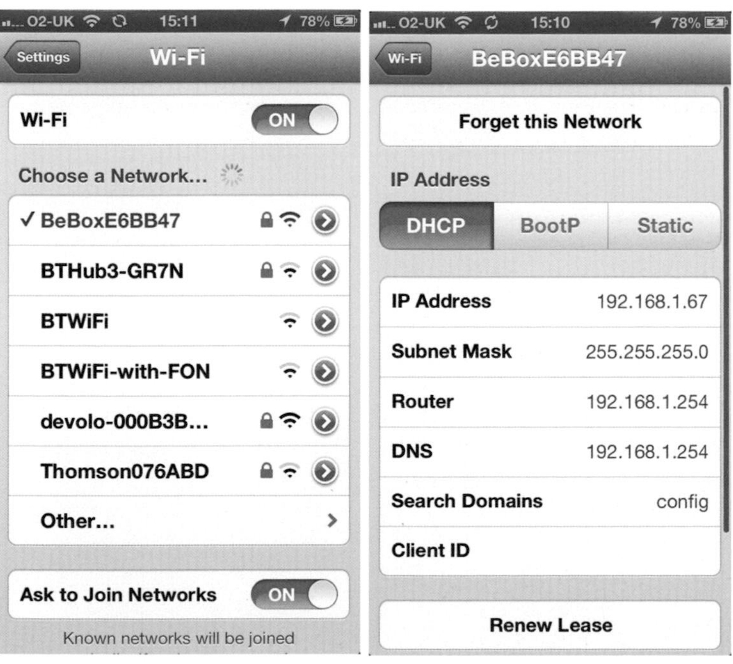

Bluetooth

1. Go to **Settings** > **General** > **Bluetooth**
2. Tap **ON** if it is off
3. Go back and switch off when not needed in order to conserve battery power

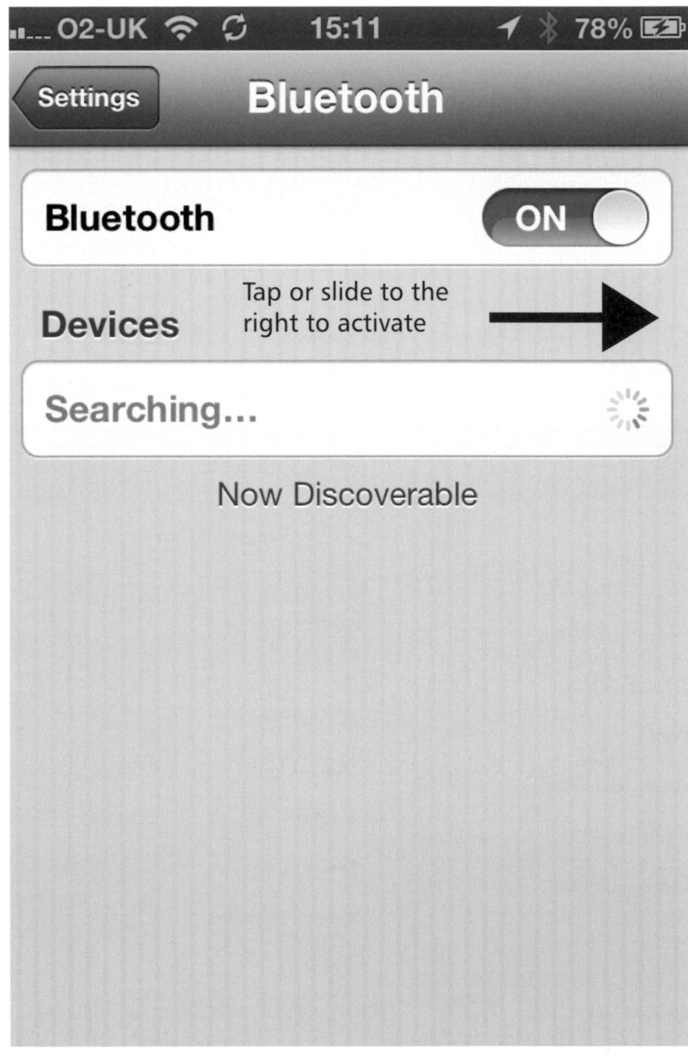

Tap or slide to the right to activate

Switch All Networks Off

1. Put the iPhone in **Airplane Mode**
2. Go to **Settings** > **Airplane Mode**
3. Tap **ON** if it is off
4. Use this on the plane or when you want to conserve power

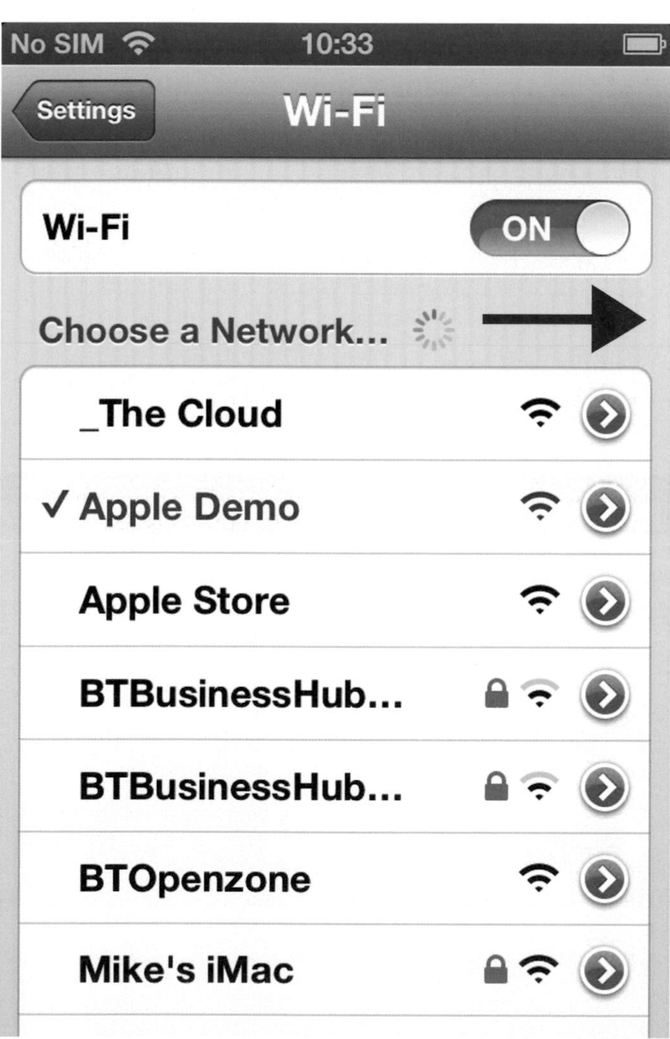

Put your iPhone in Airplane mode before you get on the plane. Then switch the power off for take-off and landing.

Browse the Internet

Safari is Apple's browser on the Mac and also on the iPhone. It is clean and uncluttered, which makes it ideal for mobile devices such as the iPhone.

1. Tap the **Safari** browser to open it
2. Tap the **address field** to enter the URL
3. Tap **Go**
4. To erase the URL, go to the address field and **tap the cross** which clears the text
5. **Browse** in portrait or landscape
6. To **scroll**, drag your finger up and down the screen
7. To **enlarge** the text, double tap the screen or stretch the text by pushing two fingers apart whilst placed on the screen

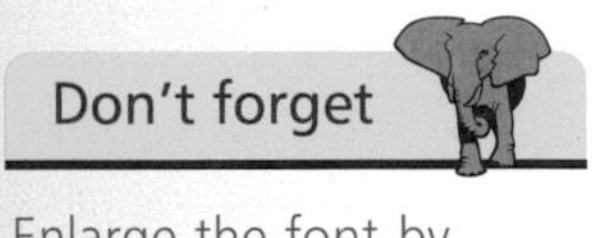

Enlarge the font by tapping twice on the screen.

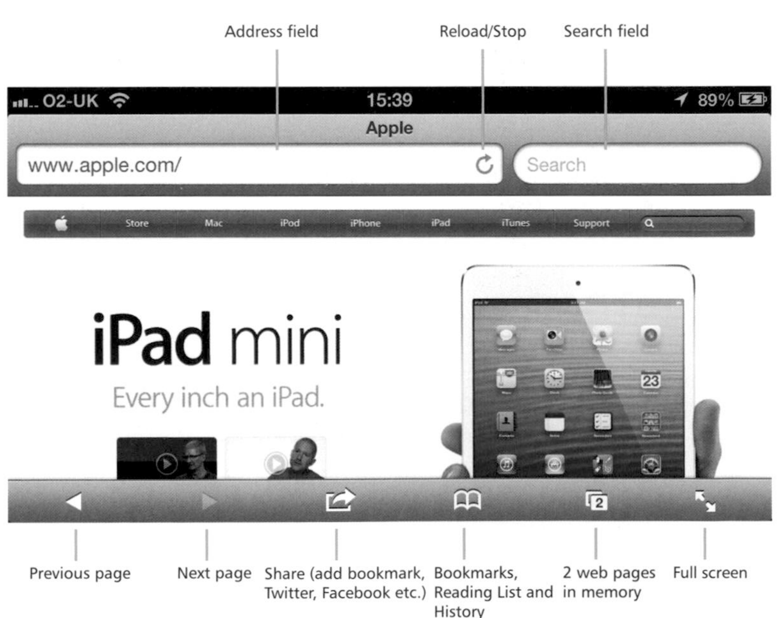

Safari Bookmarks

You can add, delete, and organize bookmarks in Safari. In addition, you can sync bookmarks between your desktop and iPhone using iCloud.

This shows the bookmarks in bookmarks folders

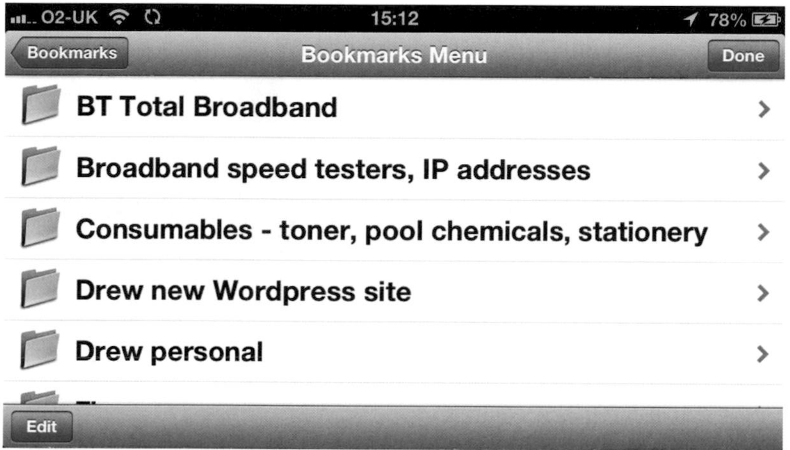

Tap Edit to delete entries, shift up or down and create new folders

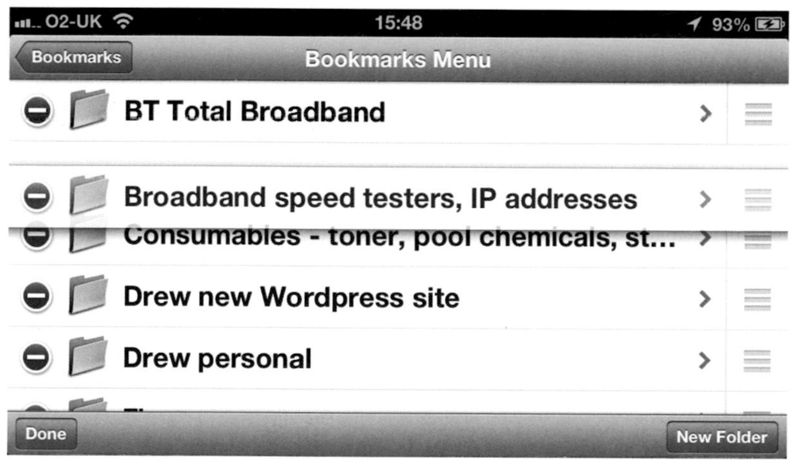

To clear History: tap **History**, tap **Clear History**

Hot tip 

Add Safari bookmarks by tapping the Share icon (center icon at bottom of Safari screen).

To sync across devices make sure Safari Bookmarks is checked in your iCloud settings on your iPhone, Mac, PC or iPod Touch.

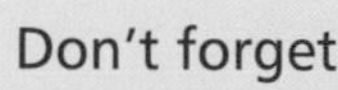

Clear your browsing history from time to time to help maintain privacy.

Zooming & Scrolling

Because of the small screen there is a limit to how much of the web page you can see.

Scroll

Place your finger on the screen and drag up or down, and left or right.

To scroll, place your finger on the screen and move the content up and down or side to side

Zoom

1. Place your index and middle finger on the screen
2. Push them apart to zoom in
3. Pinch them together to zoom out

Don't forget

You can also zoom in by placing two fingers on the screen and pushing them apart (pull them closer to reduce the size).

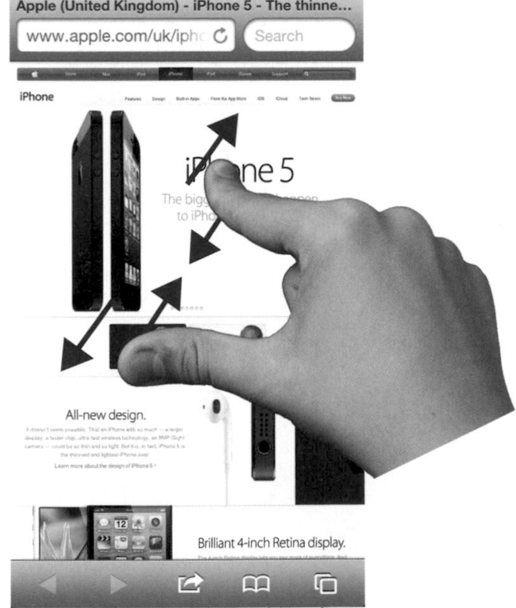

Pinch two fingers while touching the screen (zoom out) or pull your fingers closer together (zoom in) or double tap the screen (enlarge)

Add Web Clip to Home Screen

If you find a site that you want to revisit, but not add to bookmarks, you can add it to the home screen:

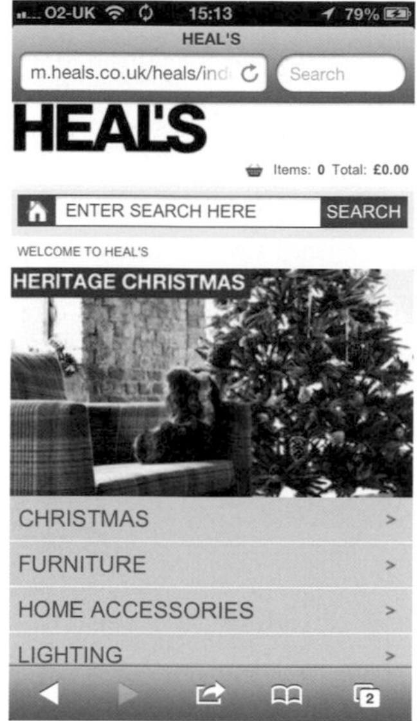

Find the site you want, tap the "share" icon (center)

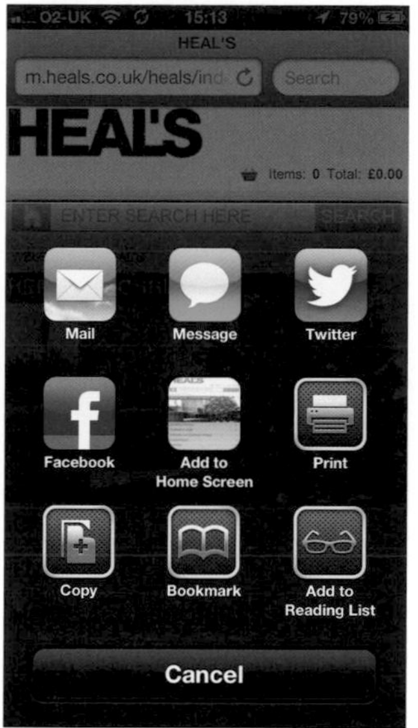

Tap "Add to Home Screen"

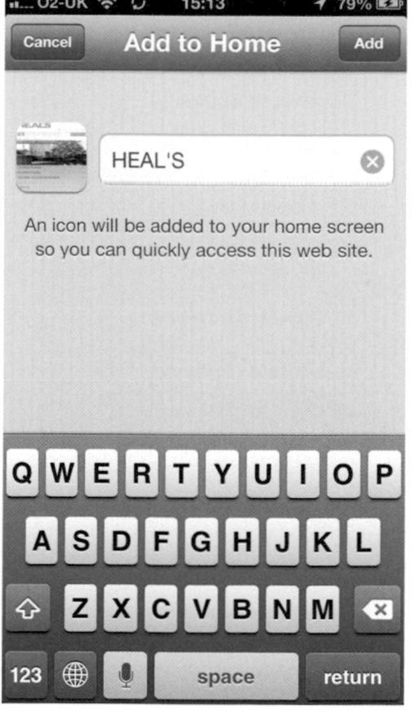

Give the link a name

The link is now on the Home Screen

Add regularly-visited websites to your Home screen to save you having to look for the bookmark.

Private Browsing

It's a good idea to clear your browsing history and other data from time to time.

1. Tap **Settings** on the Home Screen
2. Locate **Safari**, tap its button
3. Tap **Clear History**, **Clear Cookies** and **Clear Cache**
4. All private browsing data will be erased
5. Alternatively, download a browser that *only* works in private mode from the App Store
6. One example is the app *Privately* – this stores no data so there is nothing to clear later

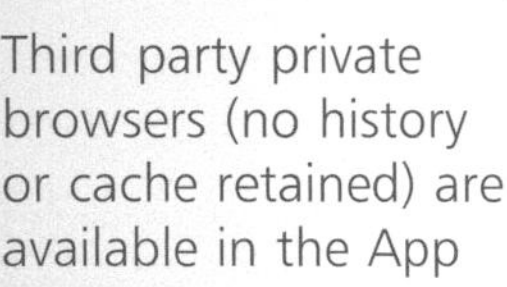

Third party private browsers (no history or cache retained) are available in the App Store.

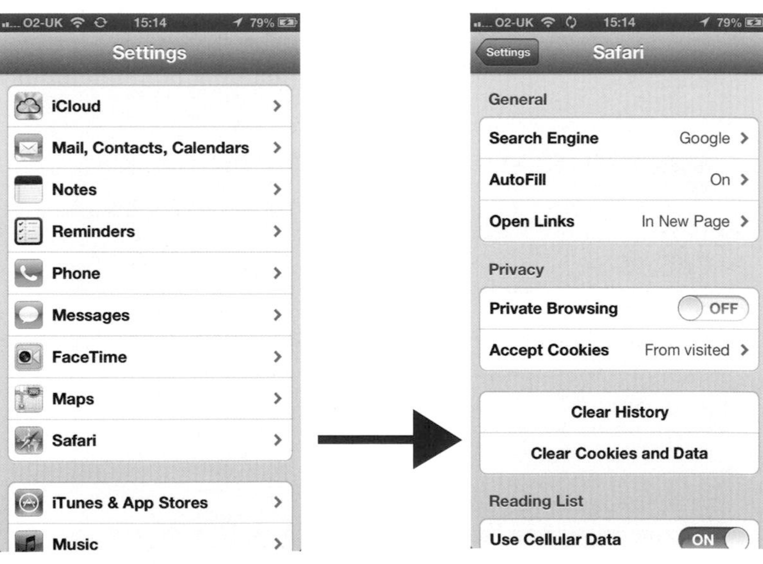

Go to **Settings** > **Safari**
Tap Safari and tap Clear History, Clear Cookies and Clear Cache by tapping their buttons

Copy Text from Safari

With Copy and Paste you can easily grab text and graphics from Safari and paste into an email or other app.

This can be a bit hit-and-miss, and takes practise.

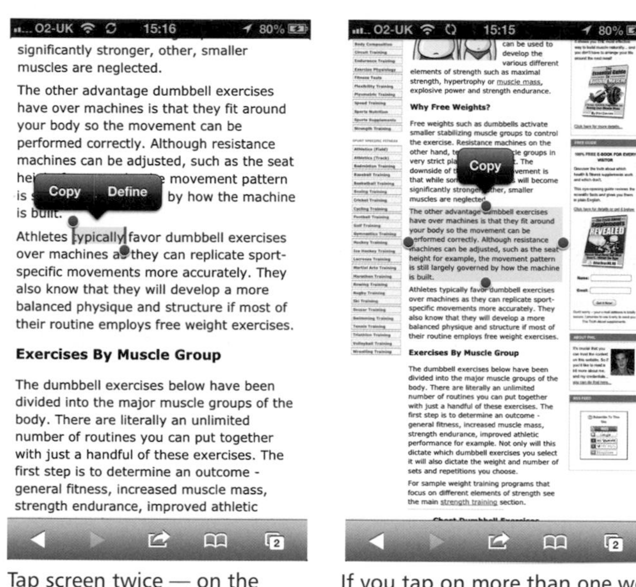

Tap screen twice — on the second tap keep finger on the screen. If you tap on one word, it will be selected for copying

If you tap on more than one word it will select a paragraph to copy. To extend the text to copy drag the blue circles to enclose the text

You can copy text and images from web pages and paste into emails or other apps.

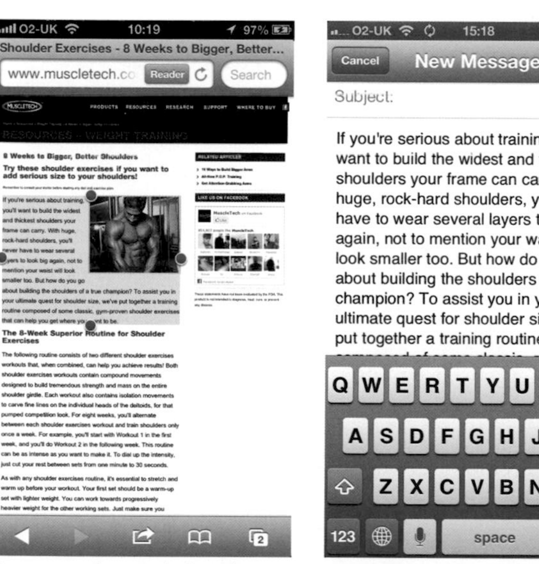

Tap copy, close Safari and open an app such as Mail. Touch the text area and "Paste" will appear. Tap "Paste" to paste the copied text

Tricks

Remove and add Safari pages

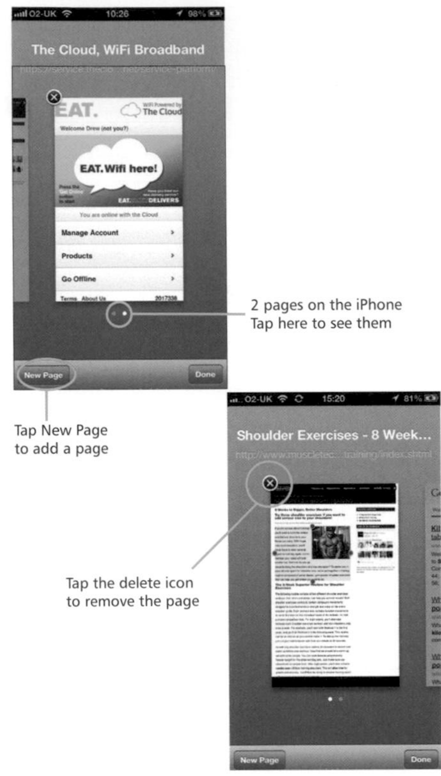

Keyboard shortcuts when entering URLs

You don't need to type *.co.uk* or *.com*. On the Safari keyboard, press and hold the *.com* key. Alternatives will pop up (the *.kr* options are showing because the Korean keyboard is active).

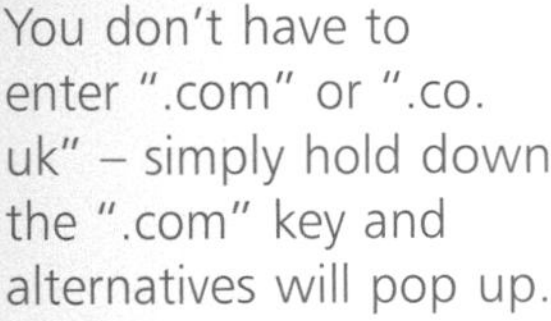

You don't have to enter ".com" or ".co.uk" – simply hold down the ".com" key and alternatives will pop up.

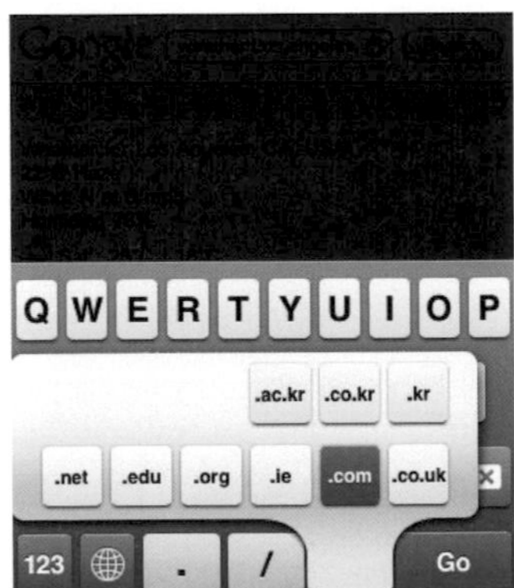

Fast Safari Scrolling

You can scroll up and down through web pages in Safari using your finger to flick up and down. But there is a very quick way of getting to the top of any web page.

Tap the time! (this works with text messages too).

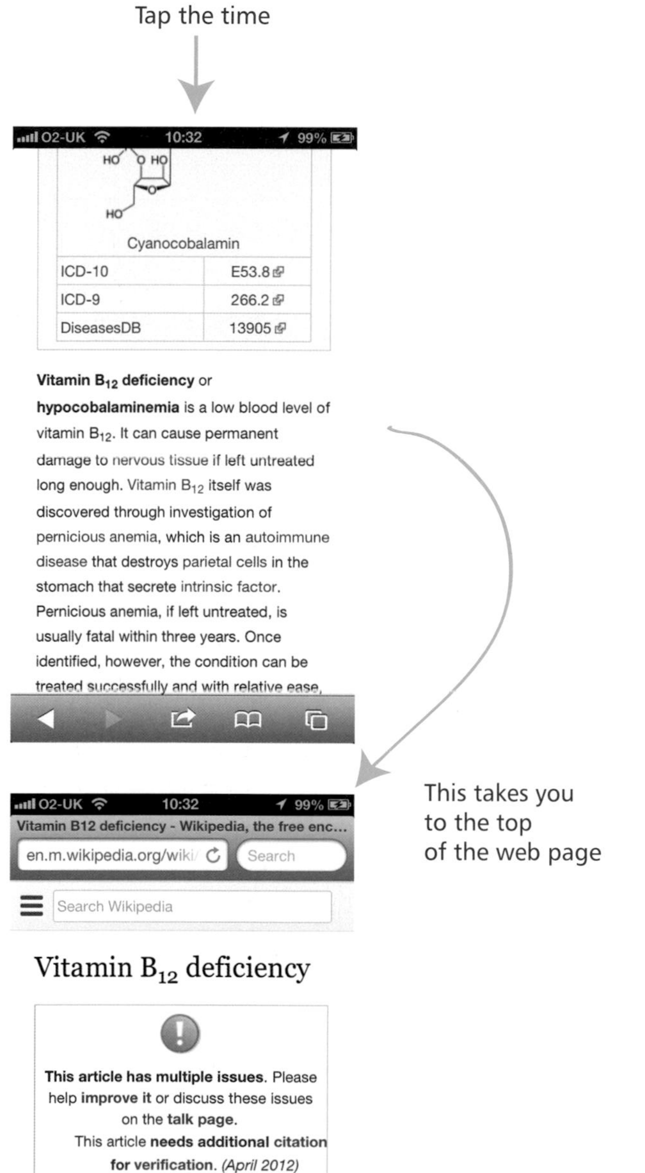

Hot tip

Zoom to the top of the browser window by tapping the time at the top of the screen.

Set Default Search Engine

Safari has Google as the default search engine. You may be happy to keep Google or you can change to another search engine.

How to switch to another search engine

1. Go to **Settings** > **Safari**

2. Look for **Search Engine**

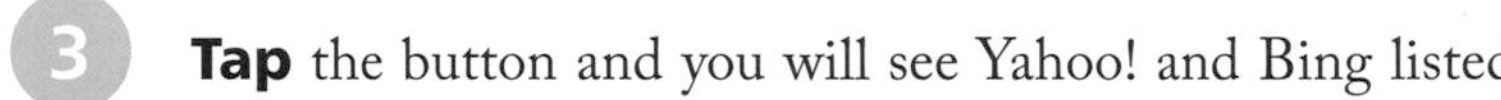
3. **Tap** the button and you will see Yahoo! and Bing listed

4. **Choose** either Google, Yahoo! or Bing

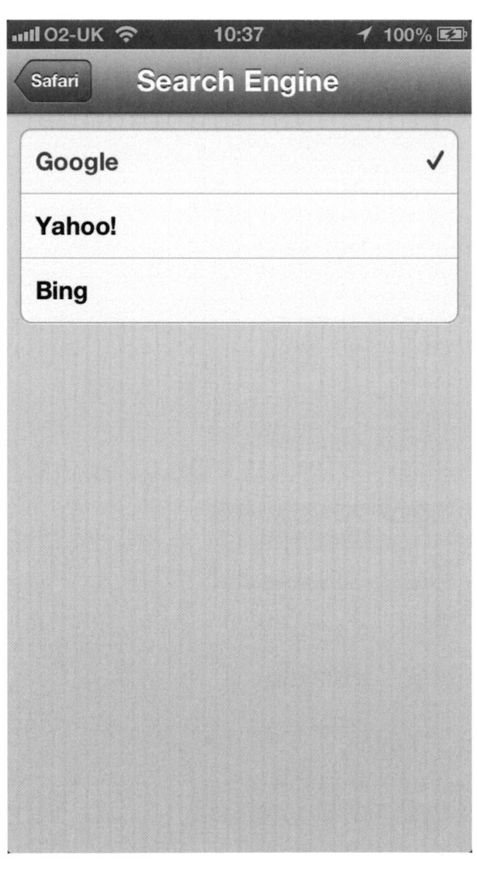

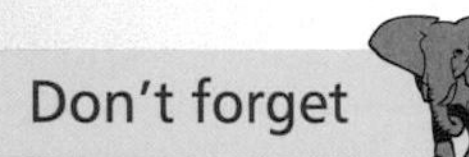
Don't forget

You can set your default search engine to Yahoo! or Bing, instead of Google.

8 Email

Most of us spend a great deal of time reading and composing emails. We will look at how to get email up and running on the iPhone.

Setting Up Email

The iPhone handles email well, and works with iCloud and Microsoft Exchange. It handles POP3, IMAP and can work with Yahoo! Mail, Google Mail and AOL.

The iPhone can handle many types of email account. IMAP accounts are useful since you can see all your folders on the server, and can save email to specific folders easily.

Setting up a Gmail account

Go to **Settings** > **General** > **Mail, Contacts, Calendars**

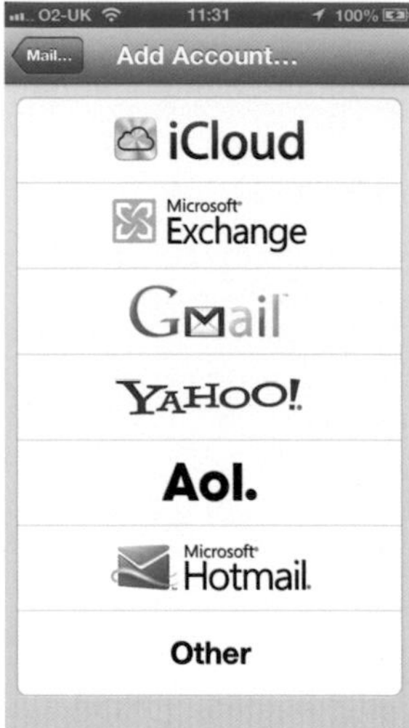

Tap the Gmail icon

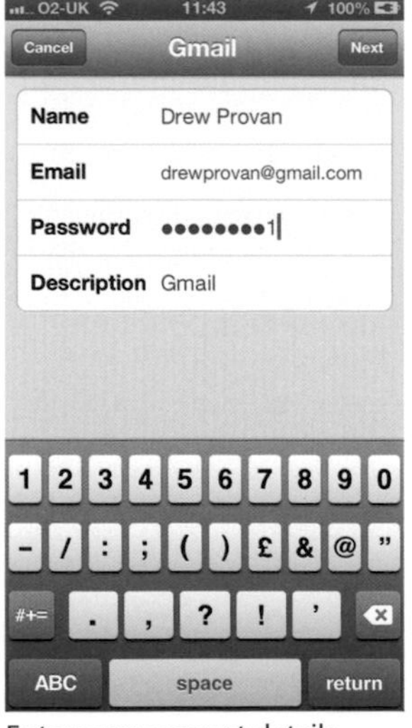

Enter your account details

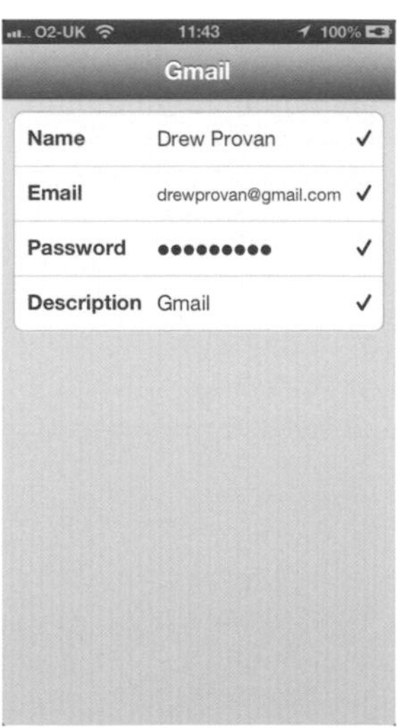

If successful you will see check marks down the right side

You will need to set up the Push frequency, security settings and other features to make your email work correctly.

Decide when you want deleted email removed from the server

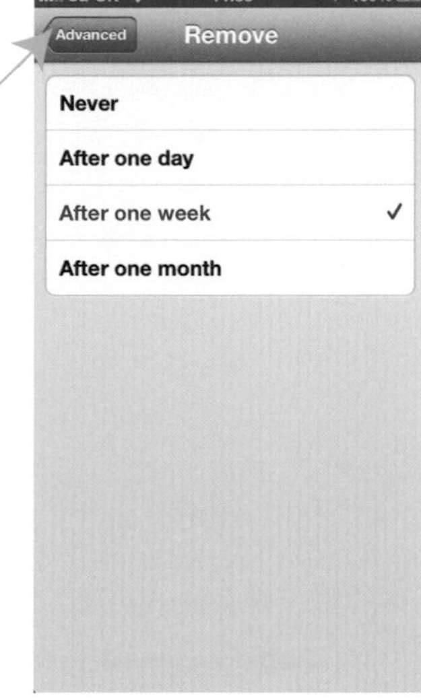

O2-UK 11:43 100%
Account
Advanced
Mailbox Behaviors
Drafts Mailbox Drafts >
Deleted Mailbox Trash >
Incoming Settings
Use SSL ON
Authentication Password >
IMAP Path Prefix /
Server Port 993
S/MIME
S/MIME OFF

You may have to check the **Advanced** tab to set up how long to keep deleted messages on the server, and other settings

Choose the authentication method

Beware

If you want to see your messages on the iPhone and your computer, make sure Delete from server is set to “Never”.

Using Exchange Server

Mail can collect email, and sync calendars and contacts using Microsoft Exchange Server, which is great news for businesses.

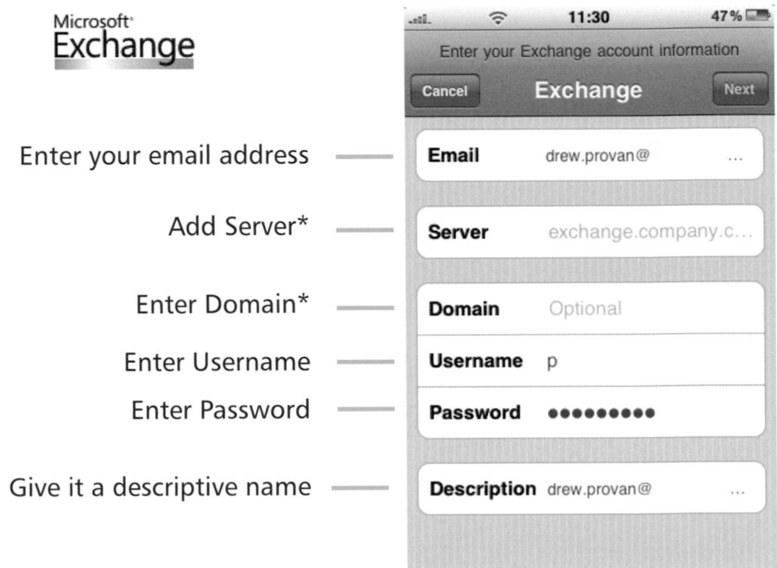

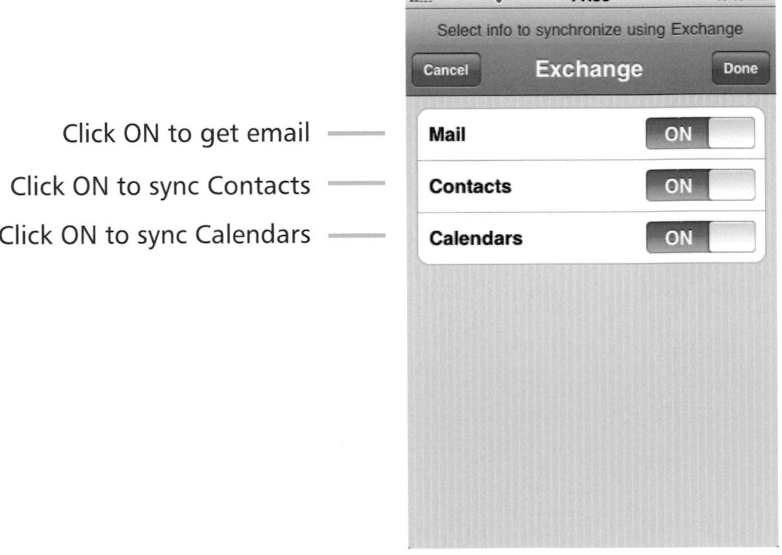

* You will need to ask your IT Administrator for these details

Email Viewing Settings

1. Go to **Settings** > **Mail, Contacts, Calendars**
2. Scroll down the list until you see **Mail**
3. **Adjust** settings for **Show**, **Preview**, **Minimum Font Size**, **Show To/Cc Label**, etc.

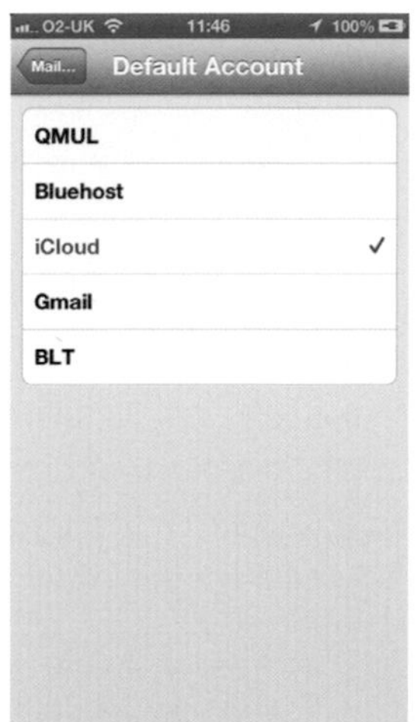

Decide which email account to use as your default account

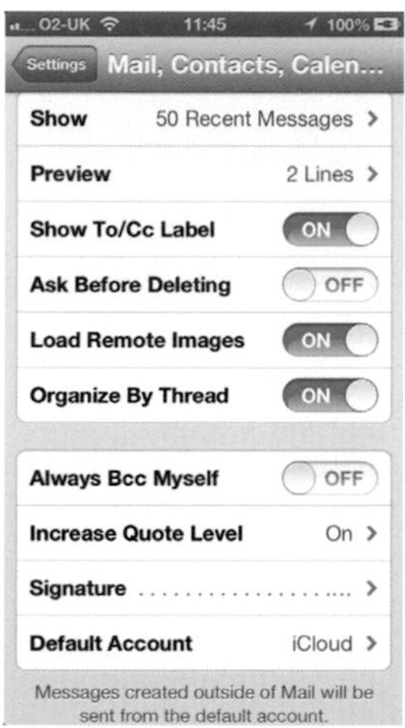

Do you want a copy of every email you send? If so, make sure **Always Bcc Myself** is **ON**

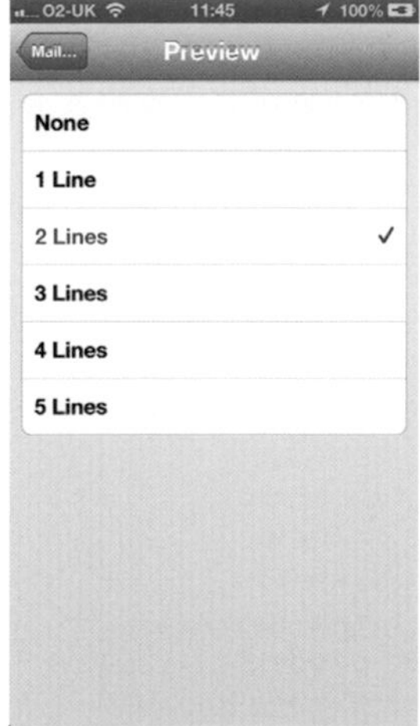

You can change the preview from **None** to **5 lines** of text

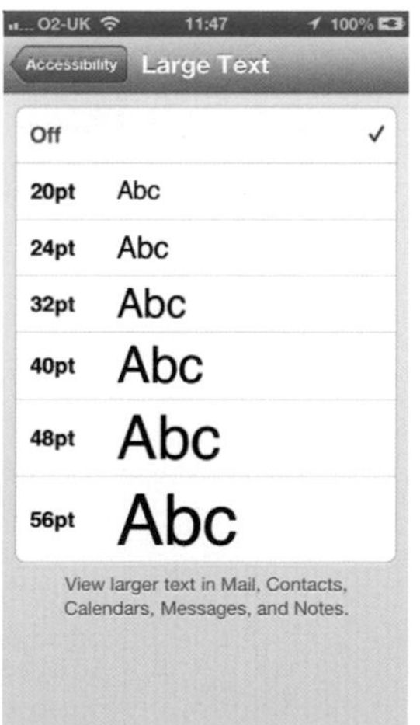

How large do you want the font? Change in **Settings > General > Accessibility**

Hot tip

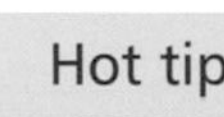

If you want to see more text on the screen set the font size to small.

Composing Email

1. Tap the **Mail** icon to open the app
2. Tap an **email account** to open it
3. Tap the **New Email** icon (bottom right). A new email will open
4. Tap the **To:** field and type the name of the recipient
5. Tap the **Subject:** and enter a subject for the email
6. Tap the **email body** area (below Subject:) and start typing your email
7. Insert a photo by selecting from Photos (touch and hold until you see **Copy** then touch and hold finger on email body until you see **Paste**). You can do the same with images in other apps, e.g., Safari
8. Once complete, hit **Send**

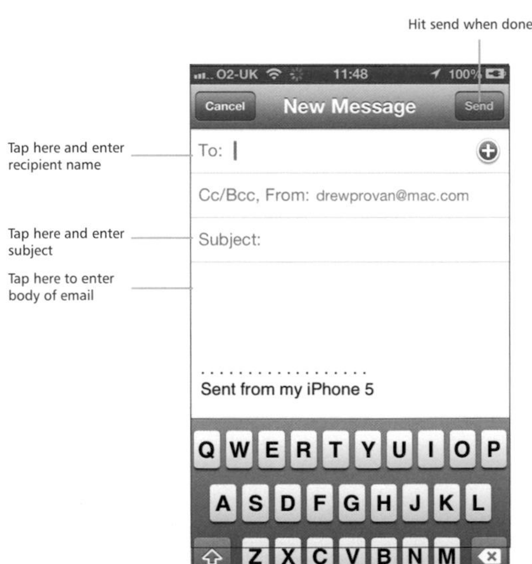

Reading Email

1. Check Mail icon for fresh mail – represented by a red circle. The number refers to the number of unread emails

2. Tap **Mail** to open

3. Tap the **Inbox** to open the email and if there is an attachment, you can tap to download

The red "1" above Mail shows you have one unread email. Tap Mail to open

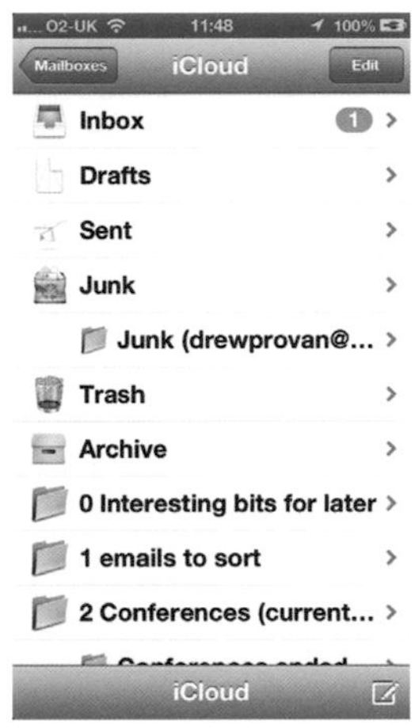

Tap Inbox to open the email

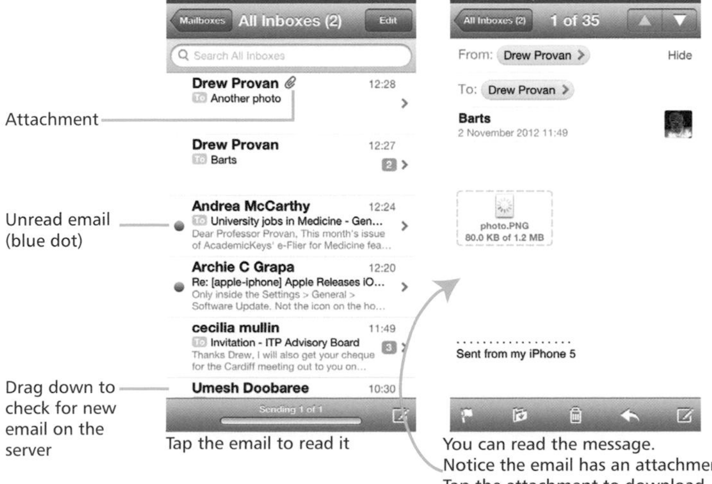

Tap the email to read it

You can read the message. Notice the email has an attachment. Tap the attachment to download

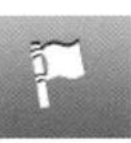

Flag important emails so you can find them again easily. Tap the Flag icon (bottom left of your email).

The paperclip icon shows you have received an attachment with an email.

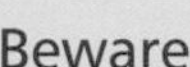

Beware

Often, attachments do not download automatically. Tap the icon and you will see the attachment download. After downloading, tap to open.

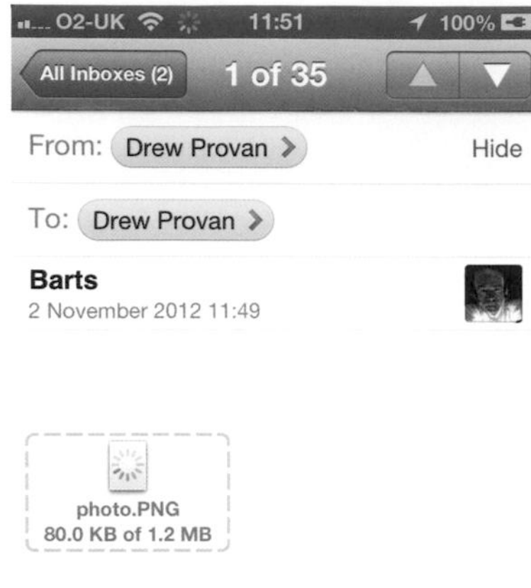

Attachment is downloading

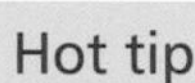

Hot tip

To save a photo from an email, touch and hold the photo until you see Save Image. Tap this, and the photo will be added to the Camera Roll.

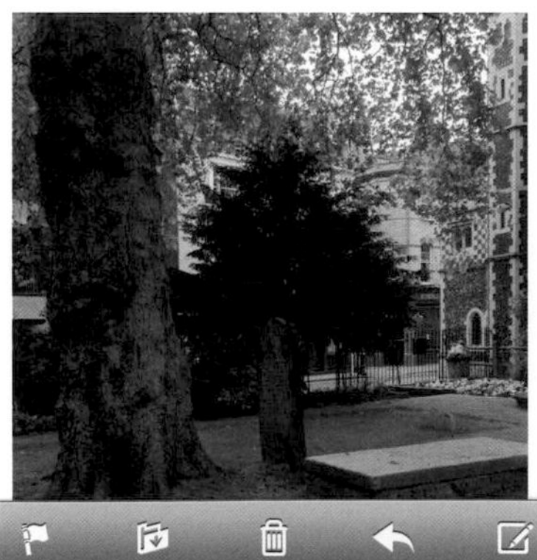

Attachment opened

Forwarding Email

1. **Open** an email
2. Tap the **Reply/Forward** icon at the bottom right of the screen
3. Select **Forward**
4. **Enter the name of the recipient**
5. In the body of the email, enter any message you want to accompany the forwarded email

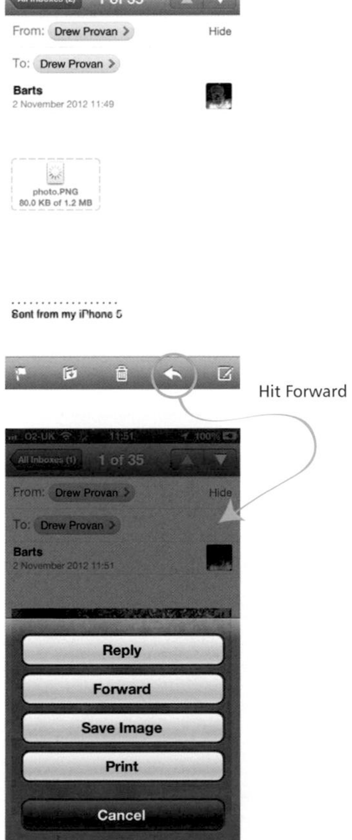

Deleting Email

You can delete email a couple of different ways

1. Tap the email to read it

2. When finished, tap the trash icon at the bottom of the screen

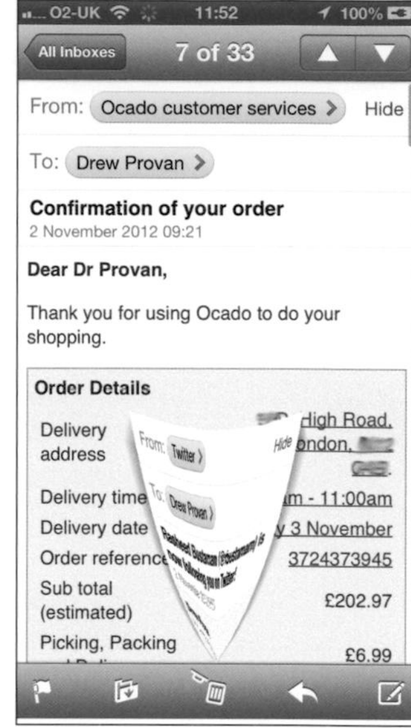

Hot tip

You can either delete emails as you read them (tap the trash can) or you can view the inbox and slide your finger left to right across the email, then hit "Delete".

Alternative method

1. In the email list view slide your finger across the email (do not open it)

2. A red **Delete** box should appear

3. Tap delete and the email will be deleted

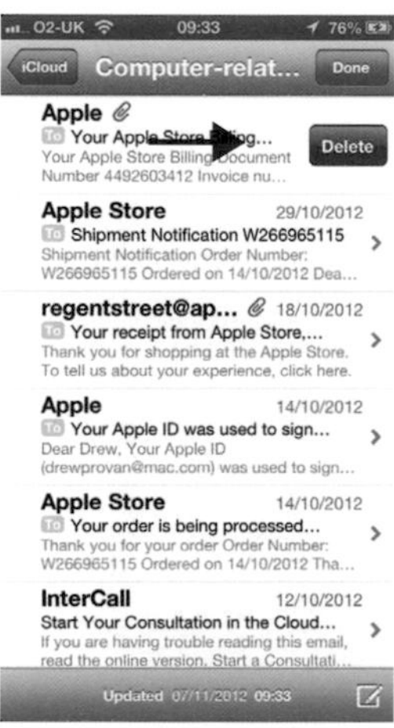

Yet another way of deleting email is

1. Go to **Inbox** and tap the **Edit** button at the top right
2. Tap each email you want to delete and a red circle will appear in the left column
3. Hit **Delete** when you are ready to delete

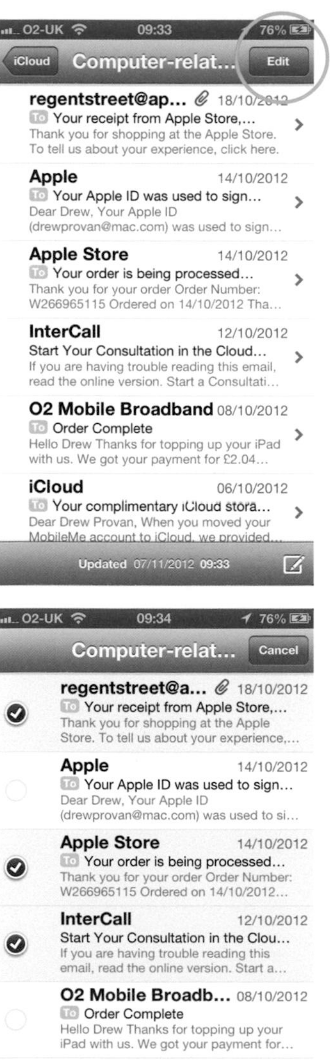

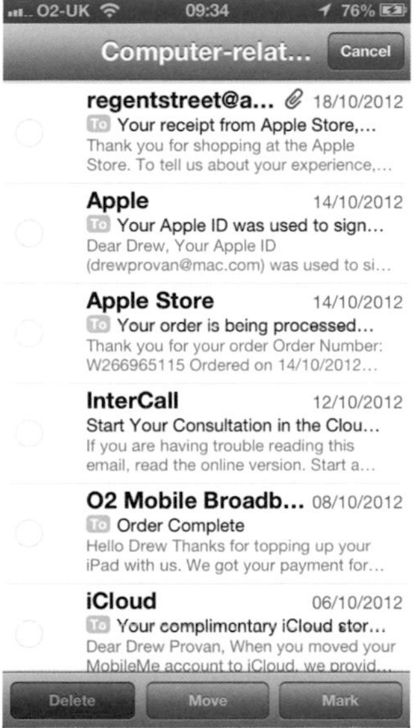

Tap **Edit**

Tap the email you want to delete
A red circle with a check mark
will appear

Hit **Delete**

Move Email to Folders

If you have an IMAP account, such as an iCloud account, you can see your folders on the server. You can move mail from your Inbox to another folder. This helps keep your mail organized, and your Inbox uncluttered.

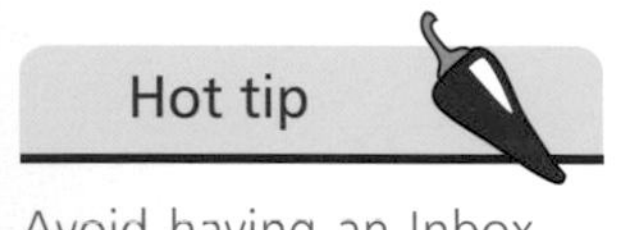

Avoid having an Inbox full of read and new mail. Move items to folders (easy with IMAP accounts) or delete them.

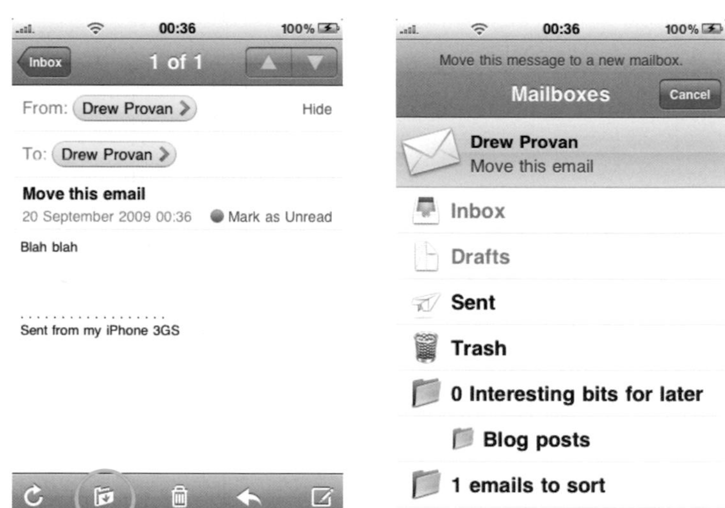

Tap the move icon and confirm you wish to move the email

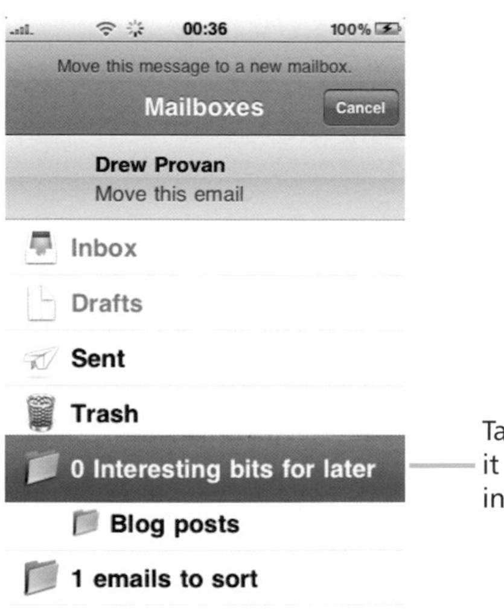

Tap the folder you wish to move it to and the email will jump into the folder

9 Accessibility Settings

The iPhone is well suited for people with visual problems. We will look at how to use Accessibility options on the iPhone.

Accessibility Settings

Many people with visual impairments should be able to make use of devices like the iPhone. With the standard default configuration they may run into problems, but the iPhone has many settings that can be modified to make them more usable.

What features are available?

- VoiceOver
- Zoom
- White on Black
- Mono Audio
- Speak Auto-text

Most of these features will work with most applications, apart from VoiceOver which will only work with the iPhone's standard (pre-installed) applications.

Switch on Accessibility

1. Plug the iPhone into your computer and make sure iTunes opens
2. Go to the **Summary** pane, check **Universal Access** in the options section
3. Within Universal Access, decide which features you want to activate

Alternative method

1. On the iPhone go to **Settings** > **General** > **Accessibility**
2. Scroll down the list of options and toggle on or off, depending on your needs
3. Switch each on or off using the iPhone or iTunes **Summary** pane

Switch on Universal Access in iTunes

Choose your options

Activate Settings on iPhone

Switching on VoiceOver

1. Go to **Settings** > **General** > **Accessibility**
2. Activate **VoiceOver** as shown below
3. When finished, you may wish to switch it off again

Switch on VoiceOver

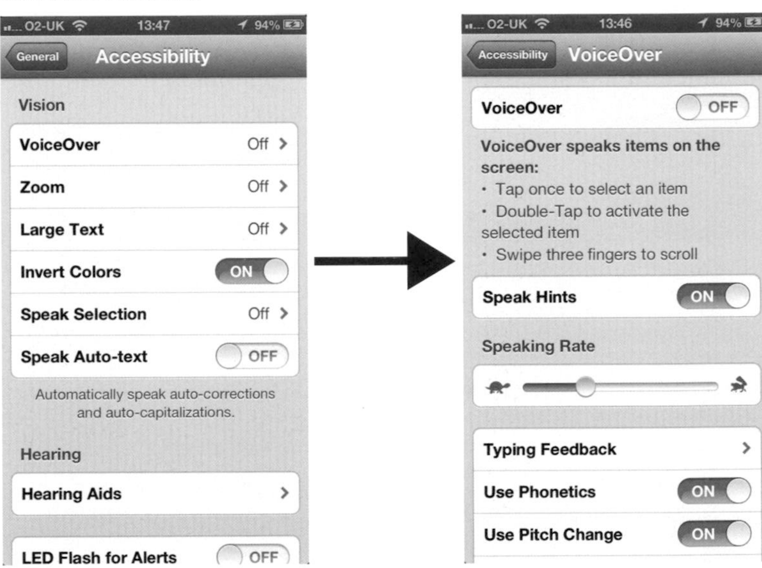

Switch on Zoom to enlarge (Zoom and VoiceOver cannot be used together)

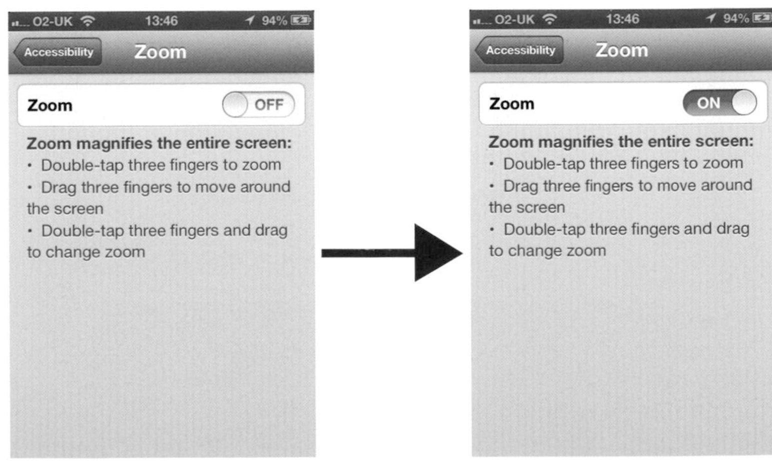

Other accessibility settings

1. Go to **Settings** > **General** > **Accessibility**
2. Activate **White on Black**
3. Activate **Zoom**

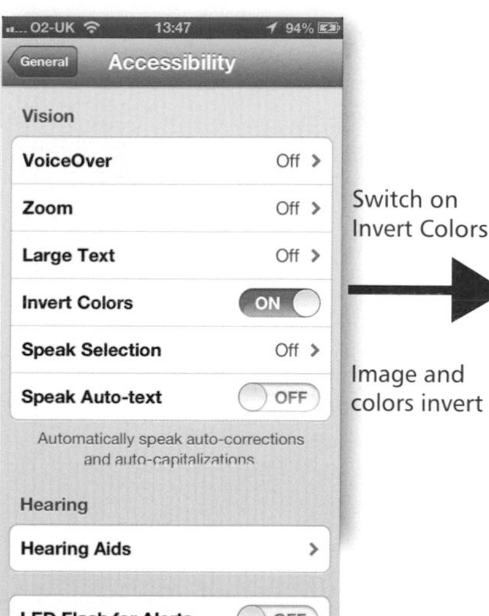

Switch on Invert Colors

Image and colors invert

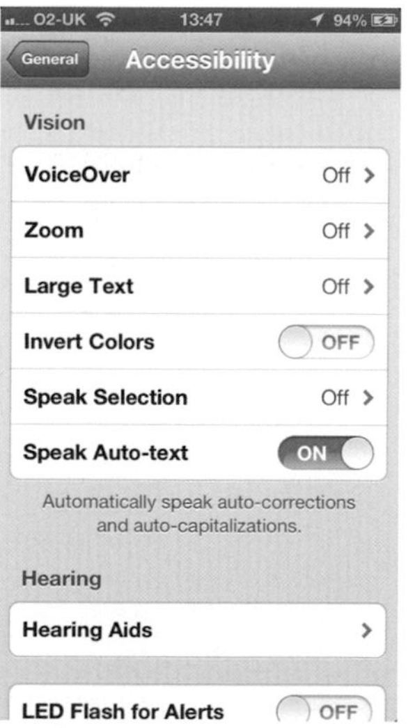

Speak Auto-text ON

Triple-Click

Triple-click the Home Button for:

- VoiceOver
- Invert Colors
- Zoom
- AssistiveTouch

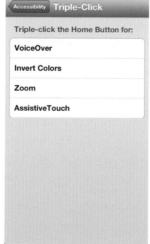

Actions on triple click Home Button

VoiceOver

VoiceOver

This speaks what's on the screen, so you can tell what's on the screen even if you cannot see it. It describes items on the screen and, if text is selected, VoiceOver will read the text.

Speaking rate

This can be adjusted using the settings.

Typing feedback

VoiceOver can provide this: go to **Settings** > **General** > **Accessibility** > **VoiceOver** > **Typing Feedback**.

Languages

VoiceOver is available in languages other than English (but is not available in all languages).

VoiceOver Gestures

When VoiceOver is active, the standard touch screen gestures operate differently:

Tap	Speak item
Flick right or left	Select next or previous item
Flick up or down	Depends on Rotor Control setting
Two-finger tap	Stop speaking current item
Two-finger flick up	Read all from top of screen
Two-finger flick down	Read all from current position
Three-finger flick up or down	Scroll one page at a time
Three-finger flick right or left	Go to next or previous page
Three-finger tap	Speak the scroll status

Apple Support for VoiceOver

See: *http://support.apple.com/kb/HT3598*.

Zoom

The iPhone touch screen lets you zoom in and out of elements on the screen. Zoom will let you magnify the whole screen, irrespective of which application you are running.

Turn Zoom on and off

1. Go to **Settings** > **General** > **Accessibility** > **Zoom**
2. Tap the Zoom **OFF/ON** switch
3. You cannot use Zoom and VoiceOver at the same time

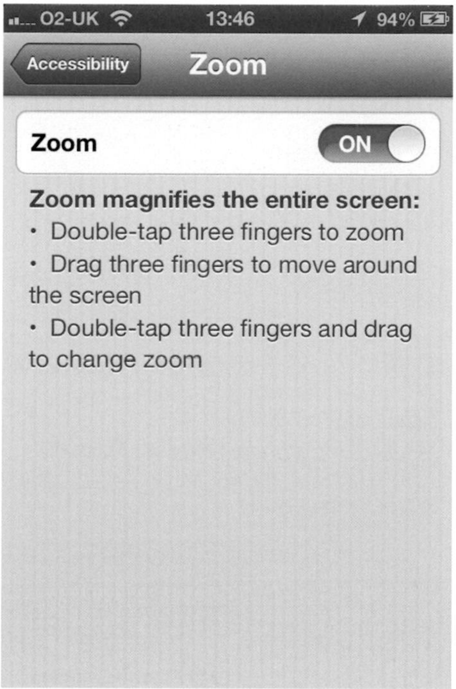

Zoom in and out

1. **Double tap** the screen with three fingers
2. The screen will then magnify by 200%

Increase magnification

1. Use **three fingers** and drag to the top of the screen (increase magnification) or bottom (decrease magnification).
2. Move around the screen
3. Drag or flick the screen with three fingers

Other Accessibility Settings

White on Black

This feature inverts the colors on the iPhone, which may make it easier for some people to read.

Activate White on Black

1. Go to **Settings** > **General** > **Accessibility**
2. Tap the **White on Black** switch
3. The screen should look like a photographic negative

Mono Audio

This combines the sound of both left and right channels into a mono audio signal played through both sides.

Turn Mono Audio on and off

1. Go to **Settings** > **General** > **Accessibility**
2. Switch on **Mono Audio**

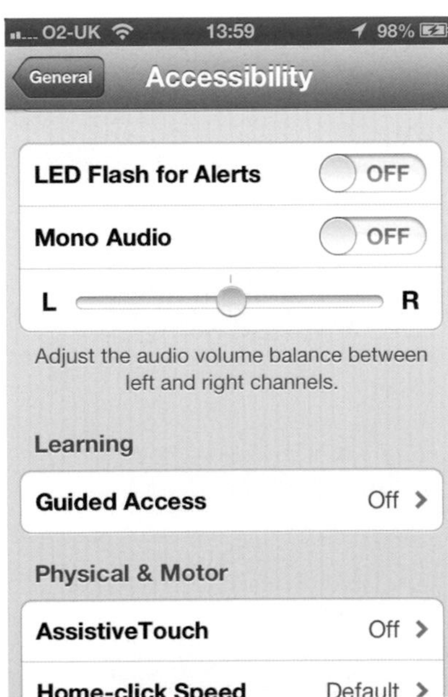

Speak Auto-text

This setting enables the iPhone to speak text corrections and suggestions as you type text into the iPhone.

Turn Speak Auto-text on

1. Go to **Settings** > **General** > **Accessibility**
2. Switch on **Speak Auto-text**
3. Speak Auto-text works with VoiceOver and Zoom

Closed Captioning

This needs to be turned on in the Music app settings:

1. Go to **Settings** > **Music app**
2. Slide **Closed Captioning** button to **ON** to activate

Hot tip

Closed Captioning adds subtitles to video content. Not all videos contain Closed Captioning information but where it is available you can access it by turning on Closed Captioning.

Large phone keypad

The keypad of the iPhone is large, making it easy for people who are visually impaired to see the digits.

1. Tap the **Phone** icon (on the dock)
2. Tap the **keypad** icon (4th icon from left)

Apple Accessibility Support

The Apple Support area is great for all Apple products, and is especially helpful for iPhone Accessibility.

Check out the FAQs and watch the videos showing you how to set the iPhone up.

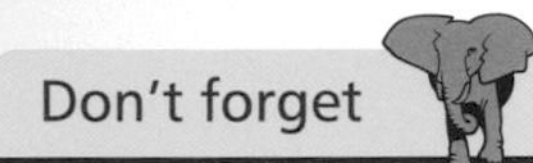

Don't forget

Apple's website has masses of information about Accessibility.

Log in to Apple support

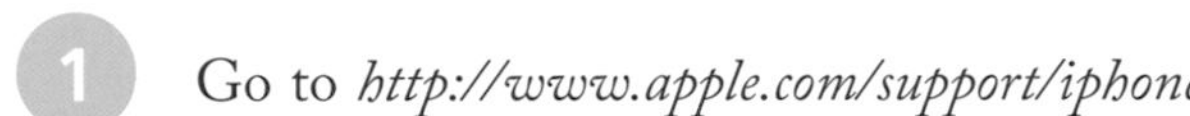

1. Go to *http://www.apple.com/support/iphone*

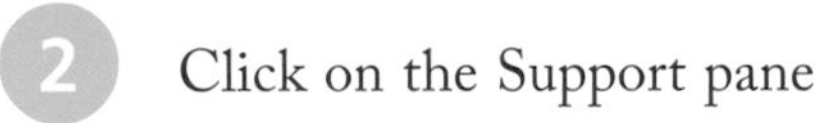

2. Click on the Support pane

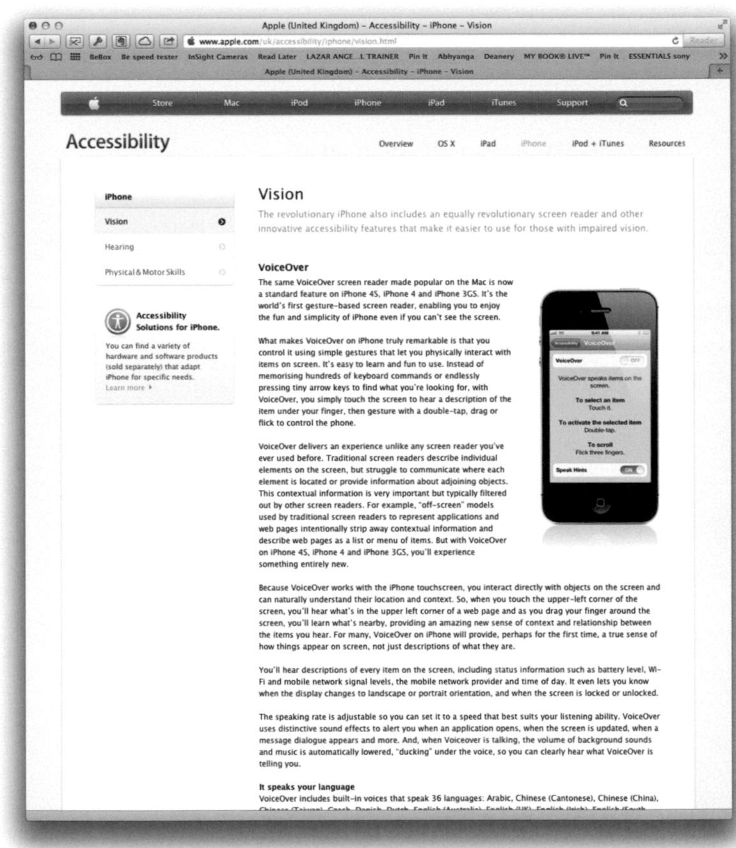

10 Working with Apps

There are thousands of apps for the iPhone, catering for every conceivable need. Here we will look at how to find apps, install them, and remove them. This chapter takes you through some of the apps in each category, to give you some idea of the range of programs available for the iPhone, both paid and free.

Installing Applications

Installing applications (apps) on the iPhone is incredibly easy, when you compare it to the cumbersome process used for installing programs onto a standard PDA. It's as simple as browsing the apps, choosing the one you want and tapping Install.

How many apps are there?

The app store was launched in January 2008, as an update to iTunes. By February 2009, there were 20,000 apps for download, and by October 2010 there were more than 300,000! At the time of writing 400 million iOS devices have been sold, and there are over 700,000 apps of which 450,000 are iPhone specific. More than 30 billion iOS apps have been downloaded.

Don't forget

You can browse apps on your iPhone or in iTunes. Installation can also be carried out using the computer or iPhone.

The App Store on your iPhone

1. On your iPhone tap **App Store**
2. Browse the apps by **Category, Featured, Top 25**
3. Or search for an app using the search function

Hot tip

Try downloading a free app to get started such as our **In Easy Steps** app. Type **in easy steps** in the Search box. You'll see:

Tap the app and follow the instructions to install the app.

Browse the App Store on your computer

1. Launch **iTunes**
2. Click the **App Store** pane
3. Find the app you want, click install
4. You will need to **enter your iTunes password**
5. The app will be downloaded and placed in the apps folder in iTunes
6. Next time you sync the iPhone the app will be copied across to the iPhone

The App Store on iTunes

This is shown below:

1. Launch **iTunes** and select iTunes Store

2. Click the **App Store** tab and look for the **Categories** drop down menu

3. Select the category you are interested in, browse and download

Open iTunes and look for the AppStore pane
Browse the apps in iTunes

...cont'd

Browsing apps using the iPhone

1. Tap the App Store icon
2. Use the buttons on the bottom to view the apps

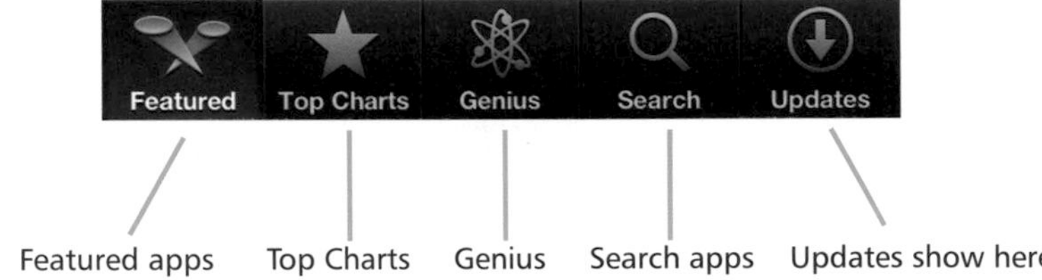

Let Genius do the hard work

Once you have installed a few apps, Genius can help you choose further apps. This works in much the same way as Genius on iTunes, where it will suggest audio that fits well together. iTunes music Genius will create playlists for you. If you don't like the playlist you just ask Genius to suggest another playlist.

Here's what Genius suggests for me based on my previous downloads

There are many ways to view the apps in the App Store

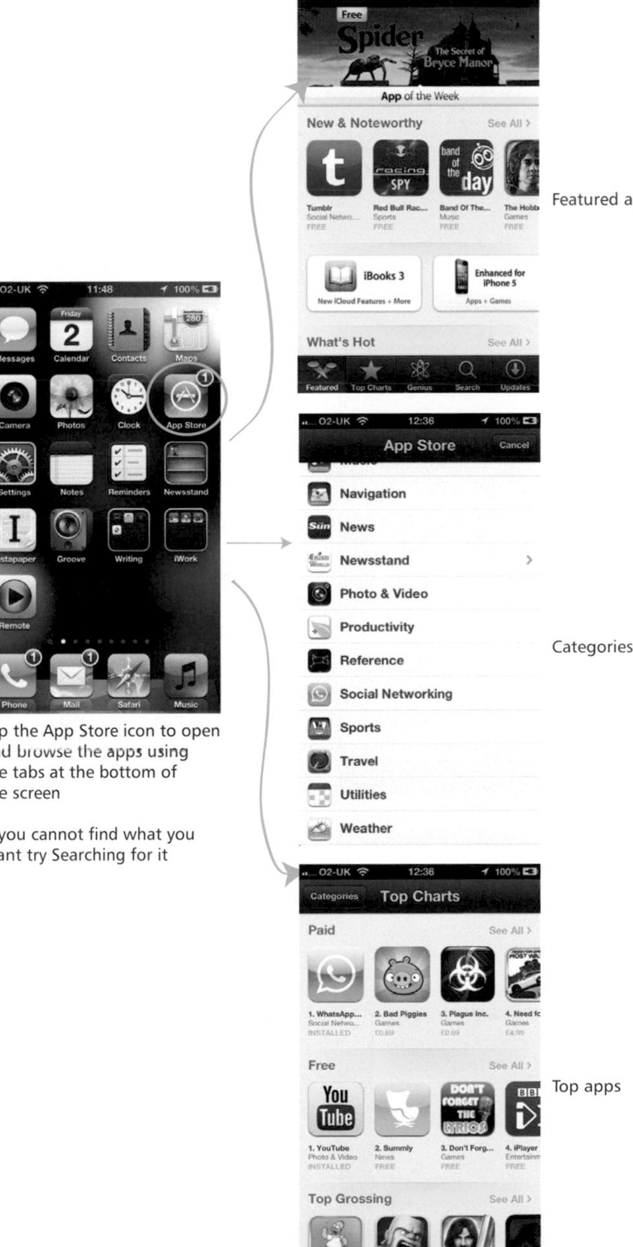

Tap the App Store icon to open and browse the apps using the tabs at the bottom of the screen

If you cannot find what you want try Searching for it

Beware

There are now so many apps, it may be difficult to find what you want. Try using the search tool and enter a word or words that describe what you are looking for.

Installation Process

1. Find the app you want using App Store on the iPhone
2. Tap the **Price** or **Free** tab
3. Tap **Install**
4. **Enter your iTunes password**
5. The app will install

You need to remember your iTunes account password – you will be asked for this each time you try to install or update an app, even if it's a free app.

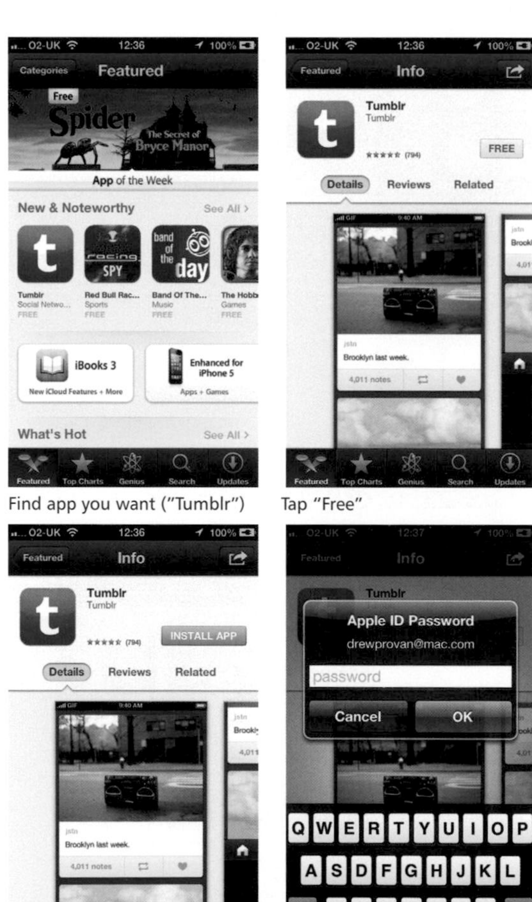

Find app you want ("Tumblr")

Tap "Free"

Tap "Install"

Enter your iTunes password

Updating Apps

The publishers of apps provide updates which bring new features and improvements. You don't have to check your apps to see if there are updates – the App Store app itself will notify you by displaying a red circle with a number in it.

To update

1. Tap **App Store** and go to **Updates**
2. Tap the app shown – if multiple, tap **Update All**
3. You should not be asked for your password but if you are, enter it

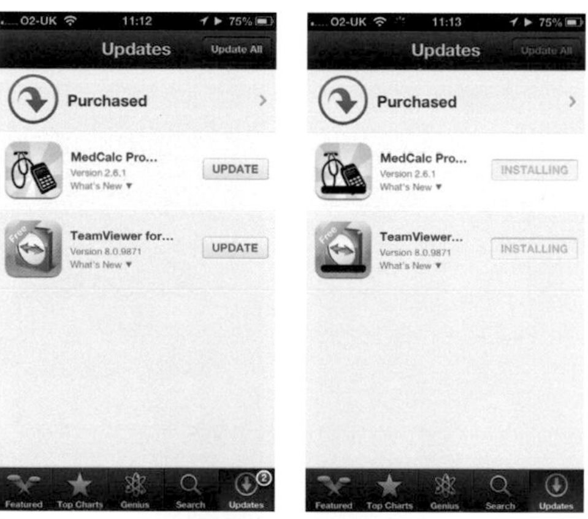

Two apps have updates ready to install

Tap Update All

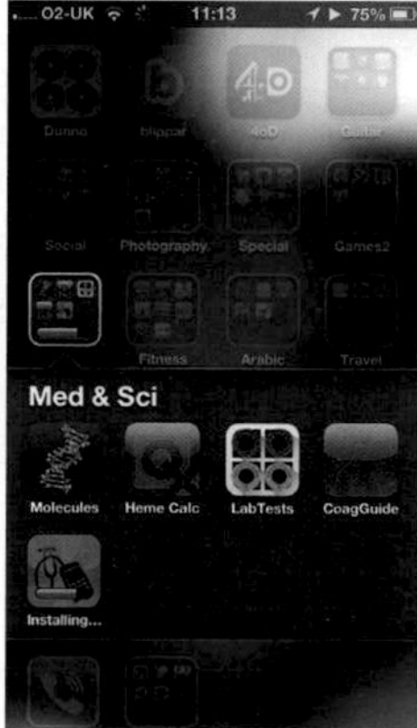

You can see the app downloading and then installing

Hot tip

If your App Store icon has a red circle with a number inside, it means there's an update for one or more of your apps. Keep them up-to-date since updated versions provide bug fixes and improvements.

Hot tip

With iOS 6 you are no longer asked for your Apple ID when you download updates or reinstall apps you have deleted.

Removing Apps

There are two ways to remove apps.

Using the iPhone

1. **Press and hold** the app you want to remove
2. All the apps on the screen will start jiggling and you will see an **x** at the top of the app
3. **Tap the x** and the app will be deleted
4. **Confirm** your action
5. Leave **feedback** if you wish

Just as you can install using the iPhone or computer, so too can you delete apps.

Tap the app but keep your finger on the icon — all the icons start to jiggle. Press the "x" on the app you wish to delete

Press Delete or Cancel

Deleting apps using iTunes on your computer

1. Plug your iPhone into your PC or Mac
2. Make sure iTunes opens
3. Click the **iPhone tab** (in left pane)
4. Go to the **Applications** pane
5. Delete by **pressing** the **x** when you hover over the app's icon in the right window, or deactivate the app by unchecking its box in the left window
6. If you deactivate, but not delete permanently, you can put the app back on the iPhone by checking the box
7. The app will be restored to the iPhone next time you sync

Apps pane
Uncheck to remove it from the iPhone when you next sync (but the app is not deleted from your iTunes)
Sync Apps
150 apps
File Sharing
To permanently delete the app, hover over the icon with your mouse pointer and click the "x"

Apps Categories

O2-UK 14:56 100%

App Store Cancel

All Categories	
App Collections	Suggested collections of apps
Books	Books
Business	Business apps
Catalogues	Various catalogs
Education	Educational apps for all ages
Entertainment	Photo editors and other entertaining apps
Finance	Financial, banking and related apps
Food & Drink	Meal planners, restaurant guides, etc.
Games ›	Paid and free games
Health & Fitness	Workout apps and other fitness apps
Lifestyle	Fashion, music, and other apps
Medical	Health-related apps
Music	Radios, other music apps
Navigation	TomTom and other satnav apps
News	News, SKY, newspapers, RSS players
Newsstand ›	Magazine and newspaper subscriptions
Photo & Video	Photo and video viewers and editors
Productivity	Notes apps and other productivity tools
Reference	Reference guides
Social Networking	Twitter, Facebook and related apps
Sports	Everything sport-related
Travel	Travel planners
Utilities	Document wallets (private) and other utilities
Weather	Weather apps

App Store is customized to local currency and language, even English spellings, e.g. catalogues v catalogs.

Games

Angry Birds Space

Description

#1 in 116 countries! Big thanks to all our fans!
...

Rovio Entertainment Ltd Web Site › **Angry Birds Space Support ›**

£0.69 Buy App

Fruit Ninja

Description

NOW WITH GAME CENTER MULTIPLAYER! -- OVER TEN MILLION FRUIT NINJA COPIES SOLD! A huge thanks to everyone out there, you have made this great game even greater because of your amazing support! #1 Paid App in Germany, Norway, Czech...

Halfbrick Studios Web Site › **Fruit Ninja Support ›**

£0.69 Buy App

Bad Piggies

Description

From the creators of Angry Birds: an all new game from the PIGS' point of view!
...

Rovio Entertainment Ltd Web Site › **Bad Piggies Support ›**

£0.69 Buy App

Plague Inc.

Description

★★★★★ #1 top iPhone and iPad game globally with 25 million+ games played ★★★★★
Plague Inc. is a unique mix of high strategy and terrifyingly realistic simulation. Can you infect the world? ...

Plague Inc. Support ›

What's New in Version 1.4

Plague Inc. Mutation 4 discovered

£0.69 Buy App

TETRIS®

Description

Thanks to everyone who has joined the One-Touch revolution. Now it's your turn to discover the Tetris® game, re-imagined.

THE CRITICS LOVE IT!...

Electronic Arts Web Site › **TETRIS® Support ›** **Application Licence Agreement ›**

£0.69 Buy App

Cut the Rope

Description

Cut the rope to feed candy to little monster Om Nom®! 250 million downloads around the world of this phenomenal puzzle game. levels and more to come!
...

Chillingo Ltd Web Site › **Cut the Rope Support ›** **Application Licence Agreement ›**

Free App

Angry Gran Run

Description

Take to the streets with ANGRY GRAN RUN!

Our Angry Gran has been locked away in the Angry Asylum, she's plotting her escape, and she needs YOU to guide her through

Angry Gran Run Support ›

Entertainment

£0.69 Buy App

Keep Calm and Carry On

Description

== The "Keep Calm and Carry On" app that hit #1 overall in the UK! ==

Keep Calm and Carry On....

Keep Calm and Carry On Support ›

Based on the old World War II posters you can create you own versions using this app.

App Store › Entertainment › Damibu Ltd

DrivingFX Pro

Description

Do you remember your childhood days making driving noises as you played with your toy car? Were you the race car driver, skidding the wheels round the corners? Now, as you sit in your family car, do you still make the same noises? If so this Ap...

...More

DrivingFX Pro Support ›

Now you can generate car noises while you are in the car, presumably better noises than your car actually makes.

Free App

Action Movie FX

Description

ACTION MOVIE FX lets you add Hollywood FX to iPhone AND iPad movies that YOU shoot!
*All the action is better! Your previous FX have been updated to HD for free. Get them now - press RESTORE PURCHASES in th

Bad Robot Interactive Web Site › Action Movie FX Support ›

Add Hollywood effects to videos you create using your iPhone (or iPad).

App Store › Entertainment › acrossair

Gyroscope

Description

An amazing visual gyroscope for your iPhone 4. This application displays a 3d gyroscope that acts just like a real gyroscope would and looks so real you'll want to touch it. And it acts as an educational tool too — flip main display over and learn about the maths and the history behind gyroscopes....

...More

acrossair Web Site › Gyroscope Support ›

This is an educational app since it emulates 3-D gyroscopes and is very realistic.

Utilities

App Store > Utilities > myNewApps.com

Battery Magic

Description

ALERT - The paid version, 'Battery Magic Elite' now has 1% Accuracy and is ON SALE for 99¢ for 2 days!!!

...

...More

myNewApps.com Web Site > Battery Magic Support >

Battery utilities are big business, and there are loads of them on the App Store. This one makes a nice sound when you have reached full charge and has a large battery display.

App Store > Utilities > Hurryforward Ltd

DIY List

Description

DIY List is a handy list maker for Do-it-yourself enthusiasts, builders, decorators and interior designers.

Quickly add or delete items from the list. Create your own categories. Email your lists to a friend....

...More

Hurryforward Ltd Web Site > DIY List Support >

Builders, home DIY enthusiasts, interior decorators and others should find this list-maker and to-do app useful.

Import birthdays from Facebook, message friends with customizable messages.

App Store > Utilities > Code Drop

Safe Note

Description

☆ Currently #6 in 'What's Hot' ☆

...

...More

Code Drop Web Site > Safe Note Support >

This app lets you keep notes, lists and reminders away from prying eyes by letting you password protect them.

Social Networking

LinkedIn

Description

For Professionals Going Places.

...

LinkedIn Corporation Web Site › LinkedIn Support ›

Popular social networking site for PC and Mac and now available on iOS devices. Useful for headhunters and those wishing to find work.

Status Shuffle for Facebook

Description

One of the most popular Facebook applications is now available on the iPhone!

With Status Shuffle, you choose a status from our huge selection. We have funny statuses, sad statuses, crazy statuses and every!

Social Graph Studios Web Site › Status Shuffle for Facebook Support › Application Licence Agreement ›

This app updates your Facebook status using random updates. Not sure why this is useful but seems popular.

App Store › Social Networking › Skype Software S.a.r.l

Skype

Description

With Skype on your iPhone, iPod touch or iPad, you can make and receive calls, and instant message anyone else on Skype, wherever they are in the world. You can also save on international calls and text messages to phones. Skype is free to download and easy to use. With the latest version, you can now call over 3G*, and keep Skype running in the background....

...More

Skype Software S.a.r.l Web Site › Skype Support › Application Licence Agreement ›

The ubiquitous Skype has now found a home on the iPhone with this great Skype app.

App Store › Social Networking › WhatsApp Inc.

WhatsApp Messenger

Description

WhatsApp messenger is a cross platform smartphone messenger currently available for iPhone, Android, BlackBerry and Nokia phones. The application utilizes push notifications to instantly get messages from friends, colleagues and family....

...More

WhatsApp Inc. Web Site › WhatsApp Messenger Support › Application Licence Agreement ›

This is a cross-platform smartphone messenger (iPhone, Android, BlackBerry and Nokia) which lets you message your friends and receive push notifications.

Music

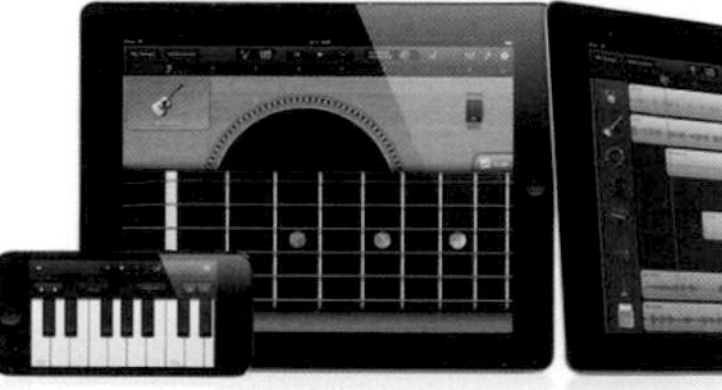

Great app on the Mac and now available for the iPhone in all its glory.

App Store › Music › WM Company LLC

Piano Chord Key

Description

Play the chords of the key or create your own key. The Piano Chord Key app makes learning chords simple! Play the chord simply by tapping the row of the chord you would like to hear. You can browse and play chords by key, type of chord, or create your own key and chord progressions from the create tab of the app. Put together some of your favorite chords and...

...More

WM Company LLC Web Site › **Piano Chord Key Support ›**

As the title suggests, this app shows you what piano keys to hit when you want to generate chords. It helps with chord progressions, too.

£0.69 Buy App

TuneIn Radio Pro

Description

Listen to and record over 60,000 radio stations including thousands of AM/FM local stations on your iPhone, iPod touch or iPad w TuneIn Radio Pro!...

TuneIn Web Site › **TuneIn Radio Pro Support ›** **Application Licence Agreement ›**

A radio app, lets you stream music using AirPlay.

App Store › Music › Synsion Radio Technologies

TuneIn Radio

Description

Listen to and record over 40,000 radio stations including thousands of AM/FM local stations on your iPhone, iPod touch or iPad with TuneIn Radio!...

...More

Synsion Radio Technologies Web Site › **TuneIn Radio Support ›**

With this app you can listen to, and record, more than 40,000 AM/FM radio stations.

Productivity

This is an amazing piece of software for the Mac and PC and now it's available on the iPhone. Because of the iPhone's small screen it is trickier to use than the computer equivalents.

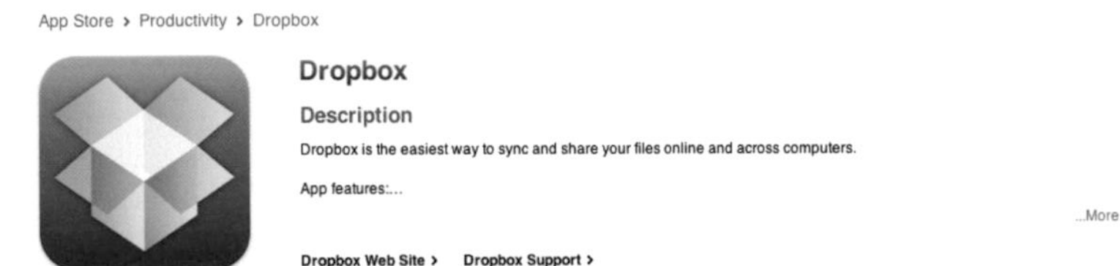

Now you can access your Dropbox files directly from your iPhone. If you don't have this for your computer – get it now!

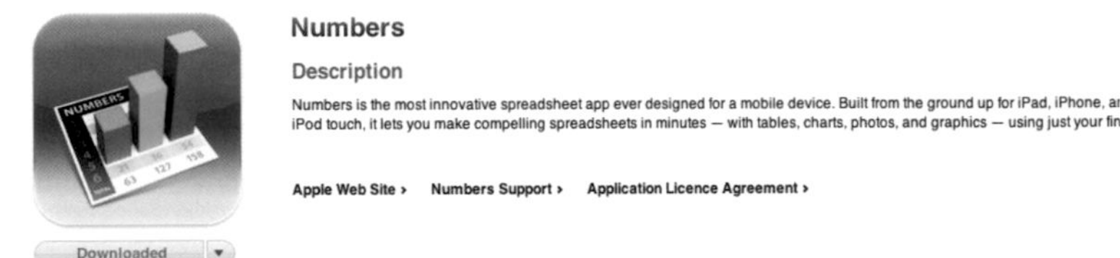

Numbers
Description
Numbers is the most innovative spreadsheet app ever designed for a mobile device. Built from the ground up for iPad, iPhone, ar
iPod touch, it lets you make compelling spreadsheets in minutes — with tables, charts, photos, and graphics — using just your fin
Apple Web Site ›
Numbers Support ›
Application Licence Agreement ›
Downloaded

Numbers is part of the iWork suite on the Mac. Useful spreadsheet with great chart options. Saves data to iCloud.

App Store › Productivity › Good.iWare Ltd.
GoodReader for iPhone
Description
Quick summary: super-robust PDF reader with advanced reading, annotating, markup and highlighting capabilities, excellent file manager, TXT file reader and editor, audio/video player, Safari-like viewer for MS Office and iWorks files.
...More
Good.iWare Ltd. Web Site ›
GoodReader for iPhone Support ›

This is one of the available PDF readers for the iPhone. Does a nice job, and has a clear interface.

Lifestyle

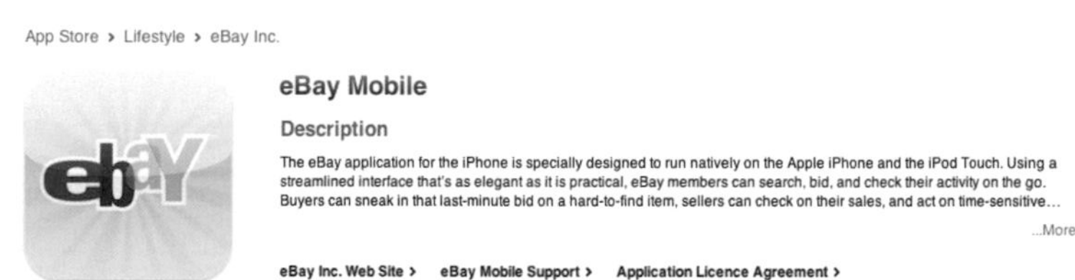

App Store > Lifestyle > eBay Inc.
eBay Mobile
Description
The eBay application for the iPhone is specially designed to run natively on the Apple iPhone and the iPod Touch. Using a streamlined interface that's as elegant as it is practical, eBay members can search, bid, and check their activity on the go. Buyers can sneak in that last-minute bid on a hard-to-find item, sellers can check on their sales, and act on time-sensitive…
...More
eBay Inc. Web Site >
eBay Mobile Support >
Application Licence Agreement >

Most of us use eBay but using a browser to check your auctions on the iPhone is not great. This app solves all those problems.

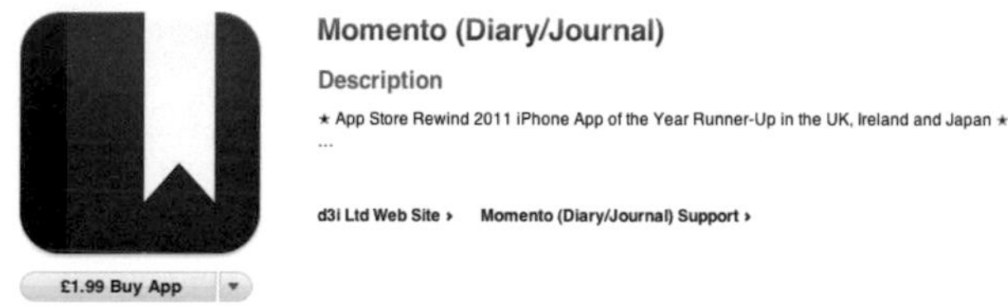

Momento (Diary/Journal)
Description
★ App Store Rewind 2011 iPhone App of the Year Runner-Up in the UK, Ireland and Japan ★
d3i Ltd Web Site >
Momento (Diary/Journal) Support >
£1.99 Buy App

Diary app lets you capture moments through the day, tag memorable events, etc.

Jamie Oliver seems to be everywhere so why not on the iPhone. The app has loads of his best recipes and cooking tips.

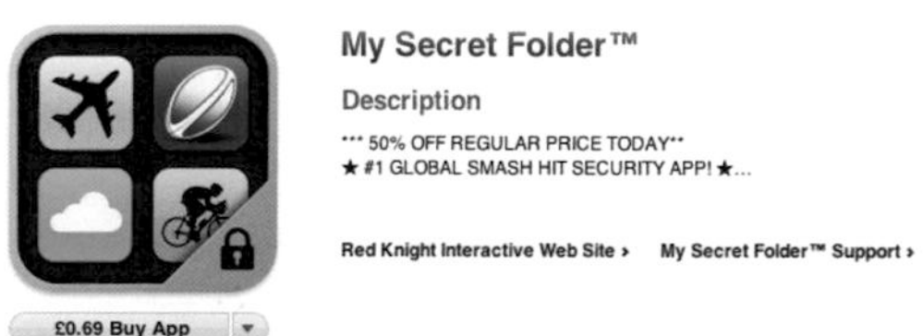

My Secret Folder™
Description
*** 50% OFF REGULAR PRICE TODAY**
★ #1 GLOBAL SMASH HIT SECURITY APP! ★...
Red Knight Interactive Web Site >
My Secret Folder™ Support >
£0.69 Buy App

Store private photos and videos. Looks like a folder but is actually an app. If someone tries to break into the app it takes a picture and will even email you if there is a break-in attempt which helps to recover stolen iPhones.

Reference

£2.49 Buy App

WolframAlpha

Description

Remember the Star Trek computer? It's finally happening--with WolframlAlpha. Building on 25 years of development led by Stepl Wolfram, WolframlAlpha has rapidly become the world's definitive source for instant expert knowledge and computation. ...

Wolfram Alpha LLC Web Site › WolframAlpha Support ›

Heavyweight reference tool for physics, chemistry, earth sciences and much more.

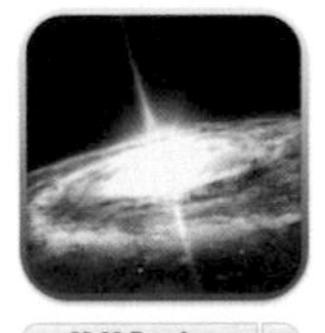

£3.99 Buy App

Brian Cox's Wonders of the Universe

Description

Take a mind-blowing 3D tour of the Universe with Professor Brian Cox as your guide. The official Wonders app by arrangement w BBC....

Brian Cox's Wonders of the Universe Support ›

Astronomy app based on Brian Cox's TV program. Explore the universe using this app. Highly rated!

App Store › Reference › Google

Google Mobile App

Description

Search Google quickly using your voice, pictures, and location. Google Mobile App includes the following features:
* New! Google Goggles - use pictures to search the web. Goggles recognizes things such as landmarks, books, wine, artwork, and logos....

...More

Google Web Site › Google Mobile App Support › Application Licence Agreement ›

This app pulls together all the Google applications into one neat app but it does take you to a browser to use the actual applications themselves. Still very useful.

App Store › Reference › Catlin Software, LLC

Dictionary!

Description

Dictionary! is an easy to use, no fluff dictionary app for your iPhone. Helps you find words when you need to without getting in your way.
...

...More

Catlin Software, LLC Web Site › Dictionary! Support ›

This has definitions of more than 200,000 words. It also has an advanced spellchecker and a thesaurus.

Travel

App Store › Travel › Malcolm Barclay

London Tube Deluxe

Description

"A must for Londoners." - London Evening Standard. London Tube Deluxe is the Most full featured & No. 1 selling guide to the London Underground....

...More

Malcolm Barclay Web Site › London Tube Deluxe Support ›

There are several Tube map apps out there but this one does it even better. It has journey planner, departure boards, and is multilingual.

App Store › Travel › Google

Google Earth

Description

Hold the world in the palm of your hand. With Google Earth for iPhone, iPad, and iPod touch, you can fly to far corners of the planet with just the swipe of a finger. Explore the same global satellite and aerial imagery available in the desktop version of Google Earth, including high-resolution imagery for over half of the world's population and a third of the world's land mass. ...

...More

Google Web Site › Google Earth Support › Application Licence Agreement ›

This remains an amazing application on the computer and the iPhone version is superb too. (It is now included in the Google Map app.)

£1.99 Buy App

FlightRadar24 Pro

Description

Turn your iPhone or iPad into an air traffic radar and see airplane traffic around the world in real-time. Discover why millions are using Flightradar24. ...

Svenska Resenatverket AB Web Site › FlightRadar24 Pro Support ›

Air traffic radar, see airplane traffic and more.

£2.49 Buy App

Live Train Times - Real-time UK Train Departures, Arrivals and Platform Information

Description

♛ Named as the Number One Train Info App by London24.com! Check out our many 5★ reviews and you can see that our thousa of users agree!...

Anecdote Software Web Site ›
Live Train Times - Real-time UK Train Departures, Arrivals and Platform Information Support ›

Provides train times for UK trains.

Sports

£1.49 Buy App

SkyDroid - Golf GPS

Description

SkyDroid - Golf GPS gives you your distance to every green on the course and more. It's easy to use, has a beautiful design, and t are no subscription, usage or course download fees....

Goldstein Technologies LLC Web Site › **SkyDroid - Golf GPS Support ›**

For golf enthusiasts. Track distance of your drives, find the distance to any point on course and many other features.

App Store › Sports › ESPN

ESPN Goals

Description

ESPN Goals is all you need to follow your favourite football team. It gives you live scores, results and latest news for the top UK and European Leagues and International Football. Plus exclusive mobile access to clips from every Barclays Premier...

...More

ESPN Web Site › **ESPN Goals Support ›**

Provides live scores for UK, European and International footballs teams.

App Store › Sports › BSkyB

Sky Sports News

Description

Get the latest sports stories as they break on the new Sky Sports News application for iPad, iPhone and iPod Touch.

With dedicated sports sections, Sky Sports News brings you all the latest news as it happens as well as keeping you up to...

...More

BSkyB Web Site › **Sky Sports News Support ›**

Live video content and interviews. However, to use the app you will need a Sky Mobile TV subscription.

£1.49 Buy App

Fantasy Premier League 2012/13 – Official App

Description

The official app for Fantasy Premier League is now available for you to download on your smartphone.
...

Appshen Limited Web Site › **Fantasy Premier League 2012/13 – Official App Support ›**

Has more than 2.5 million players. Pick your teams and play in this fantasy football game.

Navigation

Maps + Street View

Description

Get access to Street View with this handy app. The app uses the built in maps from your iPhone or iPad plus on the latest iOS 6 de
you can seamlessly switch to other maps. You can also track your location on the map as you move around.
...

Maps + Street View Support ›

£0.69 Buy App

Uses built-in iPhone maps. Provides street view (this view is not included with the iPhone's Maps app).

Waze social GPS traffic & gas

Description

Waze is a fun, community-based traffic & navigation app, 30 million strong. Join forces with other drivers nearby to outsmart traffic,
time & fuel money, and improve everyone's daily commute.
...

Waze Inc. Web Site › Waze social GPS traffic & gas Support ›

Downloaded

A Wiki app where drivers add data constantly making it very up-to-date in terms of traffic, accidents, diversions, etc. A great satnav and free!

App Store › Navigation › Tyler Bell

L.E.D. Torch

Description

#1 Sold LED Torch App in the App Store. Sold 40000 Copies In 130 COUNTRIES.
...

...More

L.E.D. Torch Support › Application Licence Agreement ›

Another app which makes your iPhone light up like a torch. Helpful when you're in a dark place and have forgotten to bring a torch with you.

App Store › Navigation › Ombros Brands Inc.

ATM Locator - Find the Nearest ATMs

Description

Find the nearest ATM (Automated Teller Machine) just about anywhere in the world! ATM Locator keeps track of the more then 1 million cash machines around the globe. You can now find cash and other services 24 hours a day, seven days a week....

...More

Ombros Brands Inc. Web Site › ATM Locator - Find the Nearest ATMs Support ›

Rather than wander for miles looking for a hole in the wall, this app will tell you where the nearest ATM is located.

Health & Fitness

App Store › Health & Fitness › Alistair Ewing

iRipped

Description

Imagine having your own personal bodybuilder/dietitian/resistance training expert in your own pocket, now you can with iRipped.
...

...More

iRipped Support ›

The ultimate app for getting the ripped look you always dreamed of. Provides great photos of the exercises, diet and sleep advice and loads more.

App Store › Health & Fitness › Medical Productions

iFitness

Description

LIMITED TIME SALE Raved about by The New York Times, Washington Post, ABC News and the countless people that have made iFitness the #1 selling fitness app worldwide! Achieve your goal of getting and staying fit with iFitness. iFitness...

...More

Medical Productions Web Site › **iFitness Support ›**

Another work-out app for those seeking the body-beautiful. Useful information in terms of workouts aimed at all levels from beginner to the seasoned pro.

Sleep Cycle alarm clock

Description

Waking up made easy.

An intelligent alarm clock that analyzes your sleep and wakes you in the lightest sleep phase – the natural way to wake up feelin

Maciek Drejak Labs Web Site › **Sleep Cycle alarm clock Support ›**

£0.69 Buy App

Monitors your movements during sleep and tells you how good your sleep cycle is. Wakes you up at the optimum time.

App Store › Health & Fitness › Chello Publishing

Carbs & Cals - A visual guide to Carbohydrate & Calorie Counting

Description

This is the Carbohydrate and Calorie Counting App you have always wanted! It contains over 1200 food photographs so you can more easily judge the carbs and calories in your food and drinks than ever before!...

...More

Chello Publishing Web Site › **Carbs & Cals - A visual guide to Carbohydrate & Calorie Counting Support ›**

This app helps you work out what to eat and what not to eat.

News

Zite Personalized Magazine

Description

Selected by Apple as #1 iPad news app of 2011!

Zite is a free personalized magazine for your iPad that automatically learns what you like and gets smarter every time you use it. Z

Zite, Inc. Web Site › Zite Personalized Magazine Support ›

Downloaded

Beautiful magazine app with personalized interface. You can share stories with Facebook, Twitter, and Instapaper.

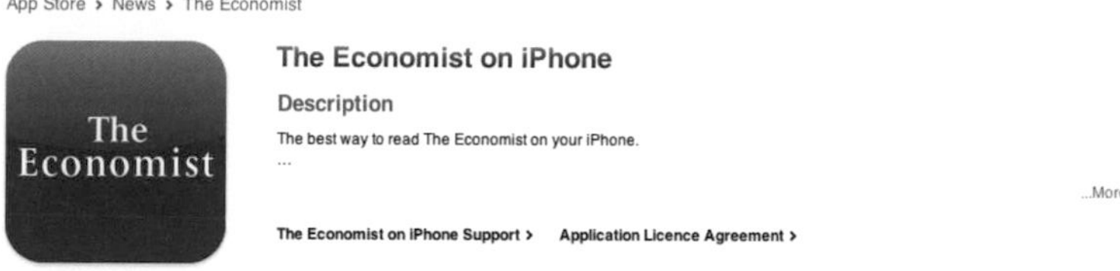

Get the Economist news stories on your iPhone. Provides the Editor's selection and must-read articles.

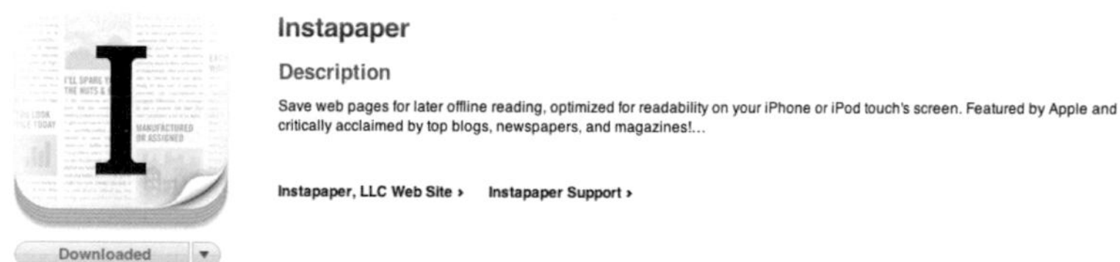

Instapaper
Description
Save web pages for later offline reading, optimized for readability on your iPhone or iPod touch's screen. Featured by Apple and critically acclaimed by top blogs, newspapers, and magazines!...
Instapaper, LLC Web Site › Instapaper Support ›
Downloaded

Cool app for saving long web pages and blogs so you can read them offline later. There are numerous user settings such as fonts, size, and others to help make the content more readable for you.

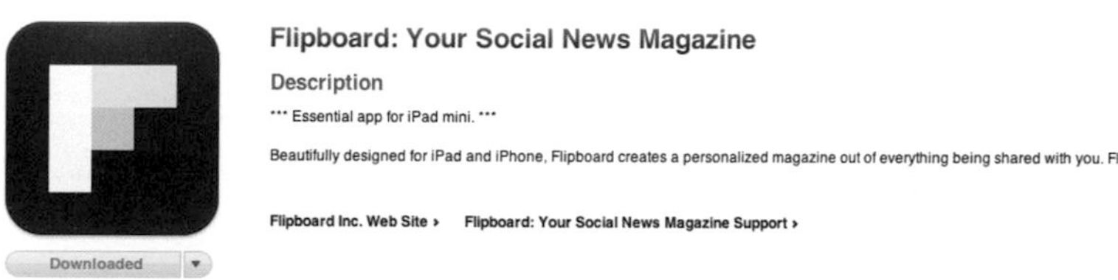

Flipboard: Your Social News Magazine
Description
*** Essential app for iPad mini. ***
Beautifully designed for iPad and iPhone, Flipboard creates a personalized magazine out of everything being shared with you. Fl
Flipboard Inc. Web Site › Flipboard: Your Social News Magazine Support ›
Downloaded

Similar to Zite, a customized reader, with sharing with Facebook, Twitter, and Instapaper.

Photography

Camera+

Description

ON SALE!
BUY NOW BEFORE THE PRICE GOES UP!...

tap tap tap Web Site › Camera+ Support ›

Downloaded

Improve your shots, high quality zoom, cropping and other tools.

App Store › Utilities › CocoaTek

Camera One : ALL-IN-1

Description

The FIRST app which supports GeoTag in iPhone photo album!
The best ALL-IN-1 iPhone Camera App! (For iPhone or iPod touch 4 Only)...

...More

CocoaTek Web Site › Camera One : ALL-IN-1 Support ›

There are loads of camera apps for the iPhone but this one seems to be several apps in one, providing color effects, zoom, antishake, geotagging and time-stamping. Very useful.

Downloaded

iPhoto

iPhoto has been popular for years on the Mac and this iPhone version has loads of great features.

iMovie

iMovie.
Make beautiful HD movies anywhere.

iMovie on the Mac makes movie editing easy and the same is true of Apple's iPhone version.

Finance

Debt Manager

Description

*** No. 1 Ranked Finance App in the UK & US ***

SALE NOW ON: 50% off for a limited time ...

MH Riley Ltd Web Site › Debt Manager Support ›

£0.69 Buy App

Get your debts under control, create plans to help you pay off your debts.

Spending Log

Description

★ Selected by Apple as 'New & Noteworthy' for Finance in the UK & Ireland ★
...

Corbenic Consulting Web Site › Spending Log Support ›

£0.69 Buy App

What's New in Version 2.5

Track your expenditure, works out where you can cut back in order to save money.

App Store › Finance › PayPal, an eBay Company

PayPal

Description

Send money to your friends, manage your account, and more, with the PayPal app. It's free, secure and more convenient than going to the ATM, writing checks, or sending gifts the traditional way.
• Send money as gifts, collect money for a group gift, or repay a friend for FREE*...

...More

PayPal, an eBay Company Web Site › PayPal Support ›

PayPal is the prefered method of payment for eBay and many websites now and it's great to have PayPal as a separate app on the iPhone.

App Store › Finance › noidentity

MoneyBook

Description

It may look simplistic, but MoneyBook is a powerful personal finance app that offers unique features in a beautiful, easy-to-use user interface. There's even an amazing free companion web app with it....

...More

noidentity Web Site › MoneyBook Support ›

Great for personal finance, and has a companion web app. You can export your transactions as emails and the app will help you with your budgeting.

Business

App Store › Business › DataViz, Inc.

Documents To Go® Premium - Office Suite

Description

"WHAT'S NEW IN 4.0" Speed enhancements, external keyboard support, Sheet To Go freeze panes and sort, multi-tasking, high resolution retina display & more! ...

...More

DataViz, Inc. Web Site › Documents To Go® Premium - Office Suite Support ›

If you ever need to edit Microsoft Office files on the iPhone this app will make the task easy. You can sync files from your desktop to your iPhone once you download the mini DTG app for Mac or PC.

Mail+ for Outlook

Description

* Highest-ranked app to securely access your Outlook EMAIL and CALENDAR *

...

iKonic Apps LLC Web Site › Mail+ for Outlook Support ›

£3.99 Buy App

An alternative mail client to the inbuilt Mail. Read, write, and reply to Outlook email.

App Store › Business › Nuance Communications

Dragon Dictation

Description

Dragon Dictation is an easy-to-use voice recognition application powered by Dragon® NaturallySpeaking® that allows you to easily speak and instantly see your text or email messages. In fact, it's up to five (5) times faster than typing on the keyboar...

...More

Nuance Communications Web Site › Dragon Dictation Support ›

Rather than type your emails and text why not dictate and let Dragon do the transcription? Easy to use.

JotNot Scanner Pro: scan multipage documents to PDF

Description

JotNot is the original and premier multi-page document scanner for the iPhone.

...

MobiTech 3000 LLC Web Site › JotNot Scanner Pro: scan multipage documents to PDF Support ›

Downloaded

Multipage document scanner. Saves files as PDF, PNG, JPEG and allows emailing of documents.

Education

App Store › Education › Milo Creative

Tiny Garden

Description

Tiny Garden is an educational game that helps children learn new words as they play. Tiny Garden delights and encourages children to explore words in an interactive musical garden that is full of animated animals, plants, fruit & vegetables. Childr...

...More

Milo Creative Web Site › **Tiny Garden Support ›**

Helps children learn new words as they play. You can record your own words and several languages are available.

£1.49 Buy App

Sakura Quick Math

Description

Kids can't put it down!

Practice your mathematics while racing the clock in this innovative iPad app. Featuring advanced handwriting recognition and a...

Sakura Quick Math Support ›

Basic math educational tool. Includes times tables.

App Store › Education › J Plimmer

Design and Technology

Description

The Design and Technology application provides students with a new way to learn, work and prepare for tests and exams in many areas of Design and Technology. Study on the bus, in your home or in school without the need to carry your books. You can even listen to your music at the same time....

...More

J Plimmer Web Site › **Design and Technology Support ›**

Now a regular school subject the D&T app helps kids get more out of their studies. The app includes quizzes and other features to help with learning in a fun way.

App Store › Education › Vito Technology Inc.

Star Walk - 5 stars astronomy guide

Description

Featured by Apple - Best Apps of 2009!
Enjoy enhanced stargazing experience with gyroscope on iPhone 4 and full iOS 4 support with multitasking!...

...More

Vito Technology Inc. Web Site › **Star Walk - 5 stars astronomy guide Support ›**

This is your personal planetarium providing all you need to know about the cosmos, with a ton of features that make astronomy even more interesting.

Weather

£2.49 Buy App

WeatherPro

Description

"Amazingly reliable seven day forecasts...we wouldn't hesitate to recommend this app." – Mac Life *****

...

MeteoGroup Deutschland GmbH Web Site › WeatherPro Support ›

Seven-day forecasting, wind direction, wind speed, sharing of data on Facebook and Twitter.

£1.49 Buy App

An Awesome Weather

Description

An Awesome Weather is ultimate desk clock and weather app in one.

The background slideshow shows gorgeous images (from Flickr) corresponding to your current weather and/or part of the day. W

An Awesome Weather Support ›

Covers more than 25,000 cities. Automatic location detector.

£1.49 Buy App

Weather Live

Description

Meet Weather Live. The most beautiful weather app. Ever.

...

Apalon Web Site › Weather Live Support ›

What's New in Version 1.9.1

Another weather app with features similar to the others. Provides freeze alerts.

App Store › Weather › Sotic Ltd

Ski Club Snow Reports

Description

The Ski Club of Great Britain snow report app, brought to you in association with Land Rover, provides you with the best and most respected snow reports from 250 ski resorts around the world, updated daily for the most current snow conditions.

...

...More

Sotic Ltd Web Site › Ski Club Snow Reports Support ›

Covers 250 ski resorts, snow depths, piste conditions, and live weather with web cams. For those who love to ski this has to be one app you can't live without.

Books

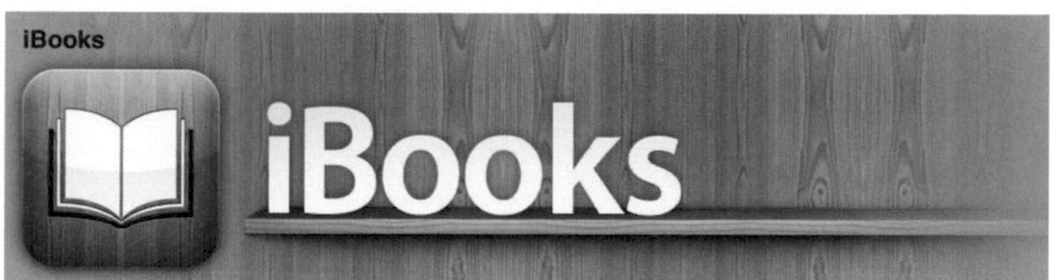

Apple's ebook app, as featured on the iPad, is also on the iPhone. You can browse, buy, read and store ebooks and PDFs for reading anywhere you want. Tons of user settings to make the reading even easier.

App Store › Books › Amazon.com

Kindle

Description

The Kindle app is optimized for the iPad, iPhone, and iPod touch, giving users the ability to read Kindle books on a beautiful, easy-to-use interface. You'll have access to over 750,000* books in the Kindle Store, including best sellers and new releases. Amazon Whispersync automatically syncs your last page read, bookmarks, notes, and highlights across devices...

...More

Amazon.com Web Site › **Kindle Support ›** **Application Licence Agreement ›**

This app is the gateway to Kindle books which you can buy and read just as you would with iBooks. There's a huge selection of books to choose from.

Free App

QI Lite for iPhone

Description

- Octopuses can open jam-jars
- The Earth has at least seven moons
- Dolphins change their skin every two hours...

Faber and Faber Web Site › **QI Lite for iPhone Support ›**

What's New in Version 1.4.1

Based on the popular quiz program.

App Store › Books › Marvel Entertainment

Marvel Comics

Description

Introducing the MARVEL COMICS app, a revolutionary new way to experience the Marvel Universe on your iPhone, iPod Touch and iPad, featuring the world's most popular super heroes! Download hundreds of comic books featuring your favorite characters -— including Iron Man, Thor, Captain America, Spider-Man, Wolverine and more -- on your mobile device with t...

...More

Marvel Entertainment Web Site › **Marvel Comics Support ›**

Features all your favorites such as Iron Man, Captain America and others You can also back up your books using the website.

Medical

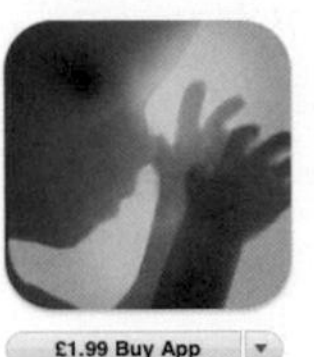

£1.99 Buy App

Pregnancy ++

Description

Congratulations on your pregnancy!

This pregnancy application is created by Health & Parenting Ltd. together with leading healthcare professionals. Highly trusted...

Health & Parenting Ltd Web Site › Pregnancy ++ Support ›

Daily information on your pregnancy. Health, diet and exercise. Weight tracker, birth planning, etc.

£0.69 Buy App

ECG Guide

Description

The most comprehensive ECG app in the iPhone App Store - over 200 examples of common and uncommon ECGs

iPad version? bit.ly/ECGiPad or search iTunes "ECG Guide iPad"...

QxMD Medical Software Web Site › ECG Guide Support ›

Largest ECG library on iPhone. ECG interpreter, 100 MCQs.

£0.69 Buy App

Blood Pressure Companion

Description

Blood Pressure Companion is a blood pressure, heart rate and weight tracker.

...

Maxwell Software Web Site › Blood Pressure Companion Support ›

Add and edit blood pressure readings. Export your data in CSV, HTML and PDF formats.

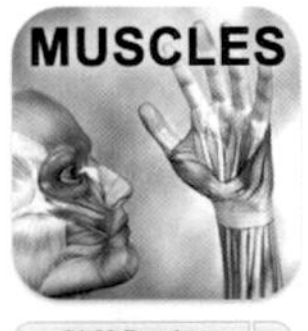

£1.99 Buy App

Learn Muscles : Anatomy Quiz & Reference

Description

A great reference, testing and education tool. Includes 141 beautiful muscle images with name, action, origin, insertion and comm
plus audio pronounciation guide, a quiz maker, an action viewer and 6 short videos to create a rich learning experience.

...

Real Bodywork Web Site › Learn Muscles : Anatomy Quiz & Reference Support ›

Beautiful reference and educational tool. Quizmaker and great graphics.

11 Solving Problems

The iPhone occasionally misbehaves – an app will not close, or the iPhone may malfunction. This section looks at how to fix common problems and provides some helpful websites. The chapter also helps you find your lost or stolen iPhone.

General iPhone Care

The iPhone is a fairly robust gadget but, like any complex piece of electronic hardware, it may suffer from knocks, scratches, getting wet and other problems.

Cleaning the body and screen

The touchscreen is supposed to be scratch resistant. In fact, there are YouTube videos showing people trying to scratch the screen by placing the iPhone into a plastic bag containing keys and shaking the whole thing around. Amazingly, the screen seems not to scratch. Then they put it in a blender and it, well, got blended. So it's definitely not blender-proof!

Hot tip

Paper kitchen towel, wetted with a little water containing a couple of drops of dishwashing liquid, is great for getting rid of heavily greased screens.

The iPhone is supplied with a small glass cleaning cloth (it should be in the small black cardboard package shown above). The best way to clean is to make sure there is no grit or sand on the body or screen and gently rub with the cleaning cloth. This should bring back the shine without scratching the glass or the back of the phone.

Occasionally the screen may get very greasy and a little soap helps to get the grease off

1. Put a few drops of dishwashing liquid in warm water
2. Get some paper kitchen towel and dip this into the water
3. Wring out the kitchen towel so it is not dripping wet and lightly wipe over the screen and rest of the casing
4. Dry off using the black iPhone cleaning cloth

Keep iPhone Up-to-Date

Apple releases updates to the iPhone operating system periodically.

These are downloaded and installed using iTunes.

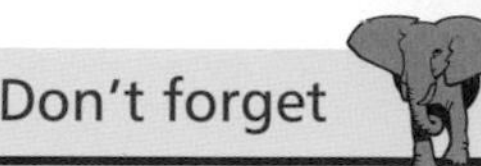

Software updates for iPhone users are provided free by Apple. If one becomes available, download and install it.

Is your iPhone fully up-to-date?

1. Plug your iPhone into **iTunes**
2. Click **Check for Update**
3. Follow any instructions

Click here to see if there are any updates

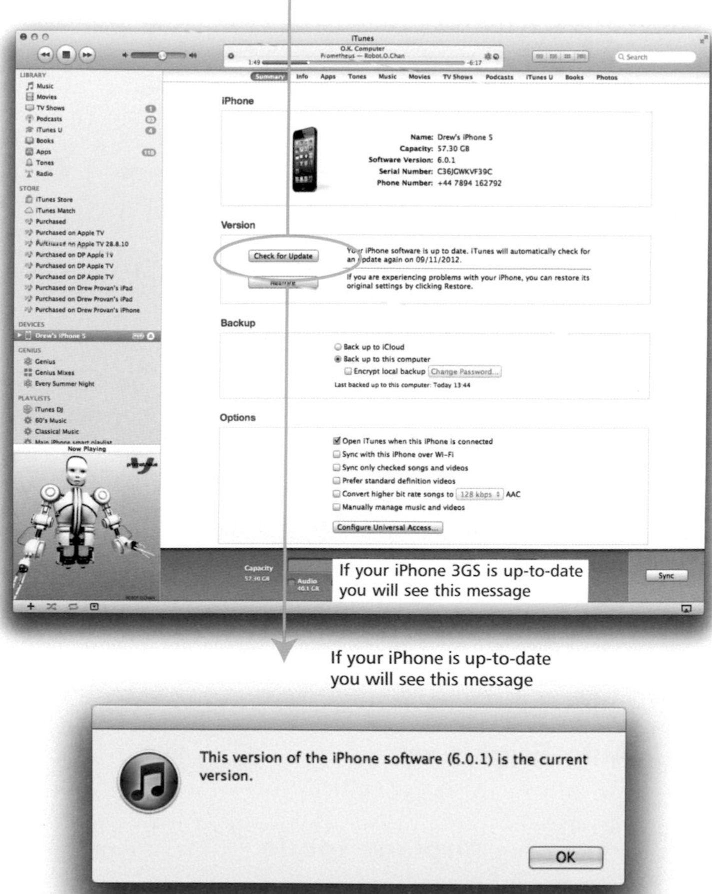

Maximize iPhone Battery

The iPhone is a bit of a power hog. Browsing the web, listening to music and watching videos drains power. If you only make a few phone calls each day, your iPhone will last a couple of days between charges. But most people use it for far more than this and their battery will last about a day.

Tweaks to ensure maximum battery life

1. **Switch off Wi-Fi** if you don't need it
2. **Switch off Bluetooth** if you don't need it
3. **Switch on battery percentage indicator**

4. **Switch off 3G** if you don't need this

5. Collect your **email manually**

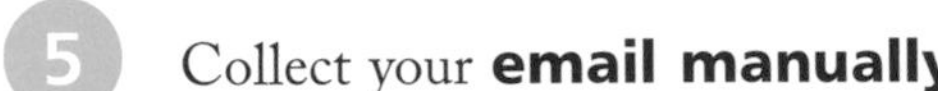

6. Set **Auto-lock** to a short period, e.g. 1 minute

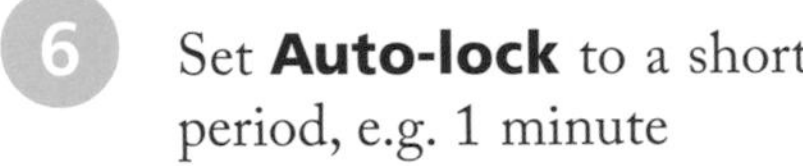

7. Always hit the **OFF** button when you have finished using the iPhone (screen goes black which uses less power)

8. Reduce the **brightness** of your screen

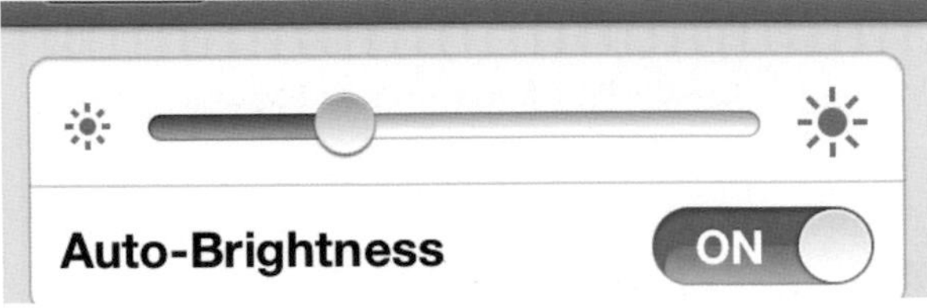

9. Consider using **Airplane mode** for maximum conservation of power!

Hot tip

You can conserve battery power by switching off Wi-Fi and Bluetooth. Instead of opting for push email, you can check for email manually.

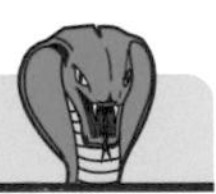

Beware

If you use Airplane mode you will not receive any calls, texts or notifications.

Restart, Force Quit and Reset

Restart the iPhone

If the iPhone misbehaves, or applications act strangely, you can restart the iPhone.

1. **Hold down** the Sleep/Wake button
2. When you see the **Slide to Power Off** appear, **push this to the right**
3. Leave the iPhone for a couple of minutes then press the **Sleep/Wake** button again and let the phone restart

Quit an app

Sometimes apps misbehave and you want to quit them and reopen. To do this, press the Home Button twice to bring up the app tray.

Touch and hold an app until they all jiggle and you see the quit icon next to each. Touch the quit icon to quit the app.

Touch and hold the apps, then touch ⊖ to quit an app

Reset the iPhone

1. Press the **Sleep/Wake** and the **Home Button** at the same time
2. The screen will suddenly turn black and the iPhone will restart

Apple Resources

Visit Apple!

The first place you should look for help is the Apple site. After all, iPhone is their creation so they should know more than anyone.

The iPhone and iPhone Support areas are packed with information, tutorials and videos.

Useful URLs

http://www.apple.com/iphone/

http://www.apple.com/support/iphone/

The first place to look for hints, tips and fixes is Apple's website, which is chock full of information and videos.

Technology Experts

David Pogue's Top 10 iPhone tips...

on the O'Reilly site are worth reading (David Pogue is always worth reading – he loves technology and loves all things Apple).

Useful URLs

http://broadcast.oreilly.com/2009/07/david-pogues-top-10-tips-for-t.html

David's New York Times blog is fantastic, and you can find it here *http://pogue.blogs.nytimes.com/*

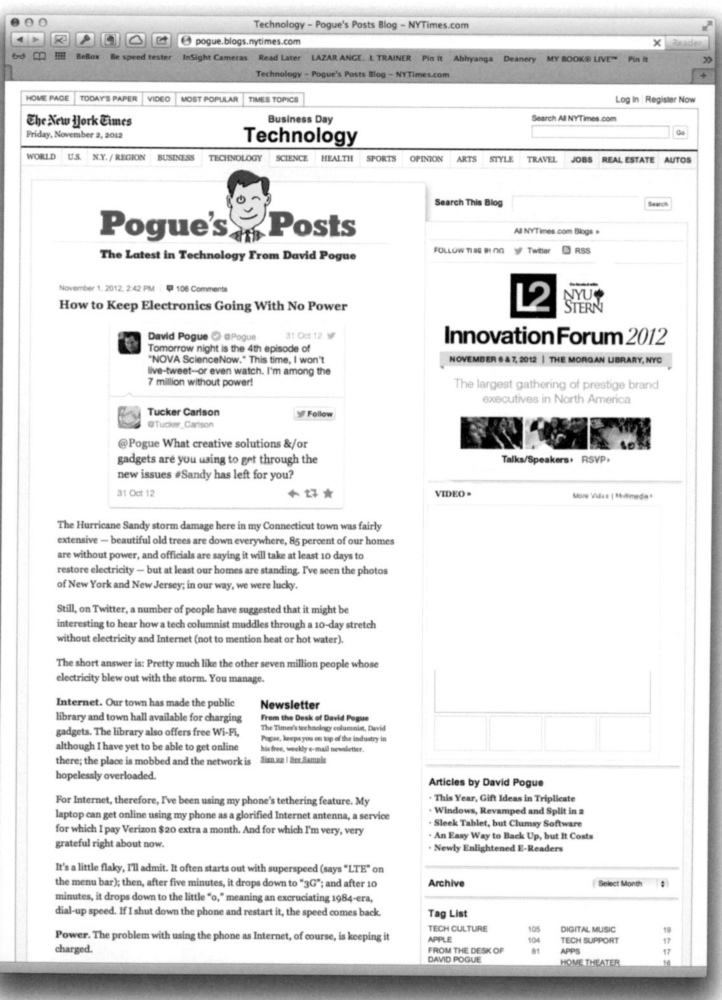

Visit the iLounge!

iLounge has long provided loads of hints and tips for iPods. These guys review hardware, accessories and provide reviews of new gear for the iPod, the iPhone and the iPad.

What does the site offer?

1. News
2. Reviews of apps and accessories
3. Forums
4. Software
5. Help
6. Articles

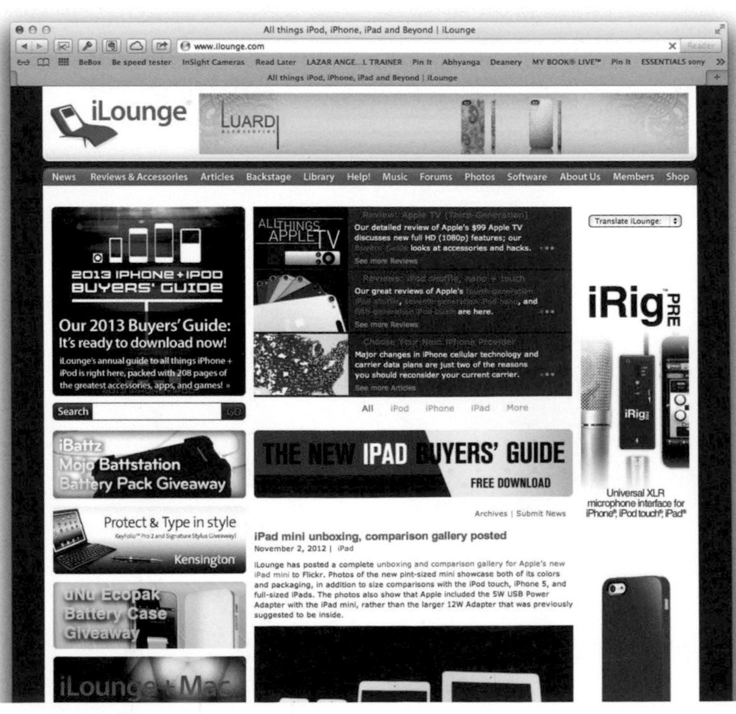

Other Useful Websites

I Use This

Provides reviews of iPhone apps, and lets you know how many people are actually using the apps.

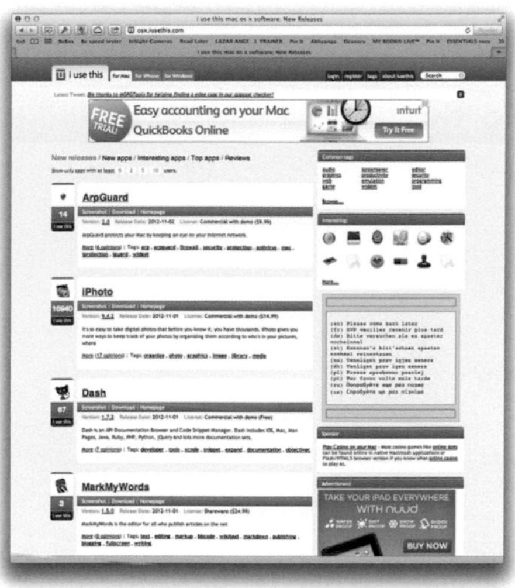

What's on iPhone

Largely a review site but it also provides information about hardware and for people interested in developing for the iPhone.

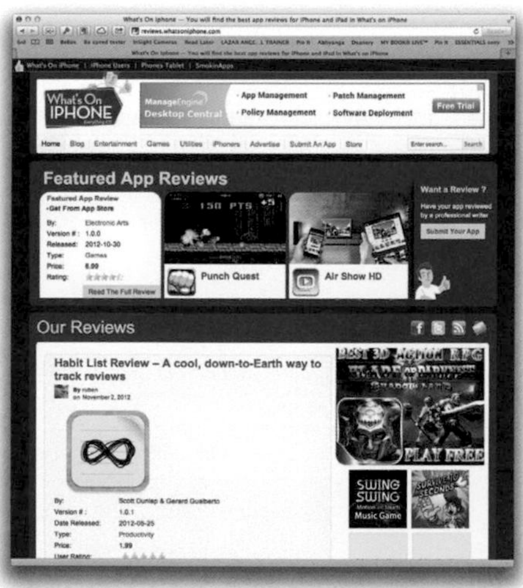

Restoring the iPhone

Sometimes things go wrong and your iPhone needs to be restored. This is similar to a PC which goes wrong – you can restore from a restore point. iTunes will make a backup of your iPhone each time you plug it in to sync.

To restore to a previous point

1. **Plug the iPhone** into the PC or Mac, open iTunes and go to the Summary pane
2. Click **Restore** and follow the instructions

Click Restore to restore the iPhone to a previous restore point

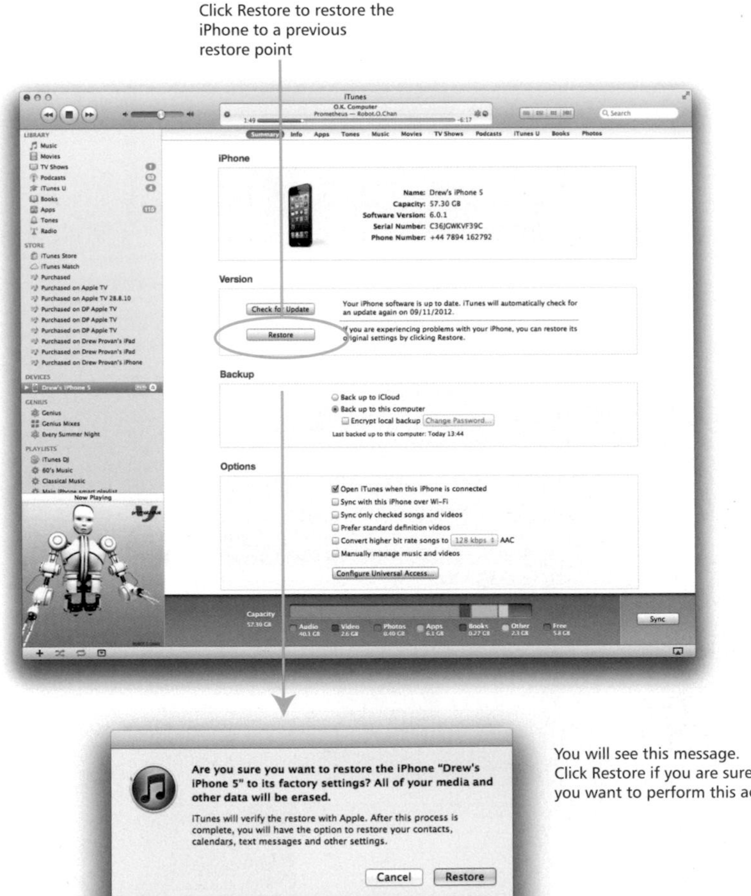

You will see this message. Click Restore if you are sure you want to perform this action

If You Lose Your iPhone

Apple has built in a new feature to the iPhone, which allows you to erase the entire contents of your iPhone remotely. This means that if it gets stolen, you can remotely erase the iPhone and prevent whoever stole your iPhone from getting their hands on your personal data.

Hot tip

If for no other reason, it is worth getting an iCloud account so you can track your iPhone and erase the contents if it gets stolen.

Set up Find My iPhone

1. **Log in to iCloud** (*http://icloud.com*)
2. Go to the **Settings** options
3. Look for **Find My iPhone**
4. **Click the tab** and set up the various options
5. If you are really sure the iPhone has been stolen, activate **Remote Wipe** to prevent any private data being viewed by the thief

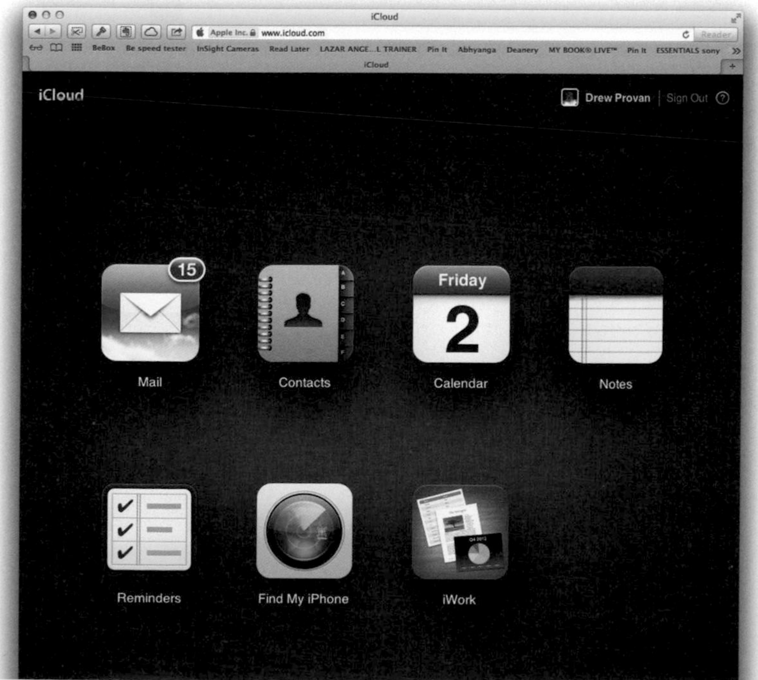

...cont'd

Locating your iPhone

Maybe you were out late and dropped your iPhone but can't quite remember where? Or perhaps it's in the house but you are not 100% sure. If you use iCloud to look for the location of your iPhone it may help you recover the iPhone. Certainly, if it's at home you will soon know, because the map location will show you where the iPhone is. The iPhone does actually have to be on, and transmitting to the cellular network, in order for Find My iPhone to work.

1. **Log into iCloud** and go to **Settings**
2. Click **Find My iPhone**
3. Check map location and recover the iPhone, if possible

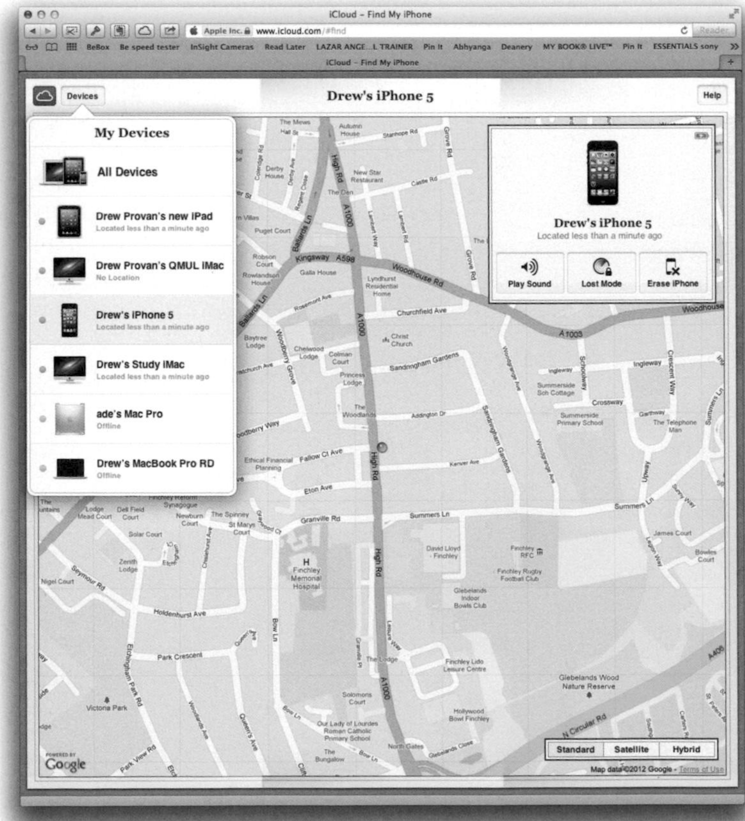

Index

A

B

C

D

K

L

M

N

O

P

R

S

T

U

V

W

Z